Collins

Cambridge IGCSE®

Art & Design

TEACHER'S GUIDE

Also for Cambridge O Level

Garry Whitehead
with Cass Bisco, Amanda Jenkins, Claire McCormack,
Rachel Richards, Joan Hutchinson and Anna White

William Collins' dream of knowledge for all began with the publication of his first book in 1819.

A self-educated mill worker, he not only enriched millions of lives, but also founded a flourishing publishing house. Today, staying true to this spirit, Collins books are packed with inspiration, innovation and practical expertise. They place you at the centre of a world of possibility and give you exactly what you need to explore it.

Collins. Freedom to teach.

Published by Collins
An imprint of HarperCollins*Publishers*
The News Building
1 London Bridge Street
London
SE1 9GF

Browse the complete Collins catalogue at **www.collins.co.uk**

British Library Cataloguing in Publication Data
A catalogue record for this publication is available from the British Library.

Lead author: Garry Whitehead
Contributing authors: Cass Bisco, Amanda Jenkins, Claire McCormack, Rachel Richards, Julia Triston and Anna White
Commissioning project manager: James Maroney
Development editor: Lucy Hyde
Commissioning editor: Lizzie Geldart
In-house editor: Hannah Dove
Project manager: Iolanda Steadman
Copyeditor: Jenny Schnetler
Proofreader: Kim Vernon
Cover designers: Kevin Robbins and Gordon MacGilp
Cover illustrator: Maria Herbert-Liew
Typesetter: Iolanda Steadman
Production controller: Tina Paul
Printed and bound by CPI Group (UK) Ltd, Croydon, CR0 4YY

® IGCSE is a registered trademark

The assessments of student case studies included in this title were written by the authors. In examinations the way marks are awarded may be different.

Acknowledgements

The publishers gratefully acknowledge the permission granted to reproduce the copyright material in this book. Every effort has been made to trace copyright holders and to obtain their permission for the use of copyright material. The publishers will gladly receive any information enabling them to rectify any error or omission at the first opportunity.

Student work
We would like to thank the following students (in alphabetical order) for giving us permission to reproduce their work:
Key: (t = top, b = bottom, l = left, r = right, c = centre)
Maddie Bentley p35b, p36; Sadie Cheesebrough p41; Helen Conley p147; Sarah El Nour p213, p214; Phoebe Farley p52t, 53t; Bella Geldart p38, p39; Tarm Hiransrisoontorn p53c, p54b; Amanda Jenkins, Camberwell College of Arts p210; Stella MacDougall p54t; Miles Mitchell p34, p37, p52b, p174; Martha Peach p232; Amika Sakchatchawan p35b; Kate Saunders p35t, p51; Joe Syrett p193; Titayatorn Utenpatanum p45r, p127; Nicha Vareekasem p45l, p53b; Prim Vudhichamnong p40; Yu Qi Wang p43.

We would also like to thank the following teachers and schools for their support:
Iain Sanderson, Harrow International School Bangkok; Kassie Gaches, Ashlyns School Berkhamsted; Caroline Ferguson, Head of Art, Berkhamsted School

CONTENTS

INTRODUCTION

Welcome to this Teacher's Guide for *Collins Cambridge IGCSE® Art & Design*.

As an art teacher, you will know the wide and varied range of subjects included in the Art & Design syllabus. It would be impossible to cover every method and approach in one publication. The aim of this guide is to support you in designing a course for you and your students.

This Teacher's Guide will help you to structure a course that gradually builds the skills and confidence of your students. Teaching art and design is a very rewarding experience. Often, you are working with individuals and discussing their ideas as they become more aware of their own direction and abilities. The aims of the Cambridge IGCSE syllabus are quite wide and intended to develop creative learners with practical and expressive skills.

Using this course with O–Level and A–Level Art & Design

The approach of this book is focused on preparing work for the Cambridge IGCSE, and much of the coursework information is specific to that syllabus. However, the majority of the book is also relevant to O–Level students, and this would also be a good support for A-Level students. The book breaks down the creative process into five main areas:

1. The use of artists to inspire student work
2. Formation of ideas
3. Experimentation with materials
4. Development of the project
5. Creating a final statement.

Any student studying art will find the examples discussed and ideas presented useful for developing their work. In addition, there are detailed suggestions and examples for how to use a wide range of material, which are useful to both students and teachers. Relating artists to themes and developing alternative interpretations of a theme are areas that are looked at in detail, and which also provide a sound basis for developing O–Level and A–Level work.

THE AIMS OF THE CAMBRIDGE IGCSE SYLLABUS

Many choices

The broad subject areas of the syllabus mean that the nature of the practical work can vary greatly. The subject skills of the staff at a centre and the facilities available will help to determine which of the following areas are offered:

1. Painting and related media
2. Printmaking
3. Three-dimensional studies
4. Photography, digital and lens-based media
5. Graphic communication
6. Textile design.

Building skills for the future

Regardless of whichever areas you are teaching, you will be helping your students to develop skills and interests that may well continue long after their IGCSE education. The foundation skills are being laid for a life-long career in art and design. By learning how to record from direct observation and personal experience, a student develops an ability applicable to any future artistic activity. Creativity, visual awareness and critical and cultural understanding can be transferred from one subject area to another. Often, as students develop their artistic career, they will draw upon the wealth of experience that started with their IGCSE Art & Design course.

Life skills and value to other subjects

Not all students will pursue a career in art and design, but many will continue using some of the skills that they are introduced to while studying for their IGCSE. The ability to identify and solve problems is valuable in many situations. For some students, the growing independence and confidence that they experience in art and design are carried across to other subject areas as their approach to education matures.

The elements of art feature knowledge and understanding that will help students in making decisions and value judgements across a wide spectrum of business environments. Each part of the world has its own unique artistic heritage and these important local influences can be incorporated into your schemes of work. By using regional artistic heritage to inspire projects, you will help students to present their personal visual response to the world.

COURSE CONTENT

The IGCSE is made of two main components:

- Coursework
- An externally set assignment.

Both components make up 50 per cent of the final mark and so are equally important to a student's success. This introduction is an overview of the whole course. *Part I: Practical Guidance* will provide further details and support in both these areas.

Coursework

- Coursework – 50 per cent of final mark
- Final outcome up to A2 in size
- Up to four sheets (eight sides) of A2 portfolio

Coursework should introduce the student to a range of inspiration, materials and techniques. The opportunity to make mistakes and learn from experience will allow the student to build their confidence and ability to make a personal response. Planning the coursework to create this outcome is an important early step for the Art & Design teacher. This Teacher's Guide includes a suggested scheme of work (page 234) to help you to structure a course for your students. It is a good idea to understand the general principles of this suggested scheme. You can then apply the concepts to your own situation and the subject areas that you are teaching.

Coursework will often start with short projects and workshops, thereby allowing students to explore a range of materials and ideas before making increasingly personal choices about their work. They will then plan and develop more ambitious finished pieces of work. A final outcome and their portfolio make up their coursework. It is essential that you allow sufficient time to sort, check and submit these materials before the submission deadline. It is important that you find out early in the course what these dates are and outline a schedule that sets an appropriate internal deadline for your students to work within.

As students will produce a lot of work, they will need advice and training in selecting from it to make their coursework submission. This submission consists of up to four sheets (eight sides) of A2 portfolio and a final piece of up to A2 in size.

Externally set assignment

- Externally set assignment – 50 per cent of final mark
- Eight-hour final outcome up to A2 in size
- Up to two sheets (four sides) of A2 supporting studies.

Sound coursework will help the student to approach the externally set assignment with confidence. Once the question paper is made available, students will have approximately 16 weeks to prepare and complete the supervised test. It consists of a list of starting points from which students select one for their own work. Helping students to make good choices at this stage can be critical to a successful outcome.

You will need to arrange times for the actual supervised test and help students plan their time in working towards this deadline. There is no time limit on preparatory work for the externally set assignment, but reference studies must be complete before the eight-hour supervised test. Students can bring up to two sheets (four sides) of A2 references to the supervised test and complete their final piece over a maximum of three sessions consisting of eight hours in total over no more than two weeks.

CONTENT OF THE TEACHER'S GUIDE

This Teacher's Guide is divided into several sections that will support you in delivering the Art & Design syllabus. At the heart of this guide is the concept of developing a scheme of work for your students. Each section contributes towards this aim, but the final section 'Scheme of Work' should be seen as the basis for constructing a sequence of activities and projects relevant to your particular situation.

The main emphasis of each section is outlined below.

Art and design in the classroom

This section features advice on best practice and tips on preparing an art and design department.

- **Resources:** This section outlines common materials and equipment, together with some alternatives. There is also a list of suggested texts to support reading on the elements of art and use of media.
- **Classroom management:** This section provides suggestions on best practice for setting up and managing an art department including storage of materials, display of work and tips for specialist areas.

Elements of art

This section looks at how to incorporate the elements of art into teaching across the entire course. Often, several elements will be included in making a work of art, but looking at them in isolation can be informative for students.

Part I: Practical guidance and checklist

This section is divided into the two elements that make up the student submission, namely coursework and the externally set assignment.

Supporting students with their coursework

This section contains suggestions for activities and ideas that relate to the different stages of coursework. The examples focus around the following:

- Themes
- Recording (ideas, observations and insights)
- Exploration
- Development
- Evaluation
- The final outcome.

Student work examples and classroom activities are used to help you think about how to direct work and assess progress.

Preparing students for their externally set assignment

The nature of the externally set assignment is explained here as it presents some new challenges.

The Assessment Objectives (AOs) are explained in relation to the externally set assignment expectations. Suggestions are given for ways to give assessment feedback to students to ensure sound coverage of the AOs. There is advice on how to read the test paper, with practice on the initial response, as well as how to set up and respond to your own design briefs in preparation for the starting points. Managing the preparation time and scheduling the externally set assignment itself are also explored.

Checklists are provided to help you manage and assess your students' output.

Part II: The creative process

This section provides an overview of how a student project may be managed to ensure that it covers all of the AO requirements. Each sub-section contains ideas for lessons that will produce work that can be used to evidence the AOs. There are also suggestions for extension material. Although your particular subject area may not be covered, the general approach to structuring lessons and activities should be clear from the examples provided. The following sections are included:

- Artistic inspiration and response
- Recording ideas, observations and insights
- Creative exploration
- Thoughtful development
- Realising your final outcome.

Part III: Media and techniques

In Part III, the broad subject areas are explored in more depth, with lesson plans provided to deliver the learning objectives from the syllabus. Both individual lesson plans and longer project suggestions are included. Each broad subject area has an introduction followed by lesson plans and a student case study, as well as further research and topic extension ideas.

Scheme of work

The scheme of work is a suggested structure for the course. The advised teaching time is 130 hours. The scheme of work is presented as a framework for individual teachers and centres to adapt to their own situations. Starting from scratch is often the most difficult part of creating a new course. After reading the Teacher's Guide and considering your local circumstances, this scheme of work can be used as the first step in building an art curriculum for your art and design students.

Glossary of terms

The glossary of terms is a useful list of vocabulary that students will come across during their studies. You can refer to this section if you want to look for an alternative way to explain a term to a student.

USING THE TEACHER'S GUIDE AND STUDENT'S BOOK TOGETHER

To reflect the nature of the subject, the *Collins Cambridge IGCSE Art & Design Teacher's Guide* and Student's Book have been designed to work slightly differently to other courses. Both books are matched to the 0400 IGCSE Art & Design syllabus and cover it fully. However, whereas the Student's Book presents student-focused guidance on the topics of the course, student activities and peer materials to guide learning, the Teacher's Guide provides guidance on best practice for teachers, and suggested lesson plans for constructing a course from both the Student's Book and Teacher's Guide. In this way, the course provides full syllabus coverage across both books and gives space for students and teachers to explore, innovate and revise work over lessons, weeks and months, and to proceed at their own pace or at that of their class.

The Teacher's Guide and Student's Book are both split into three parts – covering assessment, the creative process, and media and techniques – and follow the same order, allowing them to be used side-by-side. However, the lesson plans and guidance in the Teacher's Guide are supplementary to the Student's Book content and provide a framework for teachers to plan, carry out and develop their own teaching plan. It is hoped that in this way students can use the Student's Book to further their learning, and teachers will develop their own skills through engagement with both the Student's Book and Teacher's Guide.

Student's Book		Teacher's Guide		Teaching the course
Course content		Setting up the class		
Topic backgrounds		Building resources		Build a scheme of work
Skills explanations		Lesson plans		Teach the full course
Student activities	+	Guidance on further work	→	Explore more widely
Further research sections		Suggested projects		Plan + carry out projects
Artists with impact		Assessment guidance		Assess student progress
Student exemplar materials		Scheme of work guidance		

LESSON PLAN OVERVIEW

Introduction

These lesson plans relate to the relevant sections in *Part III: Media and techniques* (page 89). Each sequence of lessons builds from a detailed introductory lesson through a series of lesson suggestions to ideas for developing a whole project. The aim is to show how a sequence of lessons may be organised and structured. The lesson plans offer a guide that you can adapt to your own situation. Some of the main elements of these lesson plans are explored in more detail below to help explain their relationship to the aims of the Art & Design syllabus.

Classroom resources

- **Classroom arrangement:** Different activities can require different arrangements of the classroom. For example, class printmaking will need different working areas to individual drawing project work. Think about how best to use the classroom, and reassess this after you have taught the lesson for possible improvements in the future.
- **Materials and equipment:** Requirements for the lesson are suggested. Sometimes there will be alternative choices, or the lesson can be taught with a limited range of the suggested items.

Research sources

General sites, which can provide useful teacher background information and student information, are given across the topic. Sites relating to individual artists and specific works of art are listed, but it is recommended that you do your own searches to source images for your presentations.

Lesson tasks

The lessons contain a numbered sequence of tasks. Each task has two elements:

- **Demonstration:** Directions for teacher-led activities.
- **Student activity:** Suggestions for teacher input and support while students are working.

Reflection

This section considers student progress and any areas for improvement. Questions to ask include the following:

- Have the students covered the lesson's intentions?
- Could some aspects be improved on or reinforced?
- Do some areas need to be taught in a different way?

Project suggestions

A variety of ideas for projects, together with artists for inspiration and suggested materials and equipment, are provided. These examples can be used as a basis for the development of a project or as a guide to advising students on structuring their own projects. These suggestions are to promote students' own ideas, which will include many more artists, activities and possible outcomes.

Assessment guidance

Learning objectives are those that students should be learning over the course of the lesson. They are based on the examination board's Assessment Objectives (AOs). These AOs are broad and cover all aspects of art and design activity in the syllabus. Consequently, only a small section of the AOs will be covered in any series of lessons. However, it is quite normal to cover more than one AO in a lesson. For example, 'exploration of materials' (AO2) might be combined with 'recording ideas and insights' (AO1). In addition, the elements of art will often be relevant to a lesson, contributing to both 'critical understanding' and 'visual language'.

HOW TO USE THIS TEACHER GUIDE

This guide is designed to help you plan, deliver and assess the IGCSE Art & Design course. There are several features in *Part III: Media and techniques*, which are designed to help you.

Lessons and projects

Each subject area has lesson plans and project ideas showing you how to introduce the chosen media (the lesson plan structure is explained in detail at the end of this chapter). Where possible, these lessons will correspond with the content of the *Part III: Media and techniques*.

Classroom resources and research sources

The resources you will require are listed in these sections:
- Classroom layout and materials required for the lesson
- Research links to useful general references, as well as specific artists and artworks relevant to introducing the lesson, with the aim of providing detail while leaving room for you to tailor the resources to suit your own situation.

Lesson tasks

The different activities that you will engage in during the lesson are listed here. The advice is based on good practice, but should be adapted to suit your own situation and teaching style. Class demonstrations, discussions, one-to-one advice, extension suggestions and assessment all form part of these activities.

Top tip

Valuable advice for teaching is highlighted in these boxes. The information will aid in teaching the course, working with materials, assessment guidance or assisting students.

Reflection

This section allows you to look back over what you have taught and consider whether there are any elements that you need to revisit with students. Extension ideas and alternative approaches are noted here.

Key terms

At the end of each section is a list of key terms that contain simple definitions for subject-specific terms.

Assessment guidance

Assessment guidance is given at the end of each project and aims to give an overview of how the project ideas fit in with the Assessment Objectives. This advice is broken down according to the four objectives and shows the overlapping nature of the Assessment Objectives when reviewing a body of work.

When assessing work, you should have the detailed assessment guidance to hand on a day-to-day basis. It can help to think of the AOs in shorthand:

Assessment Objectives	
• **AO1**: Record	• Record ideas, observations and insights relevant to intentions as work progresses.
• **AO2**: Explore	• Explore and select appropriate resources, media, materials, techniques and processes.
• **AO3**: Develop	• Develop ideas through investigation demonstrating critical understanding.
• **AO4**: Present	• Present a personal and coherent response that realises intentions and demonstrates an understanding of visual language.

At the end of each subject area, a student example is discussed in relation to the Assessment Objectives.

ART AND DESIGN IN THE CLASSROOM

This section gives advice on how to resource your classrooms and departments. This list is only a broad description of typical equipment and materials, and it does not matter if you do not have a wide range of these resources; in some instances alternatives are suggested. The list is not exhaustive or definitive, and is intended as a foundation from which you can compare and assess your own situation.

The list is based on materials useful for painting and related media. There is some information on equipment for other subject areas later in this chapter under 'Setting up working spaces' (page 16).

RESOURCES: EQUIPMENT AND MATERIALS

Craft equipment

A wide range of tools and equipment is useful. Quantities and storage will depend on the school and projects undertaken. It is useful to have a storage box or lockable drawer for this equipment. Equipment may include:

scissors	retractable knives	cutting boards	string	masking tape
double-sided tape	hot glue guns	modelling wire	gum strip	pliers
wire cutters	staple guns			

Glue

Glue is often used in lessons. Some direction and demonstration is recommended to avoid sketchbook pages being stuck together!

- **PVA:** Glue can be used with a spreader or strip of cardboard. Although brushes can be used, often they will be ruined if not cleaned properly. PVA is strong, reasonably waterproof and suitable for gluing heavier items.
- **Glue sticks:** Glue or paste in plastic tubes is useful for small–scale sticking down of paper items.
- **Cellulose paste:** This paste can be used to stick down paper, as well as for papier-mâché work.

Surfaces

Anything on which students can draw or paint on is a surface:

- **Sketchbooks:** Students can use sketchbooks to store smaller development work in the sequence in which it is made. Try to select a weight of paper that does not buckle too much when used with paints (140-gram cartridge works well).
- **Cartridge paper:** Students can use 80 to 100-gram paper for general drawing, but heavier cartridge or card is better for painting. Packs of A2 cartridge can easily be cut to smaller sizes. Rolls of paper can be more economical for larger-scale work.
- **Watercolour paper:** Student-grade paper is economical and helps students to improve their use of this medium.
- **Coloured paper:** This type of paper is useful for collage work and display.
- **Newspapers and magazines:** These are useful for collage and protecting tables while painting.
- **Canvas:** Acrylic painting can be successful on paper, although primed papers, boards or canvases make sustained and larger-scale work easier.
- **Acrylic primer:** Opaque white primer can be used on most surfaces before painting.

Alternative

Household emulsion paint, diluted with 10 per cent water, can be used as primer for card, boards and canvas. However, keep in mind that emulsion paint is not as flexible or long-lasting as acrylic primer.

Drawing tools

Drawing materials are generally dry materials, but inks can also be used as paints.

- **Pencils:** Students may have HB–2B pencils, but softer 3B–6B are useful for sustained drawings.
- **Wax crayons/oil pastels:** Although both materials can be used for wax-resist work, oil pastels are softer and the colours can be blended.
- **Chalks or dry pastels:** These dry materials are easy to smudge and blend. Protect them with fixative.
- **Colouring pencils:** These pencils are good for colour blending. Watercolour pencils also work well on a small scale.
- **Charcoal/graphite:** These materials provide good value when bought in bulk. Both media make soft, smudged marks.
- **Erasers/putty rubber:** Erasers can be cut to an edge, putty rubber works well with charcoal.
- **Fine liners:** These tools are good for detail/cross–hatching, but are easily damaged and dry out quickly.
- **Dipping nibs and holders:** These tools are good for expressive lines, but require more practice to use with control.
- **Permanent markers:** These tools are good for working quickly, but they can bleed through paper and be expensive.
- **Fixative:** This product, usually in an aerosol spray, is used to stop work smudging.
- **Drawing boards:** These tools are used for larger drawings and when working on an easel.

Alternatives

- Simple dipping pens can be made from thin bamboo or willow sticks using a craft knife.
- Hairspray can be used as an alternative to fixative on charcoal and chalk pastel studies.

Brushes

Brushes vary in quality and it is worth using several suppliers at first to find the best option for your department. All brushes should be rinsed or cleaned after use and stored flat or bristles up. Good-quality brushes are often handed out on a lesson basis to keep them in good condition.

Brushes are permanently damaged by:

- being left in paint or glue
- students pressing too hard when using paint blocks
- being left to dry bristles down, thereby changing the shape of the bristles.

Types of brushes include the following:

- **Watercolour brushes:** Use flat and round brushes (a suitable range would be sizes 2, 4, 8, 12).
- **Acrylic and poster paint brushes:** Choose filbert, or flat and round (small, medium and large) brushes. Synthetic bristles also can last longer and absorb less water.
- **Oil brushes:** Use hog brushes, which work well when used with traditional solvents and oils.
- **Palette knives:** Use these knives for cleaning palettes and textured painting.
- **Water pots:** Consider using stackable plastic pots, which work well.
- **Mixing palettes:** Use plastic palettes as a suitable option to traditional wood.
- **Texture brushes:** Keep decorating brushes, old brushes, sponges, toothbrushes for this purpose.

Alternatives

- Modern synthetic brushes can be of a high quality and very economical.
- Plastic palette knives are economical, but should be cleaned well after use.
- Palettes can be made from washed takeaway trays or sheets of corrugated cardboard, and disposed of after use.
- Any stable container can be used for water. Glass jars work well but are easily broken.

Paints and inks

Paint is dependent on the quality and quantity of the pigment used. It is worth testing the available options to find a price or quality that works for your students.

- **Watercolours:** Student tins of block colours can be good quality. Colour should be lifted easily from moist block. Tubes work well for larger areas of colour.
- **Poster paints/gouache:** Blocks and bottles both work well. Gouache is more expensive due to the much higher levels of pigment.
- **Acrylics:** Bottles are more economical than tubes, but very large bottles can be difficult to manage. Acrylics can dry out if not sealed and the lids on jars of acrylic can be difficult to open as the paint dries in the screw fastening.
- **Oil paints:** Tubes of oil paint are more manageable than tins in most situations. Student-quality paints can have quite high pigment strength.
- **Permanent black ink:** Acrylic or shellac–based ink is waterproof when dry. Small bottles are useful for a class set, topped up from a larger bulk container.
- **Coloured inks:** Small bottles of ink are useful in class but are easily contaminated. Larger bulk containers can replace or top up the class jars. Spillage often happens with ink so smaller containers cause less damage.

Some notes on buying colours

- A limited palette of warm and cool blue, red and yellow can be used to mix most colours, and teach colour theory. As well as black and white, the secondary colours can be added to this list but are not essential.
- White will always be used more than the other colours, so buy two or three times more white.
- Black can cause problems when developing colour-mixing skills, so keep it in reserve for particular projects.

LEARNING MATERIALS

The visual resources for art teaching have changed along with technology over the last few decades. Although traditional approaches are still valid, many have been replaced by more flexible digital alternatives.

Visual resources

Some parts of the curriculum will contain information that is useful each year:

- Examples of colour theory or chiaroscuro can be reused with new students.
- Sets of images to do with a theme may be useful in stimulating early ideas.
- Saving these references for future use prevents some repetitive resource preparation:
  - **Class sets of visual learning sheets:** Store these learning sheets in folders. Consider laminating them to make them last longer.
  - **Books:** Use art and design books in the classroom for demonstrations or one–to–one advice. (A list of suggested books for each media is contained on the introductory page of each media section in Part III).
  - **Magazines:** Collect and store magazines because they provide useful reference material, as well as contemporary art and design examples.
  - **OHP, slides and transparencies:** Use acetate projectors and transparencies, as they allow images to be shown at a large scale.
  - **Exemplar student material:** Try to retain some examples of good practice by previous students where possible. Allowing your class to see work by recent students makes the challenge of their own work more real and achievable. Sketchbooks and supporting studies can really help students to understand the concept of 'development'.

Digital reference materials

Digital storage and access have become very useful in teaching art and design. Through the internet, you and your students can look at endless examples of images for inspiration, or to use as references. It is also a good way to store more exemplar material from students. However, this material will need to be updated as students leave the school and to avoid it becoming too dated.

- **Digital slide shows:** Topic introductions and presentations are easily stored digitally. In some schools, these can be accessed by students to use for further reference. Updating digital material is simple to do, and makes your presentations much more flexible.
- **Intranet exemplar material:** Example work for themes and projects can be stored digitally. There is no limit to digital storage, and taking photographs of student work means that you do not have to retain the actual material. However, looking at real examples of work in the classroom has additional befits in the appreciation of scale, texture and context.
- **Internet visual references:** Suggested websites and image searches provide invaluable benefits in sourcing visual images. A wide range of devices enable students to view images in full colour and rich detail.
- **Visual records of site visits and class activities:** An accessible library of images from a class visit allows for further reference at a later date.

Study from life

Observational drawing remains at the heart of the IGCSE. Site visits and homework can provide many options for this work, but working in the classroom with teacher direction will give students a confident grounding in drawing what they see.

- **Still-life objects:** A store of interesting visual objects enables still-life work to be set up for a variety of themes. Collect items such as mechanical parts, organic shapes, shoes and cloth.
- **Lighting:** Control of lighting can be useful when teaching tonal values. Lamps can add stronger shadows or be used instead of natural light to maintain consistent lighting.
- **Back cloths:** A large sheet of light or dark cloth can be used to cover distracting elements or to help still-life objects stand out.
- **Plinths:** Boxes enable still-life objects to be arranged on multiple levels. This is particularly useful with large classes to give everyone a good view.
- **Green screen:** A small area can be covered with coloured paper or cloth for green screen photography. This method allows people or objects to be separated more easily from the background using digital art software.

Recycled materials store

Collecting and saving materials that might be thrown away provides a wealth of opportunities for an art and design department. Students can be involved in this collecting activity for sound environmental reasons. If you are in contact with local businesses, then you may find that they are willing to give you waste items that you can use. In some countries, there are educational charities that store waste items for reuse by the local community, including schools.

- **Newspaper and magazines** are useful for class painting, papier-mâché, collage and many other activities.
- **Containers** such as disposable containers, cartons and bottles can all be reused for mixing paint, as mixing palettes or in mixed-media constructions.
- **Corrugated cardboard and tubes** are useful for sculpture projects, printmaking and collage work.
- **Wooden off-cuts** are useful for sculpture and 3-D work. If you have a technology department, it may be able to supply you with this type of material.

Workshop materials

It is useful to have a small stock of tools and fastenings for hanging work, stretching canvases and countless unexpected jobs:

- **Tools:** General wood-working/DIY tools, such as hammers, saws, screwdrivers, awls, g-clamps, pliers, canvas pliers and staple guns
- **Fastenings:** Nails, screws, pins, picture hooks, frame–hanging fastenings and staples
- **Wood:** Various uses, such as to make stretchers and boards for painting surfaces
- **Canvas:** Cotton canvas rolls.

The supply of additional materials for projects varies according to each school. Well-resourced schools may cater for all student needs, while others will charge a small amount for these extra costs. Over a period of time, you will build up a list of local suppliers that can be used for these items.

SUBJECT AREA REFERENCE SOURCES

Painting and related media	*The Story of Art* (ISBN 978–0714832470) *The Shock of the New: Art and the Century of Change* (ISBN 978–0500275825) Urban Sketchers is a global community that explores different drawing styles and how people sketch outdoors. They can be found online. The National Film Board of Canada has examples of many animation techniques.
Printmaking	*Printmaking: A Complete Guide to Materials & Processes* (ISBN 978–1780671949) *Monotype/Monoprint: History and Techniques* (ISBN 978–0961261047) A useful website to refer to is the introduction to printmaking created by the Museum of Modern Art (MOMA). You will get an overview on the history of relief printing as well as short tutorial guides to help you with your techniques. The Encyclopedia Britannica provides a good reference for an overview of different printmaking techniques.
Three-dimensional studies	*The Elements of Sculpture: A Viewer's Guide* (ISBN 978–0714867410) *The Craft and Art of Clay: A Complete Potter's Handbook* (ISBN 978–1856697286) *Product Design* (portfolio) (ISBN 978–1856697514) For some interesting examples and information on sculpture, search for The International Sculpture Conference online. Go online for some background on world costume design.
Graphic communication	*Graphic Design Rules: 365 Essential Design Dos and Don'ts* (ISBN 978–0711233461) *Illustration* (Portfolio) (ISBN 978–1856697101) A useful website can be found by searching for 'D and AD' online. This is a great place to look at examples of the broad range of contemporary graphic communication examples, including designers working in your country or region. *Information is beautiful*, a book by HarperCollins Publishers, has some great ideas about how to do information design really well. The website of the book is an excellent resource for the same ideas.
Photography, digital and lens-based media	*Understanding Exposure: How to Shoot Great Photographs with Any Camera* (ISBN–13: 978–0817439392) The Learning Zone section of the Ilford Photo website has some good guidance on developing film and traditional print.
Textiles	*Fashion Design* (Portfolio) (ISBN 978–1856696197) *Printed Textile Design* (ISBN 978–1780671185) The Textile Study Group website has examples of contemporary textiles work by several UK makers.

CLASSROOM MANAGEMENT

Setting up working spaces

Your teaching area may range from a single classroom that is also be used for other subjects, to a well–resourced art department. Given these many possibilities, the following section provides general advice to consider when arranging a studio space or art department. Despite the limitations of space and budget, some simple changes can improve a working environment.

Access

Unless you are involved in a new-build, options for access are fixed but some changes can help with the entry of students to the classroom. Sometimes you will need to work with the school to ensure suitable access for students with disabilities.

- **Floor level:** A ground-floor level offers ease of access for heavy equipment and the movement of large work. A higher floor may offer better views, which could be used for observational drawing, as well as more natural light.
- **Delivery of supplies:** Many art supplies are heavy (paper, paint, clay) and there can be problems transporting these goods and equipment up narrow stairs, and onto higher floors. Separate access to a central store room can be useful.
- **Bags, coats and aprons:** A place to store bags and coats on entry, and to collect aprons, helps with movement around the classroom. Coat hooks are useful, and sometimes there is room for a bag store. Damage from spillages is also reduced if there are no bags beneath desks.

Movement around the classroom

Consider the placement of seating, sinks and work areas.

- **Flooring:** Materials such as linoleum or tiles that are waterproof and resist staining are ideal.
- **Student seating:** Stackable stools are flexible to use and take up less space. If you have more stools than students, they can also be used as side tables and rests.
- **Tables:** Large tables are good for bigger work and group work. However, also consider flexibility so that the layout of the tables can be changed easily (see classroom set up and activities pages 19–20). Hard, wipeable surfaces are easier to clean.
- **Sink area:** Several deep sinks and taps are ideal to provide a group of students with space to clean equipment quickly at the end of a lesson. Deep sinks are needed for larger containers and buckets. Draining areas and racks are needed to store palettes, water containers and brushes. A dispensing table near the sink provides a space for paint to be put on palettes away from student work.
- **Work storage:** Storage of work is usually in folders or large drawers. Large folders can be awkward for everyday access, and are best placed in racks to prevent them from falling over. Day-to-day work can be kept in drawers and transferred to folders when complete.
- **Drying racks:** Wire drying racks allow a lot of wet work to be stored quickly, and enable the room to be cleared, ready for the next class. Work can be hung overhead from a ball drying rack or a line of pegs.
- **Materials accessibility:** Small supplies of materials can be accessible for students in the class without being dispensed by the teacher. This will depend upon the school, but might include crayons, watercolours, paper, scissors and glue.
- **Safety:** It should be possible for access to hazardous equipment, such as knives and hot glue guns, to be restricted by the teacher. Ways to achieve this include lockable cupboards or dispensing these items on a lesson-by-lesson basis. ⚠

Safe internet use and site visits

You should ensure that student use of the internet is safe and appropriate for the school's internet-use policy. Notices in the classroom at the computers can be useful, but the increasing use of hand-held devices requires this advice to be emphasised for all internet use.

When planning site visits, ensure that the school's policies are carefully followed and that a note about safety visits is included in visit information given to students.

Demonstration area and whiteboard

An area central to most students is useful you as the teacher to demonstrate techniques. Consider lighting and sightlines for the placement of visual aids.

- **Lighting:** Natural light is ideal and very effective from overhead, but direct sunlight can be too bright and some form of shade will be required. The ability to darken or blackout a room is required for the use of projectors. Artificial light is controllable, but needs to be bright enough to allow colour choices to be made accurately.
- **Teacher desk:** A desk with visibility of the whole classroom is ideal for monitoring activity while possibly having individual discussions.
- **Chalkboard/whiteboard/projector/OHP:** Some form of large board is needed for explaining vocabulary, and giving explanatory notes and diagrams. This should be visible to the entire seated class. A clear wall or screen may be required for the use of a projector.
- **Display areas:** Walls with pin boards allow work to be displayed easily. Shelving is also useful for 3-D work. Higher spaces and ceiling hangings can make imaginative use of a classroom to display student work. Students are motivated by seeing their work on display and it can be a good start for critical discussions.

Digital work areas

Departments are using more digital equipment. This is still a fast–moving area of development and individual situations vary greatly.

- **Desktop machines:** Desktop computers, if you have them, are best placed in a separate working bay so that students can access them, but they are away from the sinks and messy areas.
- **Laptop power supply:** The use of laptops is usually dependent on a power source. Additional sockets help with this, but they should be kept away from sinks and areas of student movement.
- **WiFi:** With suitable network access, a wide range of devices can be used in class at the student's working area. With permission, students can use their own devices to collect and review images.
- **Printing:** Network printing facilities are required if you have several students working digitally. There are issues with costs and management of printed material.

Cleaning

Some equipment is needed to keep the department tidy during a busy teaching day:

- **Hand towels** – for control of paint on brushes, as well as drying hands when cleaning up
- **Soap or cleanser** – for cleaning brushes and hands
- **Cleaning cloths** – several cloths for cleaning tables and making tidying easier at the end of a lesson
- **Mop and bucket** – for dealing with major spillages quickly if they are readily at hand.

Specialist equipment

There are challenges in using a generalist room for specialist activities. Good organisation and storage can overcome many problems, but you may experience some of these issues:

- Printmaking uses a lot of space and clearing up can take longer.
- Three-dimensional studies require space for materials, storage, drying areas and possibly a kiln. Dust levels need to be controlled.
- Textiles and graphics require a clean environment.
- Photography can require extensive access to computers and printers. Wet photography requires an area that can be used as a darkroom.

Painting and related media

Some equipment is needed.

- **Easels:** These are helpful for upright drawing and painting on boards or canvas. Some storage space may be required.

Printmaking

Relief work can be successfully printed by hand, but a press is required for intaglio work. Small- to medium-sized screen printing can be achieved without using a vacuum bed:

- **Relief printing:** Cutting tools, bench hooks, rollers and ink plates, as well as barrens or spoons for printing by hand
- **Intaglio printing:** Etching plates, etching solutions, inking rollers and wiping scrim
- **Screen printing:** Printing screens, squeegees, screen-washing sink area and a jet washer.

Three-dimensional studies

Much work can be taught using construction materials such as card, wire and papier-mâché. However, casting and welding are areas that need specialist advice and equipment. More commonly, clay is often taught in generalist rooms but does benefit from specialist facilities:

- **Ceramics:** Clay bins, plaster slab, clay boards, rollers, damp cupboard and a kiln.

Photography

Many digital devices can be used for photography and much of the processing and presentation of images can be digital. Film cameras can be obtained cheaply, but processing materials are required as well as darkroom facilities.

- **Digital printing:** Larger format inkjet printers and quality papers need to be budgeted for.
- **Studio equipment:** Back drops, lights, reflectors, tripods and flash guns are needed.
- **Dark room facilities**: These include developing chemicals and trays, an enlarger and a darkroom.

Graphic communication

Printed materials and card construction often only require simple materials and a clean working environment but there is an increasing reliance on digital tools to produce very high-quality results:

- **Sundry materials:** Layout paper, tracing paper, marker pens and foam board
- **Machines:** Digital printers, digital cutters and 3-D printers.

Textiles design

Storage and maintenance of textiles machines in a non-specialist room requires good planning. Power points need to be accessible for sewing machines.

- **Large tables** are needed for cutting of patterns and laying out material.
- **Sundry equipment** includes a tailor's dummy, ironing boards and irons.
- **Machines** include those for sewing (with an overlocker), knitting and weaving.

Storage of materials

Materials can be stored in individual classrooms or a central stock cupboard, and there are advantages to both approaches. Storage space is essential for a busy classroom used by several classes. Regular stocktaking will ensure that you know which supplies need to be reordered. Student access to materials helps the flow of creativity, especially at more advanced stages of the course, but needs to be monitored to avoid wasteful use of resources.

Some of the following points will be relevant to your department:

- Lockable cupboards or storage will be required for hazardous materials or equipment.
- Climate control can prevent paint containers from drying out in hot countries.
- Strong, wide shelves are required for paper storage.
- Spare paint stocks are best kept locked away, or students will keep taking the unopened bottles of paint.
- Lockable cupboards are useful for expensive items such as cameras and digital tablets.
- Craft boxes are good for storing class sets of tools.
- Shadow boards (lockable) are common in technology departments. They help keep equipment organised and secure.

Student work

Storage and display of student work needs to be considered. This includes past student's work and display around the school. The rotation of display work keeps the classroom up to date and makes sure that student work is correctly stored. Consider displaying work in other areas of the school. Locations directly outside the art department are good showcase areas for the subject. Your school may have a small art gallery space, but the school entrance foyer and other communal areas are also excellent places to show student work.

- Current work will need storing in drawers and/or folders.
- Display boards can be used to show work-in-progress, or examples of completed projects. Displays of current students' work will boost their confidence and interest in the subject.
- Display plinths are useful for many purposes including display and still life.
- Shelving is useful for storage of 3-D work and equipment such as drawing boards.
- Space is required for work retained for assessment and submission, as well as older work used as exemplar material.

Classroom set up and activities

Movement around the classroom depends upon the activity, group size and teaching style. There are many different ways to arrange furniture and make full use of the space available. Try not to see the furniture as fixed. Instead, try to move it around to suit your lesson and activity. The lesson plan sections in Part III contain specific guidance on layouts for activities.

Individual working

Students can work independently using the space available at their table. However, with large-scale work and a small classroom, this can require some teacher management. Arrange the tables to maximise student movement to sinks and materials, but ensure that you retain sight of everyone's work areas.

Paired working

For discussions, students can work well next to their neighbour. However, often you may want students to draw each other and they will need to be seated opposite each other to do this effectively. This often requires teacher direction.

Group projects

IGCSE Art & Design work is assessed on the work of individual students, but group work can be very effective for workshops and discussions. A table, or several small tables, can be used to create an area to work around. A group of four or five students might work well around a medium-sized table. Large groups work well for quick activities, but can lead to some students not working effectively over longer periods of time.

Still life/figure drawing

When drawing a still life or doing some figure drawing, move the tables to create a central space for the objects or person. This space may be a circular or U–shaped arrangement that ensures all students can see what they are drawing. Some students will enjoy helping to make these changes to the classroom. By planning around other classes, a still life could remain in the classroom for the duration of the project.

Clearing up

Without organisation, a classroom can be left in quite a mess at the end of a lesson. By giving specific jobs to students, you can avoid congestion at the sinks, and brushes and palettes being left uncleaned. Monitors can be appointed, or responsibilities rotated over a series of lessons.

Specialist activities

Some subject areas involve messy processes. More preparation and thought need to go into the arrangement of a room for these lessons. Printmaking and sculpture often require plenty of space and the use of a range of materials. Plan these lessons so that the room can be arranged suitably and allow more time for clearing up.

Demonstrations and presentations

A visual and practical subject requires a lot of demonstration by the teacher. Choose a space in the room to use regularly for this purpose, so that students can move to the area quickly and see the activity clearly. A large table will work for most situations. Some teachers use a digital camera to video their demonstrations and project them on to a larger screen. This method allows students to remain in their seats while seeing the task being demonstrated.

A chalkboard or whiteboard is useful for diagrams and specialist vocabulary. Digital projectors are widely used and work well for showing examples of artwork.

Tips for subject areas

Below are some tips and advice for particular subject areas.

Painting and related media

- Drying areas are important for the storage of wet work. A drying rack is very useful for larger classes in a busy school.
- Oil paint introduces unpleasant solvents into the classroom, so consider using water-soluble oil paints to avoid hazardous fumes.
- Spray booths make aerosol paints and glue sprays much safer for indoor use.
- Paint wastage can be high if the paint area is not monitored or students have free access to new stocks of paint.
- Disposal of acrylic paint can block sinks. It is best for students to scrape the majority of the paint onto some newspaper and place it in a waste bin.

Printmaking

- There are now solvent-free methods and materials for most printmaking techniques. The use of these methods and techniques allows work to be made without worrying about toxic materials or fumes.
- Space requirements for printmaking can be considerable. With several students producing multiple prints, make sure that you have enough drying space available.

Three-dimensional studies

- Clay recycling can reduce the cost of buying new clay, but requires time and organisation.
- Working space, drying space and firing space are all required for ceramic work.
- Dust can be a health hazard and ceramics rooms should be regularly washed down to remove this problem.

Textiles

- A clean environment is important to keep fabric clean. Dust, ink stains or unwiped tables from other activities can easily ruin expensive textiles.
- Textile machines are delicate and need to be stored away at the end of a lesson. This can take time, as well as a considerable amount of space.

ELEMENTS OF ART

INTRODUCTION

The elements of art are very useful in helping students to analyse and discuss both their own work and that of others. In terms of the Assessment Objectives, these elements can be valuable for students in addressing the following:

- **AO1:** The elements of art can be useful in guiding students to compose and arrange their observation recording work.
- **AO2:** The elements of art can enable students to make more informed decisions when experimenting with materials and assessing the most effective approaches to develop further
- **AO3:** The elements of art give students a vocabulary they can use to discuss works of art and decisions in their own work.
- **AO4:** Knowledge of the elements of art enables students to demonstrate an understanding of visual language in their written work, and helps with discussions in class.

Definitions

The elements are described below. Often students will only be concerned with one or two of these elements at any one time:

- A **line** is a clear path created by an object or tool in space, varying in thickness, direction and length.
- **Tone** or 'value' describes light and dark qualities in an artwork. A tonal scale shows a gradient of tones from lightest to darkest.
- **Texture** describes a surface quality. Actual texture is something you can feel. Implied texture is communicated visually.
- **Colour** can be explained as reflected light. A 'hue' is another word for a pure colour. Colour 'saturation' refers to the intensity of colour in an image.
- **Shape** describes the contour or outline of something. Shapes are two-dimensional.
- **Form** relates to the length, width and height of an object in space. Therefore, forms are three-dimensional.
- **Space** refers to a three-dimensional feeling in an artwork. Positive space denotes the area that an object takes up. Negative space is the area between objects.

WHEN TO INTRODUCE THE ELEMENTS OF ART TO STUDENTS?

The elements of art can seem abstract and irrelevant to students if they are not presented in context. By introducing the elements as they come up in practical work, students can see how they relate to their own work. The order of introduction will depend upon the subject area. For example, shape and form may be introduced in three-dimensional studies ahead of colour or texture. For painting and related media, the following order might relate to the projects you introduce to students:

- **Line, tone** and **texture** can easily be demonstrated using a pencil and paper. Drawing is an easy and immediate way to demonstrate these properties to students.
- **Colour** provides an opportunity to introduce students to paints and colour mixing. Pastels and colouring crayons can also be used but limit the range of colour properties that can be explored.
- **Shape** can be explored in line, but scissors and paper cut-outs provide an alternative way to do this.
- **Form** and **space** may be introduced during observational drawing. Otherwise, another good time to introduce these concepts is when students are composing their designs.

Line

Continuous line drawings

Free-flowing unbroken lines are created by maintaining constant contact between the drawing tool and the paper. It can be hard to avoid the temptation to erase 'mistakes' at first, but after a short time this drawing method develops confidence, drawing speed and encourages hand, eye and brain co-ordination. The example by Picasso, (see *Portrait of Igor Stravinsky* on page 14 in the Student's Book), shows how much information can be conveyed simply by using line. It is a direct way to work that most students feel comfortable with.

Skills activity A	• Continuous line drawing
Materials	• Fine-liner pen or ballpoint pen (this prevents students from using their erasers)
Description	• Students look at a seated figure, or still life. They draw with the pen without lifting it from the paper. They can stop and start, but will feel pressured to complete their drawings quickly. The completed drawings may be out of proportion but will have a spontaneous quality.

Mark-making techniques

Line can be used to apply tone (light and dark) to a drawing. In the drawing by Vince Low (see scribble drawing style on page 15 in the Student's Book), scribble lines have been overlaid to create depth and shadow. Fine lines add subtle shadows to the skin and facial features.

Skills activity A	• Scribble drawing
Materials	• Ballpoint pen or fine-liner pen on smooth cartridge
Description	• Ask students to find or bring in a celebrity portrait that contains good light and shadows. Students can draw the image for themselves by varying the spaces between lines, the thickness of the lines and the weight (lightness/darkness of the line). They can also try using small dashes, hatching, cross-hatching, stippling (dots) and scribbling.

Top tip
- Contour drawings can lead to making wire sculptures. Light-weight wire is easily bent into shapes to create three-dimensional 'drawings'. Pliers may be needed to help with twisting, bending, cutting and joining pieces of wire.

Artists and line

Sir Michael Craig-Martin (CBE, RA) is an Irish contemporary artist and painter. His minimalist style often references the 'readymade' concept inspired by Marcel Duchamp. Craig-Martin's later works employ a stylised drawing technique depicting everyday household objects. There is no differentiation in treatment of objects and surfaces. Lines of equal mechanical width combine with brightly coloured images. Some paintings are simple, while others are complex, produced by many overlapping lines and shapes. Craig-Martin has broken down the demarcations between 'painting' and 'sculpture'. See page 15 of the Student's Book for some examples of Craig-Martin's work.

Skills activity A	• Line drawings of overlapping objects
Materials	• Pencil and black marker pen
Description	• Using real objects or photographs, students can draw in pencil a series of kitchen objects on a large sheet of paper (A2). The objects can be drawn from different angles and at different sizes so that they overlap and fill much of the paper. • Students can decide which object is at the front of the drawing and erase overlapping items inside its shape. They repeat this until there are no overlapping lines in the objects on the paper. • Students use a thin marker to go over the pencil lines and create a bold line drawing. • This work can be extended to digital colour by photographing the drawings and working on them in a bitmap program to fill each object with a different colour.

Tone

Developing an understanding of tonal value (variations of light and shade) is important. Mastering the effects of light and shade can be challenging, but with practice it becomes easier, and drawings become more sophisticated when tone is added. Most compositions have light, dark and a range of mid-tones or values. Contrast is created by differences in tonal value, particularly in drawing and photography. See page 16 in the Student's Book an example of tonal value scale.

Skills activity B	• Make a tonal scale with pencil(s)
Materials	• Pencil, ballpoint pen, fine-liner
Description	• Draw a pencil grid to fit tonal shades similar to the value scale example shown. • Use a pencil to shade the boxes from very dark to white. • Use scribbled biro to create a different set of tonal values that use overlapping line rather than graduated shading. • Use a fine liner with dots or cross-hatching to create an alternative tonal scale.

Light and shade

Sometimes everyday objects can distract students from looking at tonal values, as colour and reflection are hard to ignore. By making some simple geometric objects from card and painting them matt white, a series of abstract still-life objects can be used to focus on tonal values. Chiaroscuro drawing can be demonstrated by using a strong light source such as an angle poise lamp.

Skills activity C	• Chiaroscuro drawing
Materials	• Charcoal and eraser
Description	• Outline shapes drawn in charcoal. Rub down the drawing with a cloth to make a ghost image. Use charcoal shading and an eraser to create a tonal drawing. • Spray the drawing with a fixative to prevent smudging.

Artists and tone

Georges Seurat (1859–1891) was a French painter and draughtsman. He is famous for his paintings using the pointillist technique where small dots of colour make up the painting. He often worked on textured paper when drawing, using the raised surface to break up the tone of his shading in a similar way to his paintings. In *A Woman Fishing* (see page 17 in the Student's Book), graduated shading has been used to show a woman fishing. The effect is quite dreamlike, as if looking through a screen or a mist.

Skills activity D	• Tonal magazine drawing
Materials	• Large magazine image of a face, pencil
Description	• Find an interesting image in a magazine. • Tear or cut out a section. Sketch out proportions lightly. • Use tone or mark-making to describe tone and texture within the area.

Texture

Texture is the feel, appearance, or consistency of a surface or a substance. It refers to the tactile qualities of an object or surface – in other words, how this work feels to the touch. Texture is one of the most fundamental elements of three-dimensional art. It is an element that is carefully considered by artists and particularly sculptors.

In *The great forest* by Max Ernst (see page 18 in the Student's Book), the artist has used rubbings to create an ancient forest. This technique of taking a rubbing from an uneven surface is also called frottage.

Skills activity E	• Frottage drawing
Materials	• Graphite stick or wax crayon
Description	• Experiment with making rubbings of textures in the environment around you. This could mean human-made objects or natural forms such as tree bark. Use media such as chunky wax crayons. • Make a composite image from the rubbings you have made. You can cut them up and arrange as you would a collage.

Observation

Textures often need to be viewed close-up to appreciate their structure and understand how to draw them. A magnifying lens or macro photography can help students to see the repeated patterns in many manufactured textures such as the image of woven cloth on page 18 in the Student's Book.

Additional skills activity	• Macro photography
Materials	• Camera or tablet with macro facility
Description	• Collect a range of organic and human-made objects with textures; cloth, wood, metal, shells, bones and sliced vegetables. • Use a square format and take close-up images of the objects, printing them out as mini pictures of about six to an A4 sheet. • Present this research in a sketchbook, grouping similar textures.

Artist and texture

The Boyle Family is best known for their series of 'Earth Studies' (see *Olympia Station*, London Series on page 19 in the Student's Book). This series are three-dimensional casts of the ground, which record unremarkable sites with great accuracy.

The works combine natural and human-made materials from the site (stones, dust, tarmac) with paint and resins, preserving the qualities of the ground surface to make unique one-off pieces that interpret the environment. The Boyle Family began this series of works by randomly placing pins in a map and using this to determine the locations they recorded.

Additional skills activity	• Photography
Materials	• Camera or tablet
Description	• Photograph areas of the school where there are very different floor surfaces and textures.* • Select one image to use as a reference for an oil pastel study. • On a large square of paper, recreate the floor surface using coloured pastels. Smudge and blend them for smooth areas, and use roughly to create broken textures. * Alternatively, find a suitable area to observe and draw on location around the school.

Colour

Artists refer to a 'colour wheel' of logically arranged pure hues of **primary colours** (red, blue and yellow) and **secondary colours** (purple, green and orange) made from mixing the primary colours (see the colour wheel on page 20 in the Student's Book).

Analogous colours are colours next to each other in the colour wheel. They are often called **harmonious** colours.

Additional skills activity	• Colour mixing
Materials	• Watercolours
Description	• Paint a colour wheel using lemon yellow, ultramarine blue and light red. • Repeat using warm yellow, dark blue and scarlet or crimson red. • Some colours produce better oranges, purples and greens. Use all the colours to make a more accurate colour wheel.

Warm and cool colours

Warm colours are considered to be reds, oranges and sometimes yellows or browns (earth colours). Cool colours have a blue base, but may be green or purple in colour.

Additional skills activity	• Warm and cool colours
Materials	• Acrylics
Description	• Start with swatches of yellow, light blue and brown in the middle of a sheet of paper. • To the left add small amounts of red to the colour and paint a swatch, increasing the amount of red in the colour each time. • Repeat to the right using blue. • The subtle colour changes at first show you how a small amount of warm or cool colour can affect your colour mixing.

Complementary colours

Complementary colours are opposite each other in the colour wheel, for example, a combination of yellows and purples, or reds and greens or oranges and blues. When mixed together, these colours create different types of grey. Using a complementary colour can help to dull a colour that is too bright in a painting, but this is a concept that students only understand after some painting experience.

Additional skills activity	• Complementary greys
Materials	• Acrylics
Description	• Mix some purple with lemon yellow and a small amount of white, painting small swatches of test colour. Eventually a mid-grey will be mixed. • Compare this with greys mixed from cadmium red and mid-green, ultramarine blue and orange.

Artists and colour

'If you put paint on to a canvas with a brush, you know what it will do. But what if you use something else to apply the paint? It's going to do something different, perhaps something you never expected.

Recently I've been applying paint with a syringe, which is an incredibly precise instrument for controlling liquid. It has allowed me to concentrate on colour and the sequence of colours rather than focusing all my attention on the paint and how it flows.'

Ian Davenport – *The Guardian*, Sunday 20 September 2009

Ian Davenport, English abstract painter, uses colour literally by the bucket load! Many of Davenport's works are made by pouring paint onto a tilted surface and letting gravity spread the paint over the surface.

Skills activity G	• Make a painting by using tools other than a brush.
Materials	• Ready mixed tempera paint, analogous colours (slightly diluted poster paint)
Description	• Collect a range of alternative tools for experimental painting: toothbrushes, old rough brushes, sponges, palette knives, thick card and crushed newspaper. • Place the colours on flat palettes so that crushed paper and sponges can be dipped in them. • Work with paper on the floor to drip, sponge, splatter and spread different-coloured paints. • Try the same effects with paper raised on a board to see the effects of gravity.

Shape

Humans develop an ability to analyse shape from a young age. We recognise two major types of shapes:

1. **Geometric or inorganic shapes**
* These shapes are angular and frequently appear in human-made objects.
* These shapes are typically made up of straight lines or shapes, and fixed and definite shapes.
* Most geometric shapes have names, which is a clear difference when compared to organic shapes.
* Examples of geometric shapes are circles, ovals, triangles, rectangles, squares and so on.

2. **Organic or irregular shapes**
* These are more irregular in shape.
* Each one is different and they are bounded by free-flowing curves that suggest fluidity.
* Organic shapes are commonly found in nature.

An example is *Star (Etoile)*, a plaster sculpture by Hans Arp. The organic star shape is balanced on a large plinth, which is a geometric cylinder.

Skills activity H	• Cut paper collage
Materials	• Coloured paper, pencils, scissors
Description	• Draw and cut out several sets of geometric paper. Fold the paper over so you can cut two or three shapes at a time. Create the following: a triangle, square, rectangle, trapezoid, semi-circle, circle and oval, and any other shapes that are geometric. • Take one set of geometric shapes and alter them to make them more organic. Cut round edges at the corners, cut irregular shapes from the inside, and make the edges of circles wavy. • Make a composition that contrasts these different types of shapes. You could make the silhouettes of a sculpture, such as those by Hans Arp.

Artists and shape

An artist famous for exploring the possibilities of mixing geometric and biomorphic shapes was Henri Matisse. In the last few decades of his artistic career, he developed a new form of art-making: the paper cut-out. At this time, Matisse was confined mostly to his bed and to a wheelchair due to severe intestinal disease.

Still fascinated by the power of colour, he began cutting coloured papers and arranging them into designs. See an example of his work on page 22 in the Student's Book.

'Instead of drawing an outline and filling in the colour...I am drawing directly in colour,' he said.

Additional skills activity	• Coloured paper cut-out
Materials	• Acrylic paint, decorating brushes, scissors, A2 cartridge
Description	• Colour sheets of paper with acrylic washes in a range of primary and secondary colours. The colour should be strong but liquid so it is absorbed into the paper, • Use a collection of natural forms for observation, such as sea-shells, bones, pebbles and driftwood, as well as photographs of plant seed-heads and clouds. • Use a pencil to draw organic shapes from your references on the dry sheets of coloured paper. • Cut out the shapes with scissors and arrange the different elements to make an abstracted composition, using additional coloured paper shapes for the background. • There are videos on YouTube showing Matisse cutting and arranging his shapes with a long stick, as he was in wheelchair at this stage in his life.

Form

A shape that is given the third dimension of depth becomes a 'form'. Circles become spheres, squares become cubes and triangles become pyramids. Forms can be organic or geometric. In art, form can occupy space in a real or implied way. In a painting, a figure is just an illusion. With sculpture, form is real because it takes up three-dimensional space.

With the element of form, one has to think about things in three dimensions and this inevitably influences the selection of materials and processes used to make artwork.

The sculpture *Agricola IV* by David Smith shows an open form sculpture with lots of negative space. The original was made by welding steel tools and pipes together.

Materials and tools

Many materials and tools can be used to create sculptural forms:

- **Carving media:** Bone, glass, stone, ice, ivory, marble, wax, wood and clay.
- **Casting media:** Cement, clay, metal, plaster, plastic, synthetic resin and wax.
- **Modelling media:** Clay, card, papier-mâché, plaster, sand and Styrofoam.
- **Assembled media:** Beads, corrugated card, foil, found objects, glue, paper-board, foam-board, textiles, wire, wood, edible material and materials in nature.
- **Tools:** Brush, chisel, hammer, mallet, clamp, vice, knife, pliers, potter's wheel, kiln, power tools, sandpaper, saw, scraper, snips, wire-cutters and welding torch.

Additional skills activity	• Scrap materials tower
Materials	• Small food cartons, boxes and containers, hot glue gun, thin tying wire, tape
Description	• Try building a balanced tower from some of the collected materials. • Use the glue gun or tape to help the objects stay upright. You can punch holes and tie objects with wire as well. • See whether you can make an interesting tower four or five objects high. • Photograph it with a white background to capture its silhouette.

Artist and actual form

'I enjoy the freedom of just using my hands and "found" tools…a sharp stone, the quill of a feather, thorns.

I take the opportunities each day offers. If it is snowing, I work with snow, at leaf-fall, it will be with leaves, a blown-over tree becomes a source of twigs and branches. I stop at a place or pick up a material because I feel that there is something to be discovered. Here is where I can learn.'

Andy Goldsworthy

Born in 1956, Andy Goldsworthy, OBE, is a contemporary British sculptor, photographer and environmentalist. He is well-known for his site-specific sculpture and land art. He lives and works in Scotland.

Andy Goldsworthy has made work from a wide variety of natural materials, for example: leaves, petals, twigs, branches, thorns, sticks, sand, stone, slate, ice, mud, ice, pebbles, boulders, snow, bark, grass and pine cones.

Goldsworthy's creations, such as *Leaves*, shell leafwork, (see page 25 in the Student's Book), are 'ephemeral' or limited in time and space. Goldsworthy photographs his work before it collapses, melts or gets washed away. His photography is therefore a crucial and integral part of his work as an artist.

Forms in Andy Goldsworthy's work include cones, towers, arcs, domes, eggs and spirals. Materials are piled, stacked, balanced, interwoven, grouped and arranged.

Skills activity I	• Use found materials in the natural environment to create individual small-scale sculptures using only hands and homemade tools
Materials	• Found objects, simple tools and fastenings
Description	• Decide which materials you want to use, such as leaves, twigs, stones and flowers. • Experiment with how you can arrange these elements to make an artwork in the environment. • Photograph your experiments and discuss the best ones back in class. • In class, consider the following questions: o What does it feel like to work outside? o What does it feel like to work with your hands? o What problems did you encounter? o How can art make a difference in the environment? o How can artists make a difference in the environment through art?

Space

Space is the illusion of distance on a two-dimensional surface such as a canvas, board or a sheet of paper. Artists employ tone and perspective to achieve a sense of space in their work. The element of space means the background, foreground and middle ground, and refers to the distances or areas around, between and within things.

Artists are interested in using **negative space** and **positive space** in their work.

We live in a three-dimensional world of depth. We can tell that some objects around us seem closer and others appear further away.

Theory of space

The theory of space involves these concepts:

- **Size:** Larger objects appear closer, while smaller objects seem further away.
- **Overlap:** Partially covering one shape or object with another makes the one in front appear closer.
- **Placement:** The creation of depth in a painting depends on where a shape or object is in relation to the horizon line. Things closer to the horizon line appear further away. Objects nearer to the top or bottom of the canvas appear closer in the image.
- **Atmospheric perspective:** As objects recede into the distance, they begin to lose colour, brightness and detail.
- **Shading:** Shapes mimic the way real objects would appear under the same lighting.
- **Linear perspective:** This concept was developed during the Renaissance (1400–1500). Drawn lines converge on vanishing points to achieve a more realistic illusion of space. Linear perspective is described by the number of vanishing points used – either 'one point', 'two point' or 'three point.'
- **Positive and negative space:** Positive and negative space is important in determining the overall composition in a work of art. In simple terms, positive space is best described as the areas in a work of art that are the subjects or areas of interest. Negative space is the area around the subjects or areas of interest. By understanding and applying positive and negative space, you will create more successful compositional work.

Additional skills activity	• Atmospheric perspective and placement
Materials	• Watercolours, landscape format paper and pencil
Description	• Paint a graduated wash in green that is just water at the top of the paper and becomes a mid-green at the bottom. • Draw objects in light pencil on the dry wash, for example trees, houses and people, which are very small near the top of the paper and get bigger as they move lower down and nearer the viewer. • Mix washes of another colour such as dark blue. • Paint very light washes on the small objects and use stronger washes on objects as they get bigger and nearer. • The aim is to make it look like the top of the painting is much further in the distance using size and transparency.

Artist and space

The Russian-American sculptor Alexander Liberman created artwork assembled from industrial objects (such as segments of steel I-beams, pipes, drums and so on), often painted in uniform bright colours.

There is much exploration of positive and negative space in his work. In *Sculpture* (see page 28 in the Student's Book), Liberman has used a variety of flame-like shapes to create a sculpture full of movement, but each element is a simple flat object. The sheets are welded together from tabs and slots in the metal sections.

Skills activity J	• Cardboard slot sculpture
Materials	• Cardboard and wood scraps/off-cuts if you need a base plinth, gum tape
Description	• Cut geometric or organic shapes from corrugated cardboard. • Play with possible arrangements and the draw lines where you need slots. • Cut slots and/or make tabs to attach sections. • Construct the sculpture using glue and gum tape. • If there is time, prime the sculpture with white emulsion paint and then colour with strong acrylic paint.

Summary

The elements of art are the individual parts that make up a whole artwork. They could be termed the 'building blocks' of art.

A student cannot create art successfully without them. Students can work well without this knowledge, but they will find that analysing artwork is much easier if they understand the elements of art being used. Most artworks will use at least one or two aspects of these concepts.

Knowing and understanding the elements of art enables students to analyse, describe and explain the work an artist has created and communicate their thoughts using precise vocabulary.

The elements are best taught in relation to practical art examples and revisited often to help embed the understanding.

PART I: PRACTICAL GUIDANCE AND CHECKLIST

Chapter 1 — Coursework

The coursework period lays the foundations of knowledge and skills that students require to produce personal and coherent work. The design of the course will determine how students learn to explore a range of different materials and ideas. The aim is to gradually build up students' confidence to enable them to make more informed choices later in the course.

UNIT 1: PREPARING FOR YOUR COURSEWORK

COURSEWORK SUBMISSION

The students' coursework must be submitted before the final date for the course, but time also needs to be allocated to the externally set assignment. By completing coursework before the externally set assignment period in the second year of the course, students can focus completely on the second element of their submission. The secure storage of coursework at this stage is important, as is allocating staff time for the assessment of the coursework.

The coursework submission consists of two elements:

• Portfolio	• Final outcome
• Four sheets (eight sides) of A2	• Up to A2 in size

Supporting portfolio

During the coursework period, students have time to experiment and develop their skills. Only a small selection of their coursework will be submitted for marking. This means that there is time for students to enjoy working with the new processes and skills to which you are introducing. As their interests become more focused, they will develop personal pieces of work and final pieces that reflect their own interests. When students submit their coursework for assessment, they will select examples of recording, exploration, development and evaluation that show how they came to make their final piece. They can use up to four sheets (eight sides) of A2.

Final outcome

This outcome is the final piece of work that students make based on their research and development work. It forms part of the submission and can be up to A2 in size. Students may work in any size or appropriate media, but any work that is fragile, three-dimensional or larger than A2 must be photographed, printed and mounted onto A2.

There are two examples of how students can present their final outcome in the Student's Book, on pages 54–57. These examples, on drawing and painting, and three-dimensional studies, show how students can include the Assessment Objectives clearly in their work and ensure that it displays a coherent relationship to their supporting studies. It also explains how they could record and present their work if it is larger than A2 or in a different format.

COURSEWORK: MAKING A START

There are many different ways to structure the course. A gradual approach to introducing materials and ideas will build confidence and allow students the time to reinforce knowledge as they progress on the course. Early opportunities to learn from mistakes will help students to be more experimental in their use of materials, as they begin to understand the iterative process of creativity.

At the beginning of the course, students will need clearly defined tasks and challenges as they familiarise themselves with IGCSE Art & Design. Short-term ideas or workshops that introduce students to a wide range of techniques and concepts work well at this early stage. As their skills and knowledge develop, they will work on longer-term projects and more personal ideas.

Starting with a question will focus students' attention and encourage them to think around a particular idea or problem. It is also good practice for the externally set assignment later in the course.

Theme: Open-ended questions

Open-ended questions are a way of introducing students to an aspect of art, but with an opportunity to develop work in different directions.

For example

This table shows a range of open-ended themes:

	Example question	Activity
Artist or art period	Salvador Dali or Surrealism	Students research the artist and explain what their work was about, choosing examples and commenting on the work in terms of method, technique or meaning.
Techniques	Still life using oil pastels	Students experiment with oil pastels following focused use on a still life.
Broad themes	'Stressful living'	This theme may raise issues related to the pressures of modern life or teenage life. Students could find relevant images and artists, as well as planning ideas for their own work.
Issue-based themes	Body image	Students can explore contemporary attitudes and art-based viewpoints on this theme, as well as identifying ideas for possible development.
Emotions or moods	Angry	Facial expressions and art dealing with emotions could be explored to help students find visual ways to deal with this theme.

Early in the course, these questions may be used for a single lesson and homework to familiarise students with how to approach starting their work. Later on, students can use the questions as themes for a complete project.

Theme: Closed questions

Closed questions are less common in Art & Design, but will often be used in design-based subject areas. Students are free to make design choices and develop ideas in their own way, but they must fit the design brief, which will include details that should be part of the final outcome.

For example

In three-dimensional studies, you might get the following brief in product design:

Design a milk carton with a 10 cm^2 base. The corporate colour scheme of pink and green should be used for the label design.

The student has a lot of freedom in the use of graphics and imagery, but must work within the limits of size and colour.

Theme: Artist or art period

A common theme for projects is looking at the work of an artist or designer. The artist's subject matter, themes and ways of working could all be looked at for research. As students work through the Student's Book, they are introduced to many artists and designers, and there are suggested artists for further research throughout this Teacher's Guide.

For example
A ceramics project might start with an exploration of the Art Deco period. Student research into the design aspects and artists of this period would then inform a project to design and construct a vessel with an Art Deco theme. Subject matter can be abstract or figurative, allowing for many different outcomes from a common theme.

Broad themes

A broad theme enables students to explore ideas in individual and personal directions. It is often easier for students to start their research from a focused point, rather than having a totally open-ended brief.

For example
Each of the words below has many associations and different interpretations. Students can start by looking up a definition and alternative words in a thesaurus. This will give them a variety of words to use in searching for images. Students may have information from other subjects that they can add to their ideas. The themes you set may be local to your area, which can make them more relevant to your students, for example:
- Hunger
- Celebrity
- Rebirth.

Theme: Issues

Another way to start a project is to look at issues in the modern world. This can be a good way to engage students who can feel it makes their work more 'relevant'.

For example
Each of the themes below can form the basis for research and initial ideas. Magazine and news articles, as well as artists and designers, can inform students with information and alternative visual forms.
- Environmental problems and renewable energy
- Natural disasters
- Poverty and equality

Theme: Moods and emotions

A mood can also be a great theme for a student workshop.

For example
These descriptive words below can all be associated with emotions or feelings:
- Peaceful
- Deserted
- Hectic.

A mind-map, as well as relevant artworks, can be a good place to start for students.

Top tip
- The elements of art (see pages 13 to 29 in the Student's Book) can be useful in helping students to develop colour ideas for this theme. For example, analogous and harmonious colour experiments might be valuable for the theme of 'peaceful'.

RECORDING

Recording ideas, observations and insights related to a chosen theme will help students to start their work. The many different ways to make progress will depend on the nature of their project.

Top tip
- Students often worry too early in the development stage about what their final piece is going to be. It is very important for students to use their research to suggest ideas for development.

Recording: Observation

1. Primary sources

First-hand recording should form a major part of a student's early research. This means that they need to think of what they can collect, visit or see for themselves. They can draw, photograph or makes notes on what they see. Where possible, bring objects into the art room that you or your students have collected. Still life provides an opportunity for students to look and draw with advice from the teacher. In the example to the right (see page 47 in the Student's Book for the full-colour version), drawing a pepper allows the student to explore proportion, tone and texture. These skills can be further developed for homework, and complemented with photography.

Top tip
- Students sometimes find it hard to think of how to do first-hand research for their theme. It can be helpful to discuss related imagery that students can find in the real world. For example, students cannot draw a real dragon for a fantasy project, but they can look at subjects such as lizards, birds and fire. Breaking down the elements of their theme will help students to find first-hand sources.

---

2. Secondary sources

Secondary sources include photographs and pictures by other people. It is very easy to collect images from the internet and without strong guidance students may rely too heavily on secondary sources. This reliance on secondary sources will limit how original and personal their work can be. Secondary sources are helpful, but must not replace a student's first-hand research.

In the annotated example in the margin (see page 47 in the Student's Book for the full-colour version), researched images of decorated ceramics are secondary source material as is the photograph of the vegetable. Student notes and annotations show the value of this information. The next stage might be to collect and draw or photograph a collection of vegetables inspired by this research.

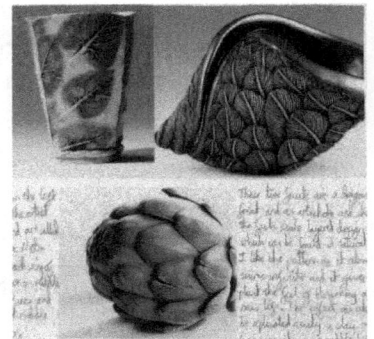

Top tip
- Students should always reference their secondary sources with clear labels to separate it from their own work.

Recording: Ideas and insights

Once students have researched a range of source material and references, they will be ready to start to generate ideas for their own work. Students all think in different ways. Encourage them to record their ideas using ways with which they are most comfortable. Students may use words, diagrams or even doodles. Some students present their ideas in organised lists, while others prefer a looser diary or collage approach.

Early ideas

A good way for students to start thinking around a subject is to use a mind-map. Starting with a central idea, they can allow alternative ideas to spread out. A single sheet of paper can cover many different possibilities for research and development.

In the example to the right, (see page 48 in the Student's Book for the full-colour version), a mind-map for the word 'natural' is explored, suggesting artists, places and objects to research. The student has pre-coloured the paper, which makes it more attractive when presented as part of their research.

For many students, simple lists work well in organising their ideas, especially when initially looking at a new theme or question. These lists could contain different ideas for a poster design or ways to use glazes on a ceramic vase.

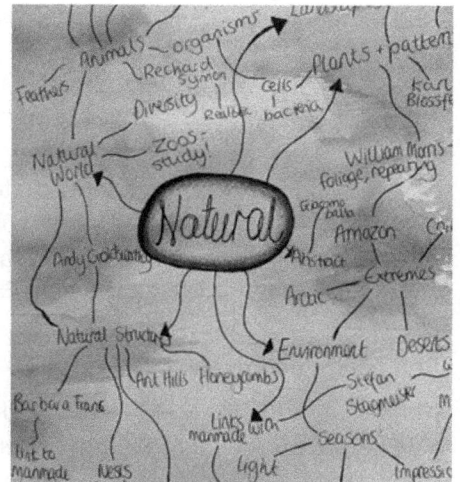

Top tip

- Small sketches can help to make ideas more real. Emphasise to students that at this stage, the quality of the drawings is less important than the quality of the ideas. Stick figures and scribbles are all helpful in showing how students intend to arrange the shapes in their design.

Insights

When relating the work of other artists and designers to their own ideas, students will often have insights that help them to develop their project. It is important that students record these insights in some way so that they can form part of the evidence showing their artistic process.

In the example to the right, (see page 48 in the Student's Book for the full colour version), the student has related their research in natural forms to the work of land artist Andy Goldsworthy. Photography, drawings, textures, notes and diagrams provide a diverse range of research sources. There are clear links between growth shapes in the vegetable forms and the spiral forms of the artist's work. The student will be able to move on with their work after evaluating these common elements.

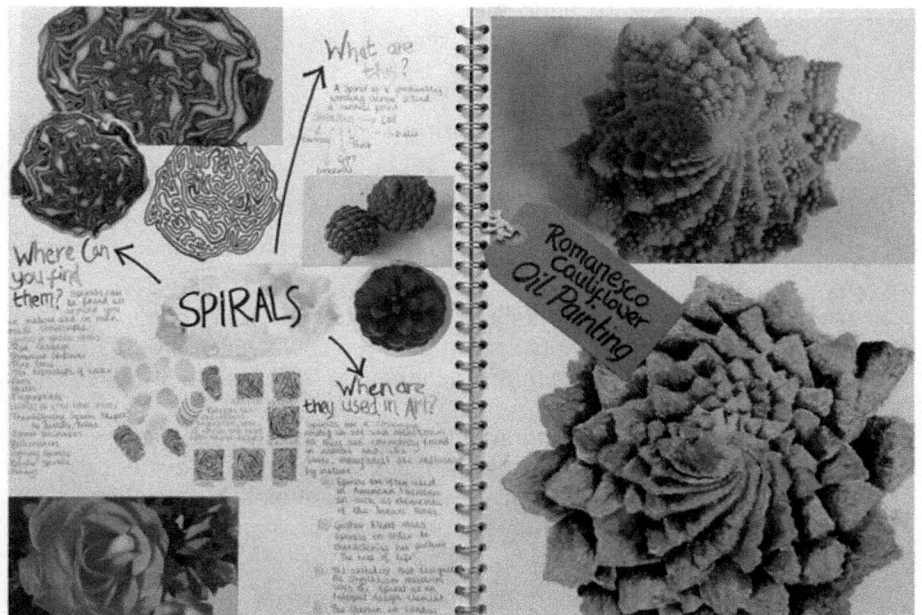

EXPLORATION

Students should be encouraged to select and explore media and techniques that are relevant to their project. Not all their experiments will be successful. It is important that students realise that this is a learning process, which will help them decide how to make their final outcome.

At the beginning of the course students will need guidance and direction in their exploration. Often teacher-designed workshops and exercises allow students to experiment with new materials and give them the experience to later make choices for themselves.

Materials

Various different materials can be used in each of the subject areas and students may not be familiar with many of them. It is important to structure projects in a way that allows students time to experiment with materials, and to choose preferred media for developing their ideas.

For example, in painting and related media, a plan for introducing students to different materials might be as follows (see Part III for detailed lessons):

1. **Introduce drawing materials**
   o Workshop 1: Line drawing (pencil, ink, biro)
   o Workshop 2: Textured drawing (pencil, ink, biro)
   o Exercise: Still-life textured drawing

2. **Introduce tonal drawing and wash**
   o Workshop 1: Tonal drawing materials (charcoal, pencil, pastels)
   o Workshop 2: Tonal wash (pen and brush with ink and water)
   o Workshop 3: Chiaroscuro portrait photography
   o Exercise: Tonal portrait (choice of materials)

3. **Introduce colour wash painting**
   o Workshop 1: Ink and watercolour washes
   o Workshop 2: Acrylic washes
   o Exercise: Abstract landscapes in wash

4. **Introduce opaque colour painting**
   o Workshop 1: Poster paint
   o Workshop 2: Acrylic paint
   o Exercise: Colour-mixing swatches and/or colour wheel

Having completed these workshops early in the first term, students will be able to attempt a more challenging project in which they select drawing and painting materials suited to their ideas.

Presentation of material experiments can include swatches or test strips with written notes. Students can select examples to evidence their learning. Encourage them to include examples of mistakes, with comments on how they improved their handling of the materials though experimentation.

In this example to the right, early experiments on the same image compare thick acrylic paint, washes and cut paper collage to explore different possible approaches. Here, the same image is used across the experiments but this is not necessary to demonstrate a student's exploration of materials.

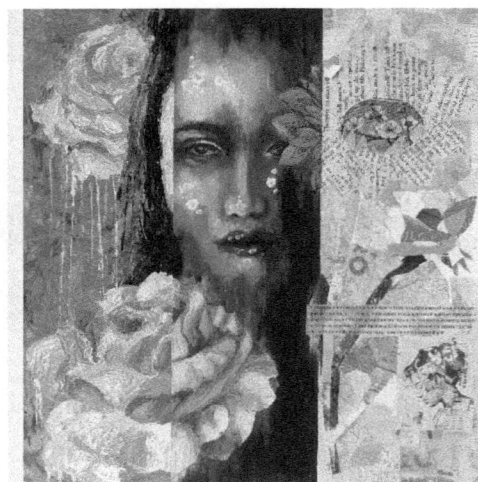

Techniques

As students explore different materials, they will use a range of techniques and processes to produce results that suit the style of their work. As with the exploration of materials, it is important to introduce techniques in a structured way so that complex methods are broken down into simple processes that help to build skills and confidence. A simple example taken from ceramics shows how building techniques might be developed along the following lines:

1. **Thumbnail pot**   (Students begin to experience working with clay)
2. **Simple slab vessel**   (Rolling clay and moisture content, use of slip)
3. **Small coil pot**   (Hand rolling and joining of coils)
4. **Larger coil pot or slab vessel** (Skills are used in a more ambitious way)

This step-by-step approach can be applied to any subject area.

Recording experiments

It is important that students record their progress with the different techniques. It is a good idea to develop and instil good habits early in the course by setting recording tasks to show different ways that students can evidence the techniques they have explored. There are many ways to do this:

- Taking notes while working
- Comparing and annotating small 2D examples of different techniques
- Giving a short presentation to visually explain the different techniques
- Keeping a diary with small drawings to explain the different techniques
- Keeping a visual diary of photographs taken during the experiments
- Finding artist examples for each technique explored
- Making a short video.

Presentation of evidence

Students will often prefer to get on with their practical work rather than spend time presenting evidence for their use of techniques. Examples from previous students' sketchbooks can be very useful in showing what can be done, as well as giving alternative approaches.

In the example to the right, ceramic work has been recorded and presented in a sequence of photographs showing how the vessel was constructed. Diagrams and written notes give a detailed explanation of the processes involved. Explaining the techniques in words is helped greatly by the supporting photographs. On one sketchbook page, the student has managed to explain a great deal of their ceramic process. The photographs were a useful prompt for the written notes. See page 49 in the Student's Book for the full-colour version.

Process Write-Up

DEVELOPMENT

As students begin to work on their own ideas, try to guide the development of their work so that more time is spent on the later stages where composition and technique can be refined to produce a high-quality outcome.

Early development and interim pieces

It is important that students do not spend too long on early development studies. If they try to perfect each piece of work, they will run out of time and may lose momentum. Students should work quickly at first, and not worry about the completion of pieces. There are several ways to encourage this:

- Set time limits in the lesson, such as 10 minutes per study.
- Limit the use of colour to only two colours.
- Specify the use of marker pens and fine-liners for quick sketches.
- Specify the use of cut paper shapes to quickly make simple compositions.
- Specify the use of biro for continuous scribble drawings.
- Set a homework target of a minimum amount of small studies.

Small experiments

This early sketchbook study in the margin is carefully drawn and includes some refined use of pencil crayons. The study is in an A4 sketchbook, which limits the size of the work, making it quicker to complete. Limiting the size of work as students begin to develop their ideas will help them to make quicker progress, and prevent them from being too ambitious with under-developed ideas.

> **Top tip**
> - After students have produced several small development ideas, challenge them to produce a more ambitious interim piece of work to see how some of these ideas might be further developed.

Interim pieces

After students have made multiple small-scale studies and experimented with different materials, they should consider making some slightly bigger studies. However, they should still try to work quickly. When you discuss students' early studies, try to help them decide the best way to develop their idea further and refine their techniques. Working on a study to a more finished quality will help them to assess if it is an approach that they want to take further.

In the example to the right, the student has decided to develop the portrait theme using a distressed surface. The drawing shows plenty of detail and works well with the textured card areas, but scale is again limited to speed up the development process.

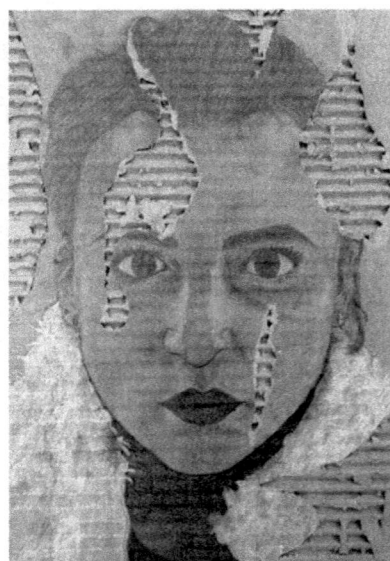

Assessment and critical understanding

Reflecting on early designs will change and develop students' ideas. This can be done in various ways:

- Teacher assessment and feedback tutorials
- Students showing examples of their work to a group or the class
- Students making presentations linking their work to other artists
- Students mind-mapping development ideas.

Looking critically at their work allows students to decide what is successful and which steps to take next. Useful questions to ask are:

1. Do they need new references to progress their designs?
2. Would looking at another artist help with their inspiration?
3. Do they need to explore a different type of material to realise their ideas more clearly.

Further development

After a period of assessment, students should be more focused when they return to their practical work. Development requires students to move forward with their work without being too repetitive. Discuss with students how they can begin work on a larger or more ambitious scale. As they do this, there should also be a more finished quality to their work as they try to refine their use of materials. There is still the opportunity to make major changes in terms of subject, colour or media but, with each piece of work, students should be trying to find the elements that will be used in their final outcome.

Top tip

- The concept of iteration is important to the development of artwork. Students should stop to assess their progress several times during this stage of their work. In this example to the right, the student has begun to make more substantial development work. A wooden board has been prepared and cut. The painting is of a more refined and finished quality. However, the piece is also quite small and areas of the image are unfinished. This is an intelligent use of time as the student has decided they have already achieved enough from the study. Written notes added to the piece show the student assessing and considering their own progress.

Compositional studies

Regardless of whichever subject area students are working in, they will need to make some final designs or plans before starting work on their chosen outcome. Alternative designs or compositions will give them the opportunity to balance the elements of their work in different ways. The final design will also help them to prepare materials and references before they begin work on the outcome.

> **Top tip**
> - Careful planning of design and compositions is another area in which teacher intervention can be helpful. Students are often reluctant to spend too much time on this area, and do not see the value in small compositional studies.

Design activity

The easiest way to get students to focus on this problem is to ask them quickly to draw how they think their final piece will look in the end. Such sketches can form the basis for a discussion of size, composition, surface preparation and other considerations for use of materials. These studies will demonstrate some students' use of the formal elements of art (see elements of art on pages 13 to 29 in the Student's Book). Encourage students to:

- think about the overall impression
- avoid detail in their sketches
- create loose or thumbnail sketches.

By exploring different compositions, students can make a final decision about the best arrangement of the elements in their design.

In this example to the right, a wide range of compositional ideas are considered. The final work will be in 2D and the student looks at many different formats for the work including portrait, landscape and square. The boxes overlap and divide the possible choices of subject. Pencil sketches zoom in on the subject to different levels and written notes by the student add non-visual thoughts and other comments.

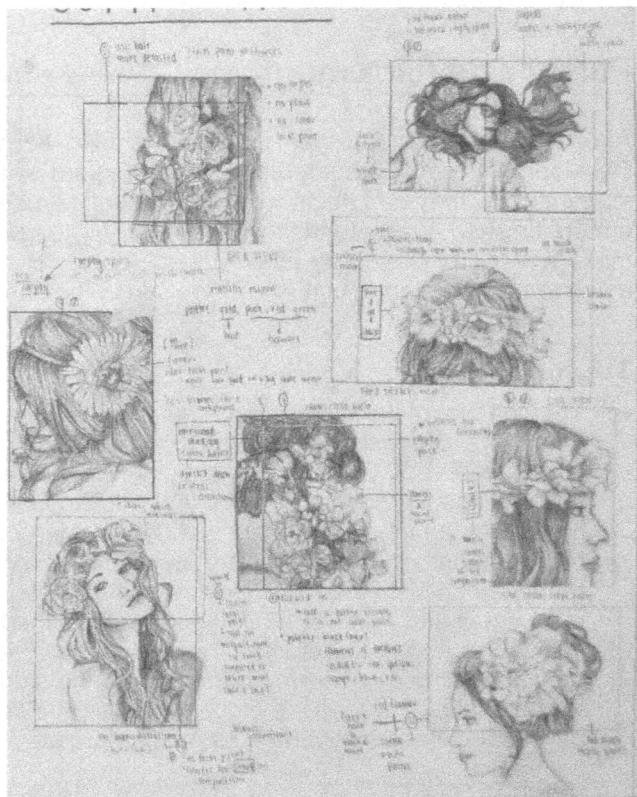

Final development work

Once students have a final composition, they may need to work on sections of it to increase their confidence with materials, or to decide which type of colour palette to use. These final development pieces can be important in linking their composition to the work they complete as a final outcome. After the students have decided upon a composition, they could consider the following questions:

- Have you finalised your colour choices?
- Does the final design clearly relate to your supporting work?
- Are there any materials you need more practice with?

UNIT 2: THE FINAL OUTCOME

The final outcome may be for coursework or the externally set assignment. The areas that your students need to consider are very similar, but there is a strict time limit for the externally set assignment work.

PLANNING AND ORGANISATION

It is useful to ask students a series of questions in preparation for their final outcome:

- **Materials:** Ensure that students make a list of the materials that they need. Are these materials all available? Are there any special materials required that need to be obtained, or used in specialist rooms?
- **Surface preparation:** What size are they going to use for their work? Which type of surface are they going to use? Do they need a stretcher or need to prime a board? Considerations for other subject areas will vary according to their choice of media.
- **Use of time:** How much time do they have to make their final outcome? How long will each stage take? How does this fit into the sessions available to them? For the externally set assignment, they should try to plan a piece of work that will use most of the available time.
- **References:** Make sure that students refer to their portfolio. They should use this as a guide when they make their outcome. Students should select supporting studies that show the development of their work and that will also help them complete their final outcome.

> **Top tip**
> - Encourage students to leave some challenges to resolve in their final outcome, so that it is not just a larger repetition of earlier work. If their later development work is made up of sections or parts of their final design, then they will still be exploring new elements as they work on the outcome.

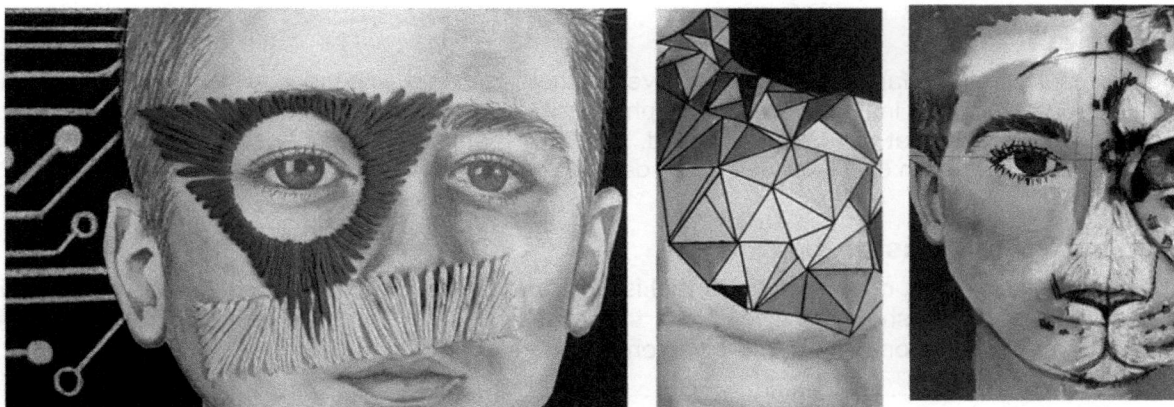

Year 11 coursework: Final piece details

The example above shows three sections from a final outcome. These sections show the range of media the student has had to prepare to use in their final piece. The media are, from left to right, stitching, marker pen and poster paint, and acrylic paint and chalks. The order of constructing the work was something for the student to consider. Drawing needed to be completed before stitching and the painted layers needed to be dry before different media could be used.

PERSONAL RESPONSE

Creating a personal response from a student can take time. Confidence in materials will help students to move on to focus on these higher-order thinking skills. Themes such as family history and location will encourage a personal response, but there are many other ways in which a student's work can be personal:

- If their designs combine artistic inspiration and first-hand resources, they will be creating work that is unique to them.
- Their interpretation of a theme, or a sustained use of a range of different media, can be very personal.
- The collection and recording of a good range of resources early in the project will be very helpful in making their work highly personal.

Strategies

Developing a student's personal response will require different strategies depending upon the student's character and interests. The following approaches can be used with individual students to encourage their responses to become more personal:

Sustained investigation

Students can work in a very traditional manner or with a limited range of subject matter and still show a personal response. Their use of lighting, composition, texture and colour can be combined to show a very individual exploration of their subject.

Detailed first-hand resources

Making a good effort to find first-hand resources is one of the most effective ways to show a personal response. Students can collect items that are personal to them, or things that just fit in with their theme. By going beyond internet images and secondary sources, they are making an effort to find more unique and personal information to inform their project.

Personal experiences

By using themselves, their family, where they live or their personal experiences, students are already showing a personal response in their work. Family photographs can be useful, but often students will need to take additional references that are better exposed, and have better detail. First-hand observation through drawing and other media is an excellent way for students to begin their work.

Communication of ideas or themes

Students' work may comment on a theme or social issue that interests them. If successful, the way in which they present their work will show a viewpoint on the issues that they have explored. Many themes that concern the younger generation can stimulate personal work, such as 'the environment' or 'identity'.

Top tip
- Knowing the interests of your students can be a big help in developing their personal response. Often your observations can encourage a student to explore something that they had dismissed because they are overly critical of their own work.

COHERENT PRESENTATION

The final outcome should have a connection to students' earlier ideas and development work. If their work jumps between unrelated ideas without reason, it will not be a coherent presentation. In a tutorial situation you can look through the supporting work and discuss links to the final outcome. The links include types of imagery, use of materials and expression of a theme. Students should not worry if their final outcome has changed from their early ideas, but try to ensure that their changes make logical sense. In helping students to assess this area, you can raise the following points for them to consider:

The supporting work tells a story

The coherent presentation of their work relies on the student telling a clear story of development that results in a successful final outcome. Useful questions include the following:

- Is the exploration of materials, subject matter and design ideas reflected in the final outcome?
- Does the outcome provide a satisfactory end to the research?

The supporting work makes logical sense

Changing their ideas and subject matter can make logical sense as long as students provide reasoning in their portfolios. Using sketchbooks and the portfolio to make connections and explain their decisions will help students to show the thinking behind their work.

Development ideas are present in the outcome

The students' final outcome should not appear to be separate from their development work. If there is no relationship with the development work, then it is hard to understand how the final outcome decisions were made. While they are composing ideas for their outcome, remind students to refer to their portfolio.

In the examples above, the student's theme for the project was 'natural forms' and the theme of studying nature is explored by looking at reference books, instruments and natural forms. Ideas for a design in abstracted sections are explored, but the student decides to work on an overhead view of a botanist's research desk. The final painting is in acrylic and includes many of the elements from the portfolio. There are clear links between the final outcome and the development work, which make a coherent presentation for this project.

REALISING INTENTIONS

The intentions of a project will be a combination of the student's early ideas and how they change during the development work. Their final outcome should sum up much of this work in a visual form. While discussing individual final outcomes with students, try to get them to consider the following questions:

- Is the final outcome connected with their supporting work?
- Does it express the elements of art they have been exploring?
- Does it show understanding of visual language (see elements of art, pages 13 to 29 in the Student's Book)?
- Is the composition of the final piece balanced in a way that suits their intentions?
- Are their responses to other artists reflected in some way in the final outcome?

Areas for student focus

Students can produce a successful project, but still find it difficult to see how they have realised their ideas through a development process. The following points can be used in student work reviews and tutorials to help them understand the concept:

Refinement of media

In their supporting work, students will have experiments in media and more substantial use of materials in later development work. The improved control and skills they have developed will be evident in their final outcome.

Refinement of design elements

Many design ideas and compositional ideas will have been explored in their supporting work. Does their final piece show development of some of these designs? Have the different arrangements they have considered been reflected in their final outcome?

Communication of ideas

Their project has a theme, which is expressed in their final outcome. Does this outcome express the ideas they have been exploring? This may be a social theme, but it may also be an exploration of formal elements. For example, if their work is about endangered species then the final outcome should visually express this.

Expressing the influence of other artists or designers

The work of other artists and designers will have been part of the student's research and inspiration. Does their final outcome show these influences? This does not mean that their work has to look like the work of others, but that elements from their art research should have clearly influenced the development of their outcome.

Top tip

- It is wise to discourage most students from using an unexplored medium in their final outcome. This medium will have no connection to their supporting portfolio and they will have had no practice in using it.

UNDERSTANDING VISUAL LANGUAGE

Some of the formal elements of art (see elements of art on pages 13 to 29 in the Student's Book) will be present in the student's final outcome. Have they demonstrated learning and understanding in their use of these elements? Different types of work and subject areas will use some of the elements of art as well as analysis of works by other artists or designers. The following areas are good themes when discussing visual language with students:

Overall design or composition

Do students have alternative compositions in their portfolio that show the possible arrangements they have considered? Their judgement in choosing a final design will help to show an understanding of visual language.

Use of colour

Colour or tonal value will be an important part of their final outcome for many students. Choice of colour will have a big effect on the mood of final outcome. Final colour decisions should relate to colour work in a student's supporting portfolio.

Other formal elements of art

Line, texture, form and other elements will be involved in the completion of different types of media and subject areas. Students' confident use of these elements will reflect further understanding of visual language.

The examples above show two outcomes for the same theme of 'Still life'. They show two very different uses of visual language.

- The painting of balls of wool and knitting needles uses lighting and shadow to show depth and form. The use of space is traditional and realistic. The colours are modelled and painted in a fairly naturalistic way.
- The painting with a bottle and glass by contrast does not use shadow or lighting. The painting is flat and relies on geometric shapes to divide up the canvas. Bright colours are not naturalistic and there is no sense of depth.

The first painting seems to be influenced by traditional still life, while the second seems to refer more to 20th-century work, especially Cubism.

UNIT 3: PREPARING FOR PROJECT WORK CHECKLIST

As your students work across their coursework, it can be useful for them to create a checklist, to ensure that they have covered everything necessary. There is a checklist on pages 60–61 of the Student's Book that students can use to help them through this process. It is suggested that you can photocopy this Student's Book checklist for students, or that they copy it out into their notebooks to use across the course. The Teacher's Guide checklist below can be used to help you monitor student progress as well. It is advised that you photocopy the table to monitor individual students.

STUDENT COURSEWORK CHECKLIST	COMPLETED/ EVIDENCE	TO DO
Theme		
• Artist or art period • Techniques • Broad themes • Issue-based themes • Emotions or moods • Design brief		
Record		
Student has collected primary sources:		
• Undertaken a site trip somewhere to record landscape or people • Collected objects related to theme • Set up a still life or interior scene • Used themselves as a model in drawings or photographs • Used friends or family as models • Visited a local museum or art gallery		
Student has collected secondary sources:		
• Collected magazine images and other people's photographs • Used the internet for image searches • Used the internet to research artists and museum collections • Watched videos on artists and designers		
Explore		
Student has organised their ideas:		
• in a mind-map • in a list • in thumbnail sketches		
Student has experimented with:		
• different materials • different techniques • evaluation of different outcomes		

STUDENT COURSEWORK CHECKLIST (CONTINUED)	COMPLETED/ EVIDENCE	TO DO
Develop		
Student has explored alternative designs		
Student has made connections in their work		
Student has avoided repetition		
Student has made smaller and larger development pieces		
Evaluate		
Student has identified successful aspects of their work		
Student has revised their work following errors		
Student has finalised their design or composition		
Final outcome		
Size of work decided		
Materials selected		
Connections to supporting work are clear		
Final outcome completed		
The submission		
Student has completed their portfolio:		
Up to four sheets (eight sides)		
Up to size A2		
Final outcome completed		
Student has attached the following using labels:		
Centre number		
Candidate number		
Name		

UNIT 1: PREPARING FOR THE EXTERNALLY SET ASSIGNMENT

Later in the course, students will need to be prepared for the externally set assignment paper. This paper presents a series of starting points for an externally set assignment project that includes supporting work and a final outcome.

STAGES IN THE TEST PREPARATION PROCESS

Guiding students through the externally set assignment can be broken down in to several stages:

Pre-planning

Working out a timetable for the preparatory period and the externally set assignment sessions is very helpful for students. Having a timetable allows students to be more organised and prepared for the externally set assignment period.

Reading the test paper

Students can find the externally set assignment very stressful. Creating a calm atmosphere and encouraging a slow, thoughtful reading of the paper can prevent students from rushing into ill-considered work.

Preparatory work

The time between reading the test paper and starting the externally set assignment sessions is for preparatory work. As with their coursework, students will need to show evidence of the Assessment Objectives:

- AO1: Record
- AO2: Explore
- AO3: Develop.

The fourth objective (AO4) is more generally applicable to the final outcome and the submission as a whole.

Supporting work

All preparatory work must be completed and presented before the externally set assignment. The two sheets (four sides) of A2 supporting studies can be taken into the externally set assignment to use as reference.

Externally set assignment sessions

The length of the externally set assignment is eight hours. The test paper will provide details on the sessions allowed, but this is usually a maximum of three sessions over no more than two weeks. The externally set assignment work should be held in a secure area.

Submission

All candidate work will need to be checked for labelling and correct administrative procedures before submitting the work to Cambridge International.

> **Top tips**
> - Encourage students to focus on research and observational recording to explore their ideas.
> - The process of developing work for the externally set assignment is the same as for the coursework. However, the deadline for the externally set assignment sessions, as well as choosing starting points from a paper can cause students to produce work that is out of character. Try to get them to continue with the same approach that they had to their coursework.

THE TEST PAPER

Make sure that students understand that the approach to the test paper is just the same as for their coursework, but they will have a limited time to do the final outcome and that all preparatory work must be completed before the test time begins. The type of work students attempt to do will depend on their subject area, although there are some common elements:

- **Imagination** should be stimulated by the starting points. There is no 'correct' answer to the starting points and students should see the starting points as a stimulus for their own ideas.
- **Personal interpretation** of the starting points will allow students to work in a more original and individual way. They should try to choose a starting point that allows them to explore ideas in which they are interested and use materials with which they have developed skills.

> **Top tip**
> - Reading the starting points slowly is important. Nervous students can rush through the paper and may miss the starting point best suited to them.

Responding to the starting points

After reading through the paper with students, they will want to absorb the information and start to record their initial reactions. The most difficult thing for many students will be deciding on a particular starting point. Initial responses vary from student to student but the following points are useful:

- Students will like some starting points more than others and it is a good idea to highlight these.
- Once they have chosen their starting point(s), they can use a separate piece of paper to start listing ideas and focus on the starting points in which they are more interested.
- If a student is having trouble finding a starting point they like, suggest that they start by crossing out the starting points they don't like. Which starting points are left? Which one interests them the most?
- Sometimes students like two starting points and want to combine the ideas in their response. As this can make their response lack coherence, they should make their response relate to one starting point.

Time limits

If students spend too long making a decision, they will waste time that they could use for developing their externally set assignment studies. Suggest the following ideas if they cannot make up their minds:

- Limit the research to a maximum of two starting points, and do some quick research into ideas and starting points for both of them. Which starting point seems to generate the best ideas?
- Explore the starting points and make a list or mind-map of ideas to research for each starting point they really like. If they cannot think of any ideas for a starting point, then they should remove it from the list.

Time is limited and students can get 'stuck' trying to decide what to do. It is important that a time limit is set for decisions on which starting point to attempt. This will ensure that students have enough time for experimentation and development.

Coursework experience

Students should respond to the starting points in an open and imaginative way but it is important that they consider the skills and techniques they have developed in their coursework. Using media that is completely new might not allow students the time to refine their skills before they attempt the eight-hour externally set assignment. When reviewing the externally set assignment starting points with students, encourage them to think back over their coursework experience:

• Are they better at a certain style of work, or do they have a favourite subject matter?
• Do any of the externally set assignment starting points allow them to work with the styles or themes that they enjoyed and are confident in?

Top tip
• Encourage students to think about the skills they have developed in their coursework. They will be more confident in the eight-hour externally set assignment if they have already used the methods and materials that they choose to work with. While reviewing their coursework earlier in the course, students can make a note of anything that they think they might really like to use in their externally set assignment.

Planning the time before the test

It is useful for students to plan how to use the time they have before the externally set assignment. This will help with their focus and organisation. The plan should only be a guideline, which remains flexible, so that it can be adjusted as students experiment with materials and develop ideas. This plan will also help students to keep stopping and assessing their progress, so that they can change ideas as they are informed by their practical work.

Skills activity L	Timetable to plan the externally set assignment preparatory work
Materials	Paper, pen
Description	• Creating a timetable can be done before the paper is given out, but often designing it after reading the paper gives students a greater sense of purpose. The table below can be adapted to suit your class's needs.

	Example	Weeks
How many weeks before the externally set assignment starts? Total number of weeks to prepare.	10 weeks	
Collect resources, research artists or designers, and so on.	Weeks 1–2	
Explore early ideas, and create thumbnail sketches and mind-maps.	Weeks 1–2	
Experiment with materials.	Weeks 3–4	
Do development work on alternative designs and refine use of materials.	Weeks 5–9	
Plan materials and working process for the externally set assignment.	Week 10	
Select and present supporting work for the externally set assignment.	Week 10	

ASSESSMENT OBJECTIVES AND SUPPORTING STUDIES

Fulfilling the Assessment Objectives is key to a successful externally set assignment submission. This is addressed in the following section.

1) Record

AO1: Record ideas, observations and insights relevant to intentions as work progresses.

Students will respond to the test paper by recording initial thoughts and ideas. This will generally be followed by observational recording and recording insights from research into artists or designers. In their supporting work, students should include examples that show their ability to record observations from first-hand sources. They should ensure that their early development work includes the following:

Ideas

When students read the test paper, they will have lots of initial thoughts and ideas. They should record them in a suitable manner such as a list or mind-map, as shown in the example to the right (see page 65 in the Student's Book for the full-colour version). As students develop their project and explore materials, they may have new ideas. Students should make sure that they record the alterations and additions to their project to ensure their work is coherent.

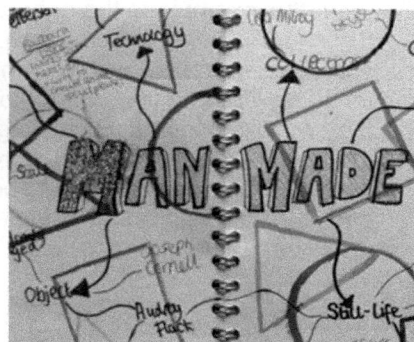

Observations

The project must include first-hand observation. Although students have limited space, make sure that they include evidence of primary observation and/or photography in their submission. They should try to fit in details of site visits, objects collected and any special arrangements they have made in sourcing their first-hand observation. (See page 65 in the Student's Book for the full-colour version of this example in the margin.)

Insights

As students combine and change their ideas, they will have insights into the artistic development of their work. Making connections with the work of other artists may inspire new insights. Mini pictures of artwork, practical studies and written analysis all help to convey the student's insights. (See page 65 in the Student's Book for the full-colour version of this example to the right.)

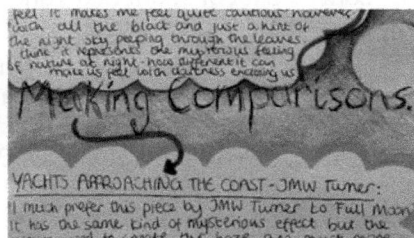

Top tip
- The presentation of work for AO1 can be difficult for students as they only have limited space on the two sheets (four sides) of A2 paper. Students should select the best work that represents the three main forms of recording above that can fit on the first and possibly second page of their supporting sheets.

2) Explore

AO2: Explore and select appropriate resources, media, materials, techniques and processes.

Once students have formed initial ideas and collected some source material, they should ensure that they explore a range of materials and techniques. The evidence for this experimentation should be clearly presented in the supporting sheets, while leaving space for development work.

Materials

Many students will have a particular material that they are experienced with and want to use for the externally set assignment. Although, this makes sense, also encourage students to show experimentation with a range of other media in their early studies to explore possibilities they had not perhaps anticipated.

In this example to the right (see page 66 in the Student's Book for the full-colour version), colour, pattern and reflection are explored in different types of paint and monoprinting. The top study allowed the student to test the range of control that they were looking for. By testing alternative possible media, the student may discover a more suitable approach to their idea, and they will definitely produce evidence for exploring and selecting appropriate media.

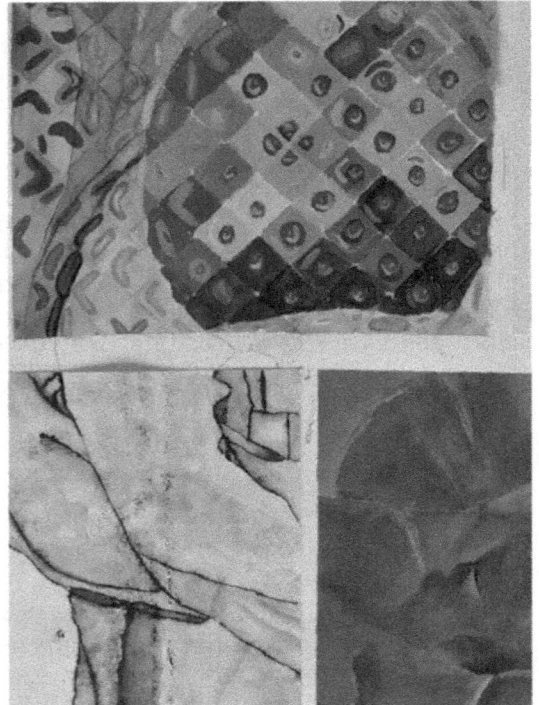

Techniques

All subject areas have their own techniques and the student's choices will determine the style of their final outcome. They will probably create many different experiments. Although work on paper can be cut and cropped for presentation, photography is also a good way to convey a lot of information and is especially helpful with three-dimensional work.

In the example in the margin, mini pictures showing stages of a technique with commentary provide a full understanding of the materials and the student's intentions. (See page 66 in the Student's Book for the full-colour version of this example.)

Top tip

- Photography is very useful for recording techniques and processes. The images provide a valuable prompt for students in adding commentary to their work and can help students explain the chronology of their work.

---

3) Develop

AO3: Develop ideas through investigation, demonstrating critical understanding.

The development of the student's project should be logical. There should be connections between the stages of their supporting work and their final outcome should be related to the development work.

Early ideas

The development of a project will start off with smaller-scale pieces as students try out different ideas. Encourage students to select a variety of alternatives to show the range of approaches and styles they have explored.

In the example in the margin, (see page 67 in the Student's Book for the full-colour version), different printmaking methods have been used on an idea about organising and arranging wool. Some of these elements were developed further, but not all of them.

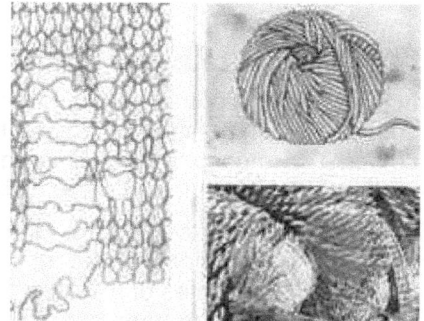

Substantial development

As their ideas and control of materials become more focused, students should start to make more substantial development pieces. These pieces do not need to be complete or all related to students' final outcomes, but they should show an increasing confidence in the arranging and presenting of ideas.

In the example to the left (see page 67 in the Student's Book for the full-colour version), a refined study explores mixing styles of work in a section of an idea for the final composition.

Composition and design

There should be a clear link between a student's development work and their final outcome. Composition or design arrangements help to show their consideration for alternative options. These studies do not need to be large scale or well developed, as long as they show how they intend their final piece to look. In showing the cohesive nature of a project, compositional studies can provide a valuable link between the development work and the externally set assignment final outcome.

In the example to the right, (see page 67 in the Student's Book for the full-colour version) simple pencil drawings show an ability to think of multiple compositions and alternative outcomes for the externally set assignment piece.

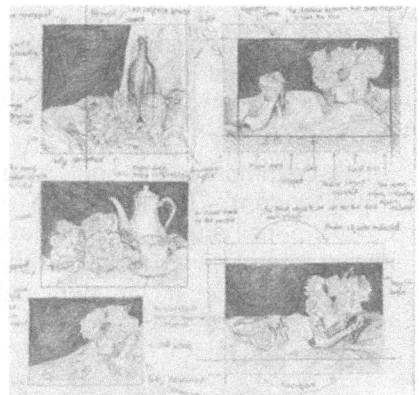

Top tip
- With the pressure of the externally set assignment, students can fix their ideas around one particular outcome at an early stage. This can lead to repetitive work that shows limited development. Encourage students to 'slow down' and explore alternative designs.

---

4) Present

AO4: Present a personal and coherent response that realises intentions and demonstrates an understanding of visual language.

Much of this Assessment Objective is concerned with the externally set assignment final outcome, but supporting studies are also relevant. Student consideration of the elements of art can be shown in various ways. When reviewing student plans for their final outcome and selecting work for their study sheets, raise these points.

In response to other artists

In their analysis of the work of other artists, students should have commented on their use of elements such as line, texture, tone and colour. These comments or diagrams will help to show that they understand how other artists use visual language in their work.

In the example to the right, (see page 68 in the Student's Book for the full-colour version), a student explores the compositional methods of an artist. Examples of the artist's work are analysed and used to stimulate design arrangements in the student's work.

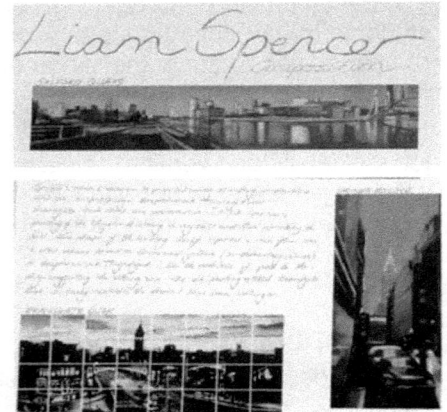

In the development of ideas

Development work will go through a variety of alternative designs. The different arrangements of students' designs should show an appreciation for many of the elements of art. Students should select work that shows a range of alternative uses of visual language, for example, line work and tonal work, or colour and monochrome development ideas.

In compositional designs

The composition of a student's work will combine several of the formal elements of art. Compositional designs in different formats and that show a variety of elements will demonstrate the candidate's strong visual understanding. While this can be seen from the design, encourage students to also add written notes and comments where they can to help explain their thinking.

In the example to the right, (see page 68 in the Student's Book for the full-colour version), pencil studies explore a variety of different formats and design arrangements. The externally set assignment outcome is based on one of these designs.

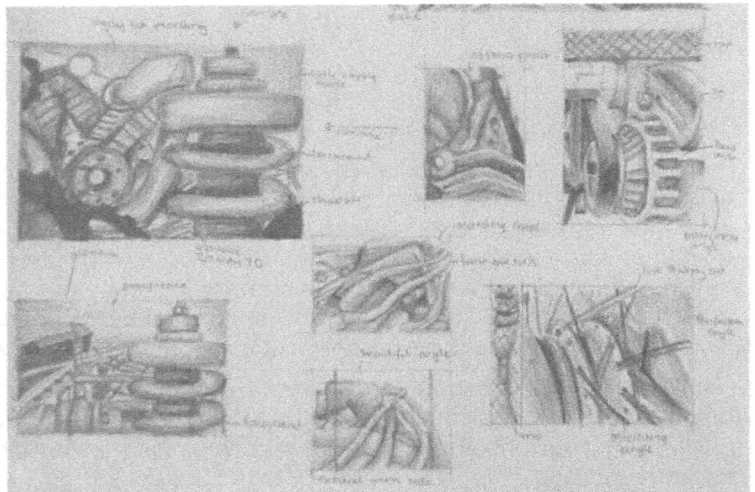

THE PREPARATORY PERIOD

The period allocated to developing ideas for the externally set assignment can appear to be a long time to students and they may think that there is no urgency in choosing a theme and developing initial ideas. This should not happen if they have a plan to allocate their time, but regular discussions or tutorials will be required to keep work on target.

Resources and ideas

During the early part of the preparatory period, students need to develop a range of ideas to explore. Once they have chosen a starting point, it is important that they explore the following aspects quickly to provide themselves with references with which to work:

- **Primary observation:** Students need to identify which places, objects or people they can observe, draw, photograph and record that are relevant to their theme.
- **Collecting objects:** This is something that may take a few days or require asking family and friends if they have objects relevant to the theme.
- **Artist research:** Early artist research will help with developing ideas and showing visual understanding.
- **Secondary sources:** Internet image searches, books and magazines can help to support the idea, especially where relevant primary sources are hard to access.

Top tip

- Students often come up with ideas that cannot be explored easily or directly in primary observation. This can cause a 'block' for students when doing first-hand observation. In this type of situation, you could make a few imaginative suggestions for parts of the idea to observe and explore. A simple example might be designing a unicorn, which cannot be observed. However, recording a horse and some form of animal horn will provide all the required visual information.

Experiments with materials

Experimenting with materials and practising techniques should be explored at the earliest possible stage. Students may put this off because they want their ideas to be more fully formed, but good experiments with materials can also provide ideas for how to construct their externally set assignment outcome. When reviewing work or discussing development, ensure that students consider the following:

- **Range of materials:** Encourage students to explore a range of materials. Often students will have a definite idea of what they want to do and can be reluctant to explore alternative media. These alternatives can include small differences, such as using ordinary and thick-bodied acrylics or applying paint with a brush or palette knife.
- **Presentation and written comments:** Space in the supporting worksheets is limited, so careful presentation of experiments is required. Written notes can provide a concise way to sum up student thinking and the reasons for choosing particular materials.

Development work

The pressure of the test can cause students to jump to a final design idea too quickly. This will prevent them from showing good development and can lead to repetitive work that simply increases in scale. Although time is precious, often students need to slow down when attempting development work. The following points can be raised with students when they reach the development stage:

- **Start small:** Large-scale ideas take a long time to complete. In early development work, keep the size small so that more ideas can be explored quickly.
- **Do not finish everything:** All work does not need to be completed. Often a part-finished study will provide enough experience for a student to move on further with the next study.
- **Create alternatives:** Although students may have a particular idea for their outcome, alternative designs will show visual understanding and can allow the student to come to the externally set assignment with a fresh outlook, rather than feeling that they are simply reproducing their studies on a larger scale.
- **Do some work at full-scale:** Full-scale work allows students to explore exactly how they will use materials in the externally set assignment. By working on a small section or test piece, they can gain this experience fairly quickly.
- **Have a final design:** Often students run out of time to clearly plan their design before the externally set assignment. This leaves a gap in the development of their work and can mean that they spend longer making a good start in the externally set assignment.

Assessing development progress

The development of the supporting work for the externally set assignment takes place over an extended period of time. If students have regular discussions with you, their teacher, it is possible to make sure that they are on target to complete all the required studies before the externally set assignment. There are several points that may need to be raised with students:

- Has artist research been shown clearly with annotations and responses?
- Is there some relevant primary observational drawing in the early recording and research?
- Is the idea changing and has this been recorded in the development work?
- Do photographs need to be printed out and presented clearly?
- Are the colours planned for the final outcome explored in the development work?
- Are all the major steps of development included in the supporting studies?
- Does the student have a clear plan of what they are going to do in the test time?

UNIT 2: THE FINAL OUTCOME

The final outcome will play a large part in Assessment Objective 04 (see page 60 in this Teacher's Guide). The outcome should show a clear connection to the student's development work and make a visual statement that is personal and relevant to their chosen theme. The eight-hour externally set assignment is a stressful time for students, but this stress can be reduced by guiding students to plan and organise their approach to the limited time available.

HOW TO APPROACH THE EXTERNALLY SET ASSIGNMENT

Being prepared

Encourage students to consider the following while preparing for the final externally set assignment time:

- The externally set assignment timetable will show the time slots that make up the eight-hour externally set assignment. Plan the use of time to ensure that the work can be completed to a good standard.
- Make sure that all equipment and materials needed are prepared and working surfaces are cut to size.
- Be at the externally set assignment room a few minutes early for each session, and think through what needs to be achieved in that session

Making a good start

Student confidence can be affected if they make a poor start to the externally set assignment. They should try to avoid this through planning and considering the following points:

- Good preparatory work is a source of confidence at the beginning of the externally set assignment.
- Students should decide what they are going to do first, for example blocking out the design or painting background colour.
- Students should start by working slowly and carefully. If they rush and make a big mistake, they will lose time fixing the problem or have to leave the mistake as part of their final piece of work.

Using supporting studies

The supporting work produced in planning for the externally set assignment is called 'the candidate's reference material'. In the externally set assignment, students should remember to refer to their supporting work and use it to help them in their composition, colour choices and use of techniques.

Assessing progress

The externally set assignment will be completed in several sessions. This can be useful as it gives students a chance to stop and assess their work. Suggest to students that they consider these questions:

- Is it going well?
- What do I need to change?
- What could be improved?
- Do I need to speed up or make changes to fit in with the time schedule?

Top tip
- Discourage students from working too quickly and with a lack of care. Remind them that quality is more important than quantity. Explain that an unfinished test piece that shows great skill will be more successful than a complete but less skilful and rushed piece of work.

UNIT 3: PREPARING FOR THE EXTERNALLY SET ASSIGNMENT CHECKLIST

As your students work across their coursework, it can be useful for them to create a checklist, to ensure that they have covered everything necessary. There is a checklist on pages 72–73 of the Student Book that students can use to help them through this process. It is suggested that you can photocopy this Student's Book checklist for students, or that they copy it out into their notebooks to use across the course. The Teacher's Guide checklist below can be used to help you monitor student progress as well. It is advised that you photocopy the table to monitor individual students.

PREPARING FOR THE EXTERNALLY SET ASSIGNMENT CHECKLIST	COMPLETED/ EVIDENCE	TO DO
Prepare		
Dates/times of the externally set assignment distributed to students		
Students have planned time allocations for the following:		
• Research and primary resources		
• Mind-mapping, ideas and sketches		
• Media experimentation		
• Developmental work		
• Review and finalising of design		
Distribute the test paper		
Students have:		
• read the paper carefully		
• selected one or more starting points		
• done quick research or mind-maps for chosen starting point(s)		
Finalise starting point choice		
Students decide on one starting point, which should:		
• give them imaginative ideas		
• allow them to use media they are confident in		
• enable them to do first-hand observation		
• include artists/designers that interest them		
• enable them to respond in a personal way		
Research and sources		
Students have:		
• made first-hand observations of people, places or objects		
• researched relevant artists/designers		
• clearly annotated their secondary sources		
Early ideas and experimentation		
Students have:		
• mind-mapped, sketched or listed their ideas		
• connected their ideas to those of other artists/designers		
• experimented with materials		
• recorded and assessed their experiments		

PREPARING FOR THE EXTERNALLY SET ASSIGNMENT CHECKLIST (CONTINUED)	COMPLETED/ EVIDENCE	TO DO
Develop		
Students have included:		
• small development pieces and alternative designs • evaluation of these studies • larger-scale studies • final composition or proposed design		
Preparatory studies submission		
Selection includes the following:		
• Recording o first-hand o artist/designers o secondary sources		
• Exploring o ideas o material experiments o evaluation		
• Developing o small scale o larger scale o reflection and evaluation o final design		
Use two sheets (four sides) of A2 to present your work ready to take into the test		
Before the externally set assignment		
• Students have planned their externally set assignment time • Students have prepared their materials		
The externally set assignment		
Remind students to:		
• be a few minutes early to the externally set assignment • bring their reference studies • not rush at the start of the externally set assignment • assess their use of time during the externally set assignment and between sessions.		
The externally set assignment submission		
Supporting work		
Up to two sheets (four sides) of A2		
Externally set assignment final outcome is complete		
Centre number		
Candidate number		
Name		
Starting point number		

PART II: CREATIVE PROCESS

A student project consists of many stages from initial ideas to the final outcome. Here in Part II, this creative process is analysed section by section, together with a series of skills activities that can be used in the classroom. The aim is to provide an overview of how the student process of developing a project relates to the objectives of the Art & Design syllabus.

The creative process is presented in five chapters. These are outlined below in relation to the syllabus Assessment Objectives listed here:

- **AO1:** Record ideas, observations and insights relevant to intentions as work progresses.
- **AO2:** Explore and select appropriate resources, media, materials, techniques and processes.
- **AO3:** Develop ideas through investigation, demonstrating critical understanding.
- **AO4:** Present a personal and coherent response that realises intentions and demonstrates an understanding of visual language.

Chapter 3: Artistic inspiration and response

Looking at works of art is often a stimulus for a project, but can be revisited throughout a project.

This response to other artists could be part of:

- **AO1:** recording insights
- **AO3:** demonstrating critical understanding
- **AO4:** demonstrating understanding of visual language.

Chapter 4: Recording ideas, observations and insights

This section clearly relates to AO1, but there will also be coverage of recording observations and insights for the other Assessment Objectives.

Chapter 5: Creative exploration

Materials and techniques are explored in relation to the student's initial ideas. This is generally covered as AO2, but will have some overlap with AO3.

Chapter 6: Thoughtful development

The development of a project is part of AO3, but some of the insights and responses may also be covered in AO1.

Chapter 7: Realising your final outcome

The final outcome, built upon the student's exploration and development work, is reflected in AO4. Again, there may be some element of recording insights that is covered in AO1.

The activities included in this section are only examples of ways to introduce students to each stage of a project. They can be adapted to your course and lesson timings, or used as a starting point for designing exercises that are more specific to your own students and subject area.

UNIT 1: YOUR INITIAL IDEA

STARTING POINT

A blank sheet of paper, with a free choice of subject, can be the most difficult way for students to start a project. It is hard for them to know in which direction to go, or which materials to use.

Inspiration

By starting a project with looking at the work of artists and designers, you can help students to focus on research and enable them to start thinking creatively. There are many ways to help students find artistic inspiration:

Artistic theme
Themes such as still life or portraiture can be illustrated with a range of examples. For example, students could explore still life through the paintings of Vincent van Gogh, or the photographs of Andre Kertesz.

School of art or design
A school or period of art makes a good starting point. For example, Surrealism could be introduced through artists such as Rene Magritte and Salvador Dali.

One-word starting point
Themes can be explored with works from different periods and cultures. For example, the theme of 'conflict' could be illustrated with works by Francisco Goya, Pablo Picasso and Roy Lichtenstein.

Design brief
A design brief can include specific artistic influences that should be visually evident in the student's work, such as a film poster influenced by the Art Deco movement.

Sources of information

The sources that students use to research artistic work can vary greatly. Art books and magazines, as well as websites, are an obvious starting point. Whenever possible, encourage students to visit museums and galleries to see the scale and physical properties of artworks. However, there are also great sources of inspiration to be found in culture magazines, film, television and literature. Artistic inspiration can be found in many places by students who are visually analysing their world.

Response
It is very important that students record their response to this work. Printed images, photographs and drawings should be accompanied by notes of the student's thoughts on the work seen. Insights into what was being communicated or how the work has influenced a student's thinking are especially valuable.

Recording their research in this manner does not come naturally to students, but, by going through this process in early projects, students will begin to see the value of presenting their analysis and understanding.

UNIT 2: WHERE DOES INSPIRATION COME FROM?

ARTISTIC INSPIRATION AND RESPONSE	Responding to an artist

This example looks at the work of an artist, together with potential development ideas for different subjects.

ARTIST

Beatriz Milhazes is a Brazilian painter who creates large, colourful collage paintings. Do some research on Milhazes' work and show examples, such as the following, to your class:

Modinha (2007)   *Rosa Nocturna (2007)*   *Manjary (2011)*
Carambola (2008)   *O Elfante Azul (2002)*   *Domingo (2010)*

ACTIVITY: Responding to an artist

1) Introduction

Demonstration	• Show the images and explain the background to Milhazes' work.
Additional student activity	• Ask students to describe what they can see. They choose their favourite work and explain their choice.

2) Response

Demonstration	• Show different ways to respond to the work in sketchbooks.
Additional student activity	• Explore work through coloured sketches, sticking down mini pictures with written comments, studying the colour palette of a work, creating a mind-map of ideas stimulated by the work, and making a list of words suggested by the work.
Top tip	• As students look at the work of an artist, they will often find connections to other artists. Encourage students to explore these links.

3) Development ideas

This initial research will need a focus to help students develop their own ideas. The introduction of additional artists can help all students find something to spark their imagination. The focus will depend on the subject area being taught. Some suggestions are outlined below.

Printmaking

A digital or screen-printing project could find many starting points in Milhazes' work, but the abstract nature of the work can make developing a theme difficult for some students. The screen prints of Eduardo Paolozzi could provide another useful reference, and suggesting ideas for making a cityscape and using contemporary imagery.

Graphic media

Students could design posters for a technology-related product. Russian constructivist images could be shown as a complement to Milhazes' work for the development of student ideas.

Textile design

In textile design, the bold blocks of colour and use of geometric shapes could inspire a fabric or clothing design. Students could look at other textile artists such as Sonia Delaunay or Catherine Kleeman.

Common themes include still life, portraits, landscapes and cityscapes. Artist inspiration adds a particular focus to these easy-to-resource subjects (see Student's Book, pages 78–83, *People, objects and places*).

Research sources

Use the following artists and works as starting points for discussions with students:

Portraits: Chuck Close

Lucas II (1987)   *John II (1993)*   *Emma (2000)*

Still life: Henri Matisse

The Goldfish (1912)   *The Blue Window (1912)*   *Still Life on a Blue Table (1947)*

Landscape: Wu Guanzhong

The Great Wall (1986)   *The Wu Village (1993)*   *Mulberry Grove (1981)*

Activity 1: Portraits

Photography and colour are explored using the student's own portraits as the subject.

1. Introduce the work of Chuck Close. Explain that he specialises in large-scale portraits from his own photographs using a grid to enlarge the image.
2. Students take photographs of each other with strong shadows (print out monochrome A4).
3. Divide the photograph into a 5-cm grid with pencil and a ruler.
4. Colour each square with oil pastels in a similar way to Chuck Close.

The study can be presented with examples of Close's work to discuss the techniques and what the student has learnt.

Activity 2: Still life

Set-up a simple still life consisting of fabric, a bowl and some fruit.

1. Introduce the still-life paintings of Henri Matisse, and emphasise the use of colour and flat space.
2. Ask students to choose a palette of oil pastel colours based on one of the Matisse paintings.
3. Let them do a 10-minute pencil outline drawing of the still life on A3 paper.
4. Use chosen oil pastels to complete the study.

Colour studies, Matisse examples and written notes would make a good visual record of this exercise.

Activity 3: Landscape

Materials are explored while responding to an artist's work.

1. Introduce the paintings of Wu Guanzhong and explain the tradition of brush painting.
2. Students dilute black ink to different tones, light to dark.
3. On A3 sheets of paper, students use different brushes and shades of ink to make marks similar to Wu Guanzhong.
4. Students add ink details to their roof top, tree and landscape studies.

These exercises will show students the skill required to control tonal washes. Next, they could work from some local landscape references to create more personal development work.

Local artists

These traditional themes are the subject for many artists' work. Student access to art in galleries and museums can be restricted by geography or the demands of a busy school. Consider contacting local artists in your area to see whether any may be suitable and interested in visiting your school. This can help to build links with the local community of artists and provide valuable opportunities for students to see work from beyond the classroom.

Taking it further

One of the aims of the Art & Design IGCSE course is to enable students to make their own, informed choices.

As the course progresses and their work matures, students will begin to make more individual choices about what to look at and develop in their projects. Some students, however, will need prompting to find their personal direction. The following are suggestions for ways to help students find that direction:

Style

Together with the students, look at work that they like. Often using a web browser makes this process quicker and more flexible. Which images do the students really like? Are there any schools of art that could be related to their interests? Can you suggest a project to students that could incorporate the style of work they admire?

Hobby

Some students respond well to ideas that relate to their own interests, such as a sport or a hobby. This can provide subject matter that makes them work with great focus on their art project. By suggesting ways to combine this theme with materials they have skill in using, they may be able to take their work in a more personal direction. Ensure that the work of other artists and designers is used to help inform the direction of a student's project.

Related artists

Sometimes the chosen artistic inspiration for a project does not really work for a particular student. However, other artists who work in a similar way or who are part of the same art movement may provide the creative spark a student is looking for. For example, Salvador Dali and Max Ernst are both surrealist artists but the slick painting style of Dali will appeal more to some students than the textured work of Ernst.

Different medium

Suggesting a change of medium can be all that is needed for student to become more motivated. Some students prefer to work physically with 3-D or printmaking processes. Many students also have considerable digital skills, which allow them to work with more speed and confidence.

Presenting a personal and coherent response is definitely something that takes time to develop. Early teacher-led projects will provide students with experience and confidence. As their work matures, the aim is to help the students become more independent in their choice of projects and outcomes.

Gallery visits

Gallery visits can provide a valuable opportunity to see work close up. Your school will have planning and risk assessment procedures to follow when organising your visit. During the visit, encourage students to take photographs where permitted, collect any leaflets and information provided, make drawings of works they are interested in and take notes of artist details and gallery commentary.

Set tasks for students such as 'compare and contrast' or 'same theme, different artist'. Once you are back in the classroom, discuss the work seen to help students develop their understanding of visual language. Students can be tasked with making a short presentation of the visit or making their assessment of 'top 5/bottom 5' artworks they saw in the gallery. These can be very useful ways to reinforce what was seen on the trip.

Summary

Looking at the artwork of creators is an essential part of teaching art and design. Although often used to inspire and start a project, the work of artists and designers can be visited at any stage in a project in the search for alternative ideas or to compare and contrast approaches. Encouraging students to describe and discuss work that they like, or don't like, will help them to become more analytical about their own work.

💡 Further research

- Vincent van Gogh: Dutch painter
- Andre Kertez: Hungarian photographer
- Rene Magritte: Belgian painter
- Salvador Dali: Spanish painter
- Beatriz Milhazes: Brazilian artist
- Sonia Delaunay: Ukrainian painter
- Catherine Kleeman: American textile maker
- Eduardo Paolozzi: Scottish/Italian sculptor
- Henri Matisse: French painter
- Chuck Close: American painter
- Wu Guanzhong: Chinese painter
- Max Ernst: German/Swiss artist

Chapter 4

INTRODUCTION

Throughout the course, it is important that recording ideas, observations and insights becomes a routine part of student activity. This can be done in many different ways: from drawing and photography to creating visual diaries and note-taking. At the beginning of the course, exercises, workshops and homework will help to direct students in this process. However, the aim is for students to see how they are making progress and the direction their work is taking, as well as to provide valuable evidence when they submit their work for assessment.

IDEAS

At the start of a project, students can find putting their ideas down on paper difficult. The ideas are in their heads, but need to be made into something they can explain and show to someone else. Exercises in collecting images, writing lists, mind-mapping and making small sketches are all ways to help students start to realise their ideas.

As their coursework progresses, students will get new ideas from investigation and experiments. Sometimes they will make big changes to what they are doing and it is important to get students to stop and take the time to record the reasons for their changes and amendments. A visual record of their work, together with written notes and annotations, will help to explain the decisions they have made. When their work is assessed, evidence from 'recording ideas, observations and insights' is one of the four marking criteria, so it is important that they build this into their work from the beginning of the course.

OBSERVATIONS

First-hand observation is a requirement of the course. In order to gather resources for their project, students may collect things, make site visits and research widely. Recording this process is important for them to be able to refer to it as their ideas develop. Drawing, photography, collage and visual diaries are just some of the processes you can introduce to students for recording their observations.

INSIGHTS

As their work develops, students will make connections and form ideas that are new to them. These insights are an exciting part of the creative process. Recording these insights will show how their creative decisions have changed during the development of their work. At different stages in their project, they will need to stop to reflect on what they have done.

> **Top tip**
> * Students are often reluctant to break from their practical work. It is useful to make reflection and assessment a regular part of class activity or homework.

REFERENCE AND OBSERVATION SOURCES

To start their project, students will need to find information that relates to their theme or idea. They will need visual information that they can record themselves or collect from a wide range of media and images. There are two main types of information they can collect:

- **First-hand or primary source material**: Anything they see and record for themselves.
- **Second-hand or secondary source material**: Anything taken from work or images made by other people.

First-hand sources

Direct observation allows students to observe and experience things that they can't get from looking at a still image or photograph. They can record objects they have collected, places they have visited or people they have observed. There are many ways to encourage students to record these observations including:

doodles	drawings and sketches	photographs
digital recordings and video	sound recordings	handwritten notes.

Observation through drawing is a simple way to make first-hand studies. In addition, students can use photography for first-hand observation, and as a reference for later studies and development.

Observational drawing and photography

Exercises and workshops can help students to develop skills in recording what they see. This simple activity can be used as an introduction. Try to control lighting in the classroom to enable students to see strong shadows.

Research sources
- Drawings of hands by Albrecht Durer
- Photography of hands by Tim Booth

ACTIVITY: Drawing and photographing hands

1) Introduction

Demonstration	• Show the images of hands and explain the use of light and dark (lighting) in both the drawings and photographs.
Additional student activity	• Ask students to describe what they can see. Ask them to choose their favourite work and explain why.

2) Response

Demonstration	• Show the students how to draw and photograph a hand in different positions with strong light and shade. Demonstrate tonal shading, and monochrome photography settings.
Additional student activity	• Students draw and photograph each other's hands in different positions and lighting conditions.
Top tip	• Hands make a good subject but controlled lighting is essential for students to create chiaroscuro elements in their drawings and photographs. • By presenting the work of artists together with their own drawings and photographs, students are linking first-hand observation to critical understanding.

SECONDARY SOURCES

Access to the internet has made it very easy for students to rely upon secondary sources. Although secondary sources are very useful to students in completing their research and references, it is important to emphasise the importance of primary observation. Secondary sources should be annotated to show where they are from and, where possible, who originally made them. Secondary sources will often be used when looking at the work of artists. Unless students can go to a gallery or exhibition, they will be using the internet or book references to source their images. Magazines, newspapers and computer image search prints are common sources for secondary references.

> **Top tip**
> - Students must not rely upon secondary sources. Their work will be better if it is based on resources that they have experienced for themselves. Additionally, the course requires the use of first-hand sources.

Activity 1: Secondary source annotation

This exercise encourages students to record the details of their secondary sources and present them in a coherent manner.

Research sources
• The Spanish architect and designer Antoni Gaudi is the subject for this activity.

Demonstration	• Show examples of Gaudi's work including his drawings and mosaics.
Additional student activity	• Students research examples of Gaudi's work and present them on an A3 sheet together with biographical details, annotations and comments in response to the work.
Top tip	• Consideration of layout can make a big difference to the presentation of secondary source materials. Although not essential, many art students enjoy designing imaginative titles for their artist research pages.

Activity 2: Mixing primary and secondary sources

In this exercise, students look at 'trees' both in the real world and those created by artists as the starting point for a research exercise that mixes primary and secondary sources.

Research sources
• Artist sources: Ai Weiwei 'Iron tree'   Singapore 'Supertrees'   Gustav Klimt   Andy Goldworthy   John Constable

Other sources
• First-hand drawings and photographs, secondary photographs and magazines

Demonstration	• Show works of art using 'trees' as the subject, as well as visit local sites to look at and observe trees. Ask students to describe some of the works and places to which they can go to observe trees.
Additional student activity	• Design a research page showing examples of first-hand and secondary source images of trees together with artist images. Try to show as many different ways to represent a tree as possible. Include annotation and design title lettering.
Top tip	• This exercise combines different sources of information. It can be useful for stimulating the imagination but, each area would need to be explored more.

UNIT 2: RECORDING IDEAS

LISTS, NOTES AND DIAGRAMS

At the beginning of a project, students can get stuck with a blank piece of paper and some loose ideas in their head. Notes, lists and diagrams can be a useful first step in getting students to visualise their ideas.

It is useful to demonstrate different ways that they can start to record ideas:

- **Lists**
  Written lists are a simple and direct way for students to put any ideas down on paper. These lists can be a useful starting point for discussions with you, the teacher, or just to make sure that ideas are not forgotten.

- **Mind-maps**
  A good way for students to record the 'thinking' process is through a mind map, or a 'brainstorm'. Usually a central theme is written in the middle of a page and as ideas come up they are linked to this theme with a line or arrow. The connections move out as each thought or idea is given more detail, or suggests further ideas.

- **Visual mind-map**
  Images can also be used to make a mind-map. By sticking down on paper any images that relate to their ideas, students make a visual mind-map of new connections for potential development.

- **Thumbnail sketches**
  Stick-figure drawings, simple diagrams or small sketches are very useful tools in starting the process of making ideas visual. Students do not need to worry about the quality of their drawing, as this process is about putting ideas down on paper.

Top tip
- Different students will prefer certain approaches, but there is no 'best' way – instead there is just the specific way that works for each individual student.

Activity 1: Starting point ideas

The theme for this exercise is 'movement'.

Research sources

• Italian Futurists – good examples are:
  Fortunato Depero – *Motorbiker*, 1923   Giacomo Balla – *The Car has Passed*, 1913
  Luigi Russolo – *Dynamism of a Car*, 1912   Umberto Boccioni – *Dynamism of a Cyclist*, 1913

Demonstration	• Show students some images that include movement such as a speeding car and an athlete. Link these images to Italian Futurist images.
Additional student activity	• Students think of words they associate with movement, themes they could use to make a work of art and images they could use to help resource their idea. The Italian Futurist examples should help to stimulate visual ideas. Students should try to develop ideas for their subject area such as sculpture, printmaking or graphic media.
Top tip	• If students find this difficult, try to get them to think of sports they are interested in, as well as places to go to photograph movement.

INTERNET RESEARCH AND PRESENTATION

The internet provides great possibilities for student research:

- The work of artists and designers can be well documented.
- Photographs to use as secondary source material can be found for any theme or idea.
- Techniques and materials can be researched.

Students often have problems when they print images from the internet. Sometimes, images print out very small, or if enlarged they are too pixelated. For detail or printing on a large scale, higher resolution images are required. An image with a 25 × 25 pixel size will be very small, but something 500 × 500 would be suitable for printing out in a sketchbook page. However, very large images can take a long time to download and print.

Top tip

- Students are often familiar with using search engines but it is useful to demonstrate the 'image' search functions of a browser. There are tools that can help students refine their search, such as searching for only photographic or black and white images.

Activity 2: Presentation from internet research

The aim of this exercise is to help students to record relevant details when doing internet research. Choose a theme that is relevant for your students. It could be a related artist or a subject to research.

Exercise 1 (collect information)

Demonstration	• Show students how to use presentation software to create a document and copy images and text information from the web browser to the document. They can 'right click' images to copy or save in a folder.
Additional student activity	• Use a web browser to search for relevant images and written information. Copy this to a presentation document that is in a 'screen' format. Encourage students to make the layout of the information readable and vary the size of images.

Exercise 2 (present information)

Demonstration	• Set students the task of preparing a two-minute presentation of their research, which they will present to the class while showing their research slides.
Additional student activity	• Make notes on what they are going to say and practise in pairs. Presentations should be in a relaxed atmosphere.
Top tip	• Simple presentations by students will increase their confidence in analysing and discussing work. Some students will find them quite challenging, but all students will see an improvement in their ability after two or three presentations during the first year of their course.

SITE VISITS

Making site visits to look at places or structures provide a valuable opportunity for students to see work close-up. Your school will have planning and risk assessment procedures to follow when organising your visit. First-hand experience allows students to appreciate scale, size and location using all their senses.

Top tip
- If you are arranging a school site visit, try to ensure that the trip will work regardless of the weather. If there are indoor and outdoor areas of interest, then students can work in shelter if needed.

During the visit

Students should bring a range of equipment for recording what they experience:

- Sketchbook
- Camera and/or smartphone
- Pencils, pens and colouring pencils.

Students should make sure that they look carefully round the site before deciding what to explore in detail. To record their visit, they can make simple maps and diagrams, written descriptions, drawings and photographs/videos. Literature and other information also may be available for students to collect.

Recording the visit

After the visit, students will have some information in their sketchbooks but may also have digital images, loose leaflets and postcards. It is a good idea to set students the task of organising all this information to include printed mini pictures, larger selected images, commentary on the images and insertion of any leaflets or other information.

Summary

Art is a visual subject and it follows that much of a student's work will be recorded visually. However, thought processes and ideas do not always fit neatly into a picture and individuals think in different ways. By combining a range of different ways of recording and presenting their ideas, observations and insights, students can show the range of work they have been attempting to explore.

Further research
- Albrecht Durer: German artist
- Tim Booth: UK photographer
- Antoni Gaudi: Spanish architect
- Marina Bay: Singapore
- Gustav Klimt: Austrian painter
- Andy Goldsworthy: UK sculptor
- John Constable: UK painter
- Italian Futurism

INTRODUCTION

Creative exploration is very much about exploring and selecting appropriate resources, media, materials, techniques and processes. Experimenting with materials and exploring techniques may take place separately, or during the same activity.

Once students have an idea to focus on, they can then explore the materials and techniques needed to realise their intentions. This is an opportunity for students to try out different ways of working. Early in the course, you may use workshops to introduce new materials before students choose how to develop their ideas. This process will produce a range of test pieces from which students can select the media they think works best to further develop their project.

UNIT 1: EXPLORING MEDIA
UNIT 2: EXPLORING MATERIALS AND TECHNIQUES

EXPERIMENTATION WITH MATERIALS

One way to begin broadening a student's knowledge of materials is through simple exercises to explore the qualities of different media. By dividing a sheet of paper into a series of boxes, students can make marks and compare different materials next to each other. These exercises introduce students to materials in a quick and efficient manner, but they need to be followed up with more imaginative activities that link the materials to artists or themes.

Research sources
• Artist sources: Paul Klee – monoprints   Guercino – ink drawings • Materials: 2B pencil, ink pen, size 3 brush and ink, inked paper for monoprinting

Activity 1: Line drawing

The aim of this activity is to experiment with pencil, ink pen, ink brush and monoprinting.

Demonstration	• Show examples of work by Paul Klee and Guercino. Divide a sheet of paper into 16 boxes. In each row, draw lines and marks using one of the four materials. Demonstrate how to use all four materials.
Additional student activity	• Students experiment with each of the materials, comparing the types of lines made, as well as ways to control thickness and tonal value. Written notes on the sheet are used to explain what they have learnt.

Top tips	• Simple monoprinting method:
	    o Roll slow-drying ink onto a thin sheet of paper.
	    o Place this paper ink-side down on another sheet of paper and draw on it.
	    o Observe as the drawing is transferred to the paper below. The line has the blurred quality associated with monoprinting.
	• Simple experiments can be made whenever new materials are introduced. Some students find these abstracted demonstrations of materials very informative, but other students will prefer to learn about materials and explore their properties by making images and small pieces of work.

EXPERIMENTATION TO SUIT THEME

Students who are trying to convey a texture or surface will find that some materials are more suitable than others. Experimentation with materials can determine which material has the required expressive property. In this exercise, students experiment with materials to create soft and graduated effects that could be used in a chiaroscuro portrait.

Research sources
• Artist sources: Georges Seurat – drawings   Frank Auerbach – charcoal drawings • Monochrome reference portraits with good lighting • Materials: Erasers, 3B pencil, graphite and charcoal, A3 cartridge paper landscape format

Activity 2: Smudging

This activity involves experimentation with pencil, graphite and charcoal.

Demonstration	• Divide the paper into three sections and draw a rough outline portrait in each section. Use each of the materials to complete each portrait, smudging the materials and using an eraser.
Additional student activity	• Start with the pencil drawing and try to create dark tones with the side of the pencil, smudging the pencil and using the eraser to draw back into the tonal areas. Compare this drawing and the tonal values with similar drawings made in charcoal and graphite.
Top tip	• Charcoal and graphite will come off on the students hands and can be a messy process. Aprons and paper towels will help to contain the materials. Allow time for washing hands at the end of the activity. Drawings will need 'fixing' to stop them from smudging further.

COLOUR AND MATERIALS

As students begin to explore colour, it is useful to look at the properties of different materials. Expressive shapes can be used in this exercise to compare the colour qualities of the different materials.

Research sources
•   Artist sources: Emile Nolde – landscapes •   Monochrome reference portraits with good lighting •   Materials: Watercolour, pencil crayon, oil pastel, acrylic, A3 cartridge, reference images of stormy skies and clouds

Activity 3: Colour mixing

The aim of this activity is to create an expressive experimental colour study of a storm incorporating different materials.

Demonstration	• Look at Nolde's paintings and discuss the use of colour. Show examples of stormy sky photographs that can be used as reference for this exercise.
Additional student activity	• Select some photographic references and draw a basic sky composition in pencil. Use a range of pencil crayons to add colour to areas of the drawing and then add similar oil pastel colours next to them. Mix up the same colours in watercolour and add to the picture. Then repeat this with the acrylic paints.

Reflection

The end result of this exercise is a colourful study comparing the qualities of the different materials. Make sure to point out areas of wax resist and expressive, but accidental effects produced by the mixture of materials.

TECHNIQUES

Students will find that much crossover takes place while they are exploring materials and techniques. Generally, when students are exploring one material, they will be looking at different techniques that make use of its properties. It is a good sign when students become absorbed in their exploration of techniques, but when the work is dry, it needs to be collated, presented and recorded to evidence what the student has learnt. Demonstrating techniques is particularly useful when a process or craft is being explored. For example, printmaking processes often have several steps and in ceramics test firing of glazes is very common. Sometimes processes are time-based or the evidence is very bulky. Photography is a good way to present these techniques through step-by-step images, or photographs of 3-D objects.

Top tip
- Encourage students to use a smartphone or tablet to regularly record their exploration of materials and techniques. This record can be used to build a diary or explanation of process in a quick and easily understood manner.

Demonstrating techniques

If you introduce students to ways of presenting their experiments in techniques early in the course, it can become a natural part of their working method.

Research sources	
• Artist sources:	
Helen Frankenthaler	*Canyon*, 1965 (wash)
David Hockney	*A Bigger Splash*, 1967 (solid colour)
Vincent van Gogh	*Wheat Field with Cypresses*, 1889 (impasto)
Paul Cezanne	*Portrait of the Artist's Father*, 1866 (palette knife)
• Materials: Acrylic paints (medium body), soft and bristle brush, toothbrush, palette knives, newspaper, strips of cartridge paper	

Activity 4: Painting techniques

This activity explores different painting techniques.

Demonstration	• Show examples of different painting techniques and demonstrate the techniques using acrylic paint.
Additional student activity	• Explore the following on cartridge paper:
	○ A wash thinning paint with water and using a soft brush
	○ Flat painting with solid colour
	○ Brush texture using a bristle brush
	○ Impasto using a palette knife
	○ Dragged brush marks using an old brush
	○ Dry brush techniques
	○ Print application using paint on crumpled newspaper.

Reflection

This exercise produces several loose sheets of different painting techniques, which will need to dry. Students can then cut them up and present them in a way that compares the different qualities. Notes can be added on problems that arose and students may have a preference for certain techniques that they want to explore further.

TECHNIQUES OF LOOKING

Research sources

• Artist sources:
    Pablo Picasso   *Still Life under the Lamp* (linocut, 1962)
    Giorgio Morandi   *Still Life of Vases on a Table* (etching, 1931)
• Materials: Pencils and white chalk, A4 paper

Activity 5: Still-life drawings

Set up a simple still life of some bottles or containers.

Demonstration	• Show the example artworks and discuss the different ways of looking at the still life. Discuss the concepts of outline, positive/negative, tonal values and working in negative with chalk on a black background.
Additional student activity	• Create four drawings of the still life exploring these alternative approaches: outline (3 minutes), positive/negative (5 minutes), tonal (10 minutes) and coloured background (10 minutes).

Reflection

Students can use these small studies to demonstrate their knowledge of the different drawing and looking techniques, as well as working in chalk on a dark background.

CONTRASTING TECHNIQUES

Contrasting techniques and materials can demonstrate alternative approaches to students, thereby enabling them to choose their own working method. In this exercise, students explore 3-D construction techniques.

Research sources

• Artist sources:
    Alexander Calder   *Medusa* (wire, 1930)
    Naum Gabo   *Head No 2* (steel, 1964)
    Giovanni Bologna   *A River God* (terracotta, 1575)
• Materials: Clay, modelling wire, thin cardboard and tape

Activity 6: Working in 3-D

The aim of this activity is to build a cup and saucer using three different techniques.

Demonstration	• Show the examples of sculpture in wire, steel and clay. Demonstrate using clay, card and wire to make three small cups and saucers.
Additional student activity	• Build three simple models of a cup and saucer using the clay, slab and coil pot technique, wire-frame construction and card construction from curved sheets and tape.

Reflection

Understanding of the techniques introduced is more important than the quality of the outcomes.

Summary

One of the reasons many students choose to study art and design is because they want to work with materials and use their hands, as well as their heads. It is important that their enthusiasm to work practically is complemented by an ability to present and analyse the results of their experiments with materials and techniques. Students mature as the course progresses and what at first may seem a chore to some students can develop into a solid foundation for the development of their project ideas.

💡 Further research

- Paul Klee: Swiss artist
- Guercino: Italian artist
- Georges Seurat: French artist
- Frank Auerbach: UK artist
- Emile Nolde: German artist
- Helen Frankenthaler: American painter
- David Hockney: UK artist
- Paul Cezanne: French painter
- Alexander Calder: American sculptor
- Naum Gabo: Russian sculptor
- Giovanni Bologna: Flemish sculptor

Chapter 6 — Thoughtful development

INTRODUCTION

The development of a project is where the student's ideas and choice of materials come together in a series of works. The development of an idea is a process with several stages. Students may jump around as they work, but the general stages with which they will be involved are the following:

Early development and interim pieces

Students should work quickly at first, and not worry about the completion of pieces. They are trying to decide on the best way to develop their idea and how to refine their techniques. If they work on a study to a more finished quality it will help them to assess if it is an approach they want to take further.

Assessment and critical understanding

By reflecting upon early designs, they will change their plans. Looking critically at their work allows students to decide what is successful and which steps to take next. They may need to find new references, look at another artist or explore a different type of material to realise their ideas more clearly.

Further development

By this stage, student ideas are more focused. They begin work on a larger scale and to a more finished quality as they try to refine their use of materials. There is still the opportunity to make major changes of subject, colour or media, but with each piece of work they are trying to find the elements that will be used in their final outcome. Students should stop to assess their progress several times during this stage of their work.

Top tip
- Students are reluctant to stop their practical work, so it is useful to build these short assessment sessions into a timetable of classroom activity.

Compositional studies

Whichever subject area students are working in, they will need to make some final designs or plans before starting work on their chosen outcome. Alternative designs or compositions will give them the opportunity to balance the elements of their work in different ways. The final design will also help them to prepare materials and references before they begin work on the outcome.

Final development work

Once students have a final composition, they may need to work on sections of it to increase their confidence with materials, or to decide what type of colour palette to use. These final development pieces can be important in linking their composition to the work they complete as a final outcome. In the following sections, these stages are explored with practical activities.

UNIT 1: EARLY DEVELOPMENT WORK

EARLY DEVELOPMENT AND INTERIM PIECES

As students begin to develop their ideas, encourage them to keep the scale small so they can work through alternatives quickly. They shouldn't worry about finishing every piece of work. If they work through early ideas quickly, they will have more time for their substantial development work.

Early in the course, students will need to develop the approaches and habits that help them to make practical work from their ideas. Teacher-set exercises and workshops will give them the experience they need to make their own decisions later in the course.

Early decisions

Making a list of activities to develop initial ideas is a good way for students to begin to organise their work, with your assistance.

Use the following questions with students to help them move forward with their ideas.

Activity 1: Questions to ask students

- What type of materials do you want to use for your early development work?
- What time limit can you set for each study?
- Can you decide when you have done enough on a study and not complete every piece of work?
- Can you decide on a main focus before you start a study?
- Can you use other materials to encourage speed in your work?

As students start to draw, sketch and paint ideas from their research, encourage them to move on when they have achieved their focus. They will produce more work and stop becoming too fixed on one particular idea or piece of work.

Stimulating imaginative visual ideas

Sometimes student ideas are vague and they have trouble finding imagery to create their own studies. By working on a surface that adds random information to their ideas, their imagination can help them add new imagery.

Research sources
• Artist sources: Collage drawings by Loui Jover. Look for examples such as: *Baby Cakes* *Deconstructing George Orwell* *Deconstructing Franz Kafka*

Activity 2: Suggested imagery

Students use a random background to suggest images to combine with their idea.

Demonstration	• Show the work of Loui Jover and demonstrate sticking down torn or cut newspaper and adding light grey ink washes.
Additional student activity	• Create a newspaper or wash surface. When dry, draw on the surface using the visual references. Look at the background to see whether it suggests any way to combine it with the drawings.
Top tip	• Half-closing the eyes can help students to see the main tonal values in the random collage and encourages imaginative connections.

INTERIM PIECES

After quickly exploring some of their ideas on a small scale, it is a good idea for students to make a more substantial piece of work. This helps them to see whether their idea is worth developing and whether they need to improve their technical skills. The interim piece is an opportunity for students to reflect on the personal response they are making. Is it coherent? What works and what do they need to spend more time developing. If the idea does not work as an interim piece, then the student can move on to develop an alternative idea.

Planning breaks from practical work for reflection is very important. This need not take up a long period of time, but it allows students to assess the progress they have made and consider the direction of the next stage of their development. There are different ways to help students to assess the work they have produced.

COMPARISON OF TECHNIQUES AND MATERIALS

Students can make a comparison of the success and effectiveness of their early uses of materials and techniques. The following questions are useful ones to ask:

- Same subject, different media – which is best?
- Same subject, different technique – which works the best?
- Which colour combinations/colour palettes suit the work?
- Which textures and surfaces best express the mood of the idea?

CRITICAL REFERENCES

Inspiration from other artists and further artistic research are important to a project:

1. Did the artist research help your own work?
2. Do you need different art influences?
3. Do the formal art elements of your work reflect your artist research?

Reflective log

After students have produced some development work, it is useful for them to compare these studies with their starting points:

- Does your work express your chosen theme?
- Does the work show a connection with your artist references?
- Have you tried alternate techniques to express your ideas?
- Does your work evolve and avoid repetition?

New materials

Early development work may be in easy-to-use materials such as card, paper and tape, or graphic materials. Once students have developed some of these ideas, they will want to use materials that need more planning or care in how they are used.

Top tip
- Exploring new materials does not mean students have to start working slowly and on a larger scale. New materials can still be treated as experiments until students are sure more substantial work is going to be useful to them.

COMPOSITIONAL STUDIES

As students near the time to complete their project with a final outcome, they will want to finalise their designs. By exploring different compositions, they can make a final decision about the best arrangement of the elements in their design. These studies will demonstrate their skills in some of the formal elements of art (see elements of art, pages 13 to 29 in the Student's Book).

Top tip

- Help students start a sheet of compositional studies by asking them to think of different shapes for the format of their design. Draw all the possible shapes they think might work and then see how their designs can be arranged in each of these shapes. Some will 'fit' better than others.

Alternative designs

Planning their composition works well if students think about the overall impression and do not involve themselves too much in detail. Loose or thumbnail sketches are ideal.

Activity 1: Compositional sketches

Additional student activity	• Draw a basic shape for the format of your composition. Using only simple geometric shapes (circles, triangles and rectangles), quickly draw a sketch of your design.
Notes and plans	• Compositions can be small sketches, but with the addition of written notes and diagrams, they can provide a map for the student's final outcome. Useful information to add includes notes on the position of colours, the order of painting or construction, areas that could benefit from further practical studies, and lighting direction and tonal values.

Visual thinking

Compositional studies are an opportunity to think about many different shapes and forms for the student's final piece.

Activity 2: Compositional sketches

Additional student activity	• Draw three alternative compositional sketches for your design. Each sketch should have a different format or changes of scale to the elements in the design (three minutes per drawing).
Top tip	• Asking students to work at speed and to a time limit can be very effective. Students will be reluctant to work so quickly, but can find the challenge enjoyable.

Artist influence

It can be useful to for students to refer to the work of other artists before planning their composition. These may not be the artists that they originally looked at. The teachers input can be very useful as their subject knowledge can guide students to look at artists they are unaware of.

Elements of art

Consideration for some of the elements of art can help students to add variety to their compositions. For example, students can try balancing opposites in their composition: big and small; busy and empty; thick and thin, and curved and straight.

UNIT 5: FINAL DEVELOPMENT WORK

While organising their development work and compositions, students will probably think of areas in which they are still not confident. Before students start their final outcome, they should practise any techniques or uses of material in which they are still unsure. This final development work should mean that when students start their final outcome, they have a good idea about how to work on each element of it, from the beginning stages to refining the final use of materials.

There are several ways in which you can guide students in this process.

Full-size section test piece

Once the final design or composition is complete, it can be very informative for students to make a trial piece which is a full-scale section. The reasons for doing this include:

- practising the painting of a complex part of the design
- assessing the size of brushes and tools required for full-scale work
- identifying the different qualities that materials have when used on a larger scale
- testing techniques for 3-D work to ensure that they will work at full scale.

Combination of materials

During the development process, students use a wide range of materials, Sometimes they may want to combine these materials in their final piece. Although this can work well, it is a good idea for students to test this on the scale of their final outcome. Sometimes smaller experiments do not work when enlarged.

Alternative colour palettes

If students are still unsure of their colour choices for the final outcome, they can explore alternatives by looking at other artists' work for possible palette choices. Colour sketches based on these ideas can help to confirm a student's ideas.

Compositional changes

When finalising their design, students may make substantial changes to their composition. If there is time, additional development studies will ensure that the student can complete the final outcome with confidence. This also has the advantage of ensuring that there is coherence between the supporting work and the final outcome.

Summary

The development process connects ideas and experiments with the final outcome. Successful decisions and judgements in this stage are very important to the overall quality of a project. Your guidance as the teacher can be fundamental in helping students to consider alternative ways to develop their work and to critically assess their own progress. In designing the course, you can create a structured approach with set targets and provide the opportunities required for students to reflect upon their work.

💡 Further research

- Loui Jover: Australian artist

INTRODUCTION

The student's final outcome may be one or several pieces of work that make a final visual statement about their chosen theme. Creating this work can be stressful for students, especially if it is within the limited time of the externally set assignment. You can increase student confidence by ensuring that they are properly prepared for the final outcome. Encourage them to make their work ambitious, but achievable, so that they produce an outcome that builds on their strengths and improves skill levels.

AREAS TO FOCUS ON

You should try to ensure that students cover the following elements in their work:

Personal response

Themes such as family history and location are obviously personal, but there are many other ways in which a student's work can be personal:

- If their designs combine artistic inspiration and first-hand resources, they will create a unique work.
- Their interpretation of a theme, or sustained use of different media, can be very personal.
- Collecting and recording a good range of resources early in the project will help to make their work highly personal.

Coherent presentation

The final outcome should have a connection to student's earlier ideas and development work. If their work jumps between unrelated ideas without reason, it will not be a coherent presentation. In a tutorial situation, look through students' supporting work and discuss links to the final outcome. The links include types of imagery, use of materials and expression of a theme. Students should not worry if their final outcome has changed from their early ideas, but they should try to ensure that their changes make logical sense.

Realising intentions

The intentions of a project will be a combination of early ideas, and how they change during the development work. The final outcome should sum up much of this work in a visual form. While discussing individual final outcomes with students, ask the following questions:

- Is the final outcome connected with their supporting work?
- Does it express the elements of art they have been exploring?
- Does it show understanding of visual language (see elements of art, pages 13 to 29 in the Student's Book)?
- Is the composition of the final piece balanced in a way that suits their intentions?
- Are their responses to other artists reflected in some way in their outcome?

The different strands of the final outcome are explained in more detail with examples in the following sections.

UNIT 1: YOUR FINAL OUTCOME

GETTING READY TO START

It is useful to ask students a series of questions in preparation for their final outcome:

- **Materials:** Ensure that students make a list of the materials that they need. Are they all available? Are there any special materials required that need to be obtained or used in specialist rooms?
- **Surface preparation:** What size are they going to work in? What type of surface are they going to use? Do they need a stretcher or to prime a board? Considerations for other subject areas will vary according to their choice of media.
- **Use of time:** How much time do they have to make their outcome? How long will each stage take? How does this fit into the sessions available to them? For the externally set assignment, they should try to plan a piece of work that will use most of the available time.
- **References:** Have they referred to their supporting studies or portfolio? Students should refer to their supporting studies or portfolio as they make their outcome. Selecting supporting studies that show the development of their work and will help them complete their final outcome.

> **Top tip**
> - Encourage students to leave some challenges to resolve in their final outcome, so that it is not just a larger repetition of earlier work. If their later development work is made up of sections or parts of their final design, then they will still be exploring new elements as they work on the outcome.

PERSONAL RESPONSE

You can guide a student's personal response in a variety of ways.

Sustained investigation

Students can work in a very traditional manner, or limited range of subject matter, and still show a personal response. Their use of lighting, composition, texture and colour can be combined to show a very individualistic exploration of their subject.

Detailed first-hand resources

A personal response can be shown in finding and working with first-hand resources. Students may collect items that are personal to them, or that fit in with their theme. By going beyond internet images and secondary sources, they are making an effort to find more unique and personal information to inform their project.

Communication of ideas or themes

Students' work may comment on a theme or social issue that interests them. If successful, the way in which they present their work will show a viewpoint on the issues they have explored. Many themes that concern the younger generation can stimulate personal work, such as 'the environment' or 'identity'.

COHERENT PRESENTATION

For the student's final outcome to be coherent, it needs to adhere to the following points:

The supporting work tells a story

The student's work tells a clear story of development and results in a successful final outcome. Exploration of materials, subject matter and design ideas should be reflected in the final outcome. The outcome should provide a satisfactory end to the research.

The supporting work makes logical sense

Students should not worry about changing ideas and subject matter as their work develops, but they do need to ensure that it makes logical sense in the supporting studies or portfolio. Making connections and explaining their decisions will help to show the thinking behind their work.

Development ideas are present in the outcome

Final outcomes should not appear to be separate from development work. If there is no relationship with the development work, then it is hard to understand how the final outcome decisions were made. While students compose ideas for their outcome, they should constantly refer to their supporting studies.

REALISING INTENTIONS

The student's early ideas and development will show the direction of their work and also create expectations for what their final outcome will be about. This outcome should resolve the lines of enquiry that they have focused upon in their later development work.

REFINEMENT OF MEDIA

Student supporting work should have experiments in materials, and refinement of media in later development work. Improved control and skills should be evident in the final outcome. Discourage students from using an unexplored medium in their outcome, as it will have no connection to their supporting work.

REFINEMENT OF DESIGN ELEMENTS

Many design ideas will have been explored in students' supporting work. Check whether their final piece shows development of some of these designs? Have the different arrangements they considered been reflected in their final outcome?

COMMUNICATION OF IDEAS

Their project has a theme, which is expressed in their final outcome. Does this outcome express the ideas they have been exploring? This may be a social theme, but it may also be an exploration of formal elements. For example, if their work is about endangered species, then their final outcome should visually express this.

EXPRESSING THE INFLUENCE OF THE ARTIST

The work of other artists and designers has been part of the student's research and inspiration. Does the final outcome show these influences? This does not mean that their work has to look like the work of others, but that elements from their art research should have clearly influenced the development of their outcome.

UNDERSTANDING OF VISUAL LANGUAGE

Some of the formal elements of art (see elements of art on pages 13 to 29 in the Student's Book) will be present in the student's final outcome. Have they shown learning and understanding in their use of these elements? Different types of work and subject areas will use some of these elements.

Overall design or composition

Alternative compositions in students' supporting studies and portfolios will show the range of possible arrangements that they have considered. Their judgement in choosing a final design will help to show a student's understanding of visual language.

Use of colour

Colour, or tonal value, will be an important part of many students' final outcomes. Choice of colour will have a big effect on the mood of the final outcome. Final colour decisions should relate to colour work in a student's supporting references.

Other formal elements of art

Line, texture, form and other elements will be involved in the completion of different types of media and subject areas. Confident use of these elements will reflect further understanding of visual language.

SUMMARY

The complete development of a project is quite a journey for a student. Much of the early part of the course will be taken up with you, the teacher, directing activity that builds the skills and understanding required to develop a personal and coherent portfolio of work.

It takes time for students to understand how the final outcome relates to their supporting work and much of the work you guide students through leads to this end result. As you plan the schemes of work, try to ensure that:

- the final outcome has grown out of the student's early ideas and research
- the techniques used should have been refined from development work
- it is clear that the supporting work formed the basis for the final outcome
- the elements of visual understanding are clear to see in the final outcome, in use of balance, or development of form, or composition, and so on.

As their teacher, you can guide your students through a series of activities and tasks that build their visual understanding.

Part III looks at the methods, materials and artists particular to different subject areas, together with examples of activities and ways to introduce these topics to your students.

Chapter 8	Painting and related media

INTRODUCTION

8.1 Drawing

8.2 Painting

8.3 Graphic media

8.4 Non-traditional media

8.5 New media

8.6 Student case study

Learning objectives

By the end of this unit students should:

- have selected and controlled a range of media, processes and techniques
- recognise the use of line, tone, colour and texture in drawing
- know how to choose and compose/organise a variety of elements
- have shown use of analytical skills
- recognise the use of form and relationships.

Classroom resources

- Student's Book Chapter 8 Painting and related media, pages 179–203
- Displays of works by some of the related artists and a colour wheel for painting reference; natural and human-made forms collection for observational drawing.

Research sources

- Books:

  From Giotto to Cezanne: A Concise History of Painting – Michael Levey

  The Shock of the New: Art and the Century of Change – Robert Hughes

Top tip

- Limit the range of colours kept in stock. Warm and cool primary colours with black brown and white should give students a range to mix 99 per cent of colours.

General lesson ideas

- Introduce painting and related media by showing examples for each sub-section of work by relevant artists. Encourage curiosity from students with questions and answers.
- Ask students to write down all types of supporting work for painting and related media that they can think of without looking at their Student's Book, and then to check. They can keep their list in their sketchbooks for reference.

Key considerations:

- What projects or topics are suggested or could you devise? Test practical activities yourself before setting them as tasks for students. Encourage students to work to their strengths and areas of interest within the limits of resources. Check that students have correctly used key terms and technical information.

Reflective log:

- What practical skills do I need to develop in order to help my students achieve?
- How can I use practical and theoretical lessons to help my students to develop their work?
- How can I structure my teaching to make the most of the resources and facilities that I have available to me?
- Are there any local exhibitions or resources that my students could visit or use?

Key terms

- **Student's Book key terms:** acrylic, charcoal, complementary colours, harmonious colours, impasto, iterative, line drawing, mid-tone, oil paint, opaque, positive and negative, tonal value, transparent, wash, watercolour

UNIT 1: DRAWING
UNIT 2: PAINTING

DRAWING LESSON	Tone

This lesson is designed to introduce students to the materials and techniques used in drawing tonal values. Students first explore pencil technique before looking at how lighting and composition affect the arrangement of a still-life. The lesson's main emphasis is on the concepts of chiaroscuro and seeing tonal values.

Classroom resources

- *Classroom arrangement:* If possible set up the lighting to come from one direction to increase the quality of shadow.
- *Materials and equipment:* Cartridge paper, range of 2H to 6B pencils, erasers, pencil sharpeners, ceramic jars, cups and saucers.

Research sources

- Fundamentals of tonal drawing
- Search for example drawings to demonstrate use of tone. Possible artists and works include:

Jim Dine	*Ten Winter Tools*, 1972
Fernando Botero	*Still life with Teapot and Lemons*, 2005
Leonardo da Vinci	*Cartoon for St Anne*, c.1499
Pablo Picasso	*Still life with a Pitcher and Apples*, c.1919
Georges Seurat	*Madame Seurat*, 1882

LESSON TASKS

1) Starter suggestions

Demonstration	• Show examples of artists' drawings using tone to define **shape** and **form**. Explain vocabulary such as **tone**, **tonal**, and **chiaroscuro**.	
Additional student activity	Ask questions such as:	
	• What materials have been used? • How do we see the edges of the objects? • Are there any lines in the drawing? • What direction is the light coming from?	(pencil, charcoal, chalk, paint, ink?) (from the contrast of light and dark) (no, mainly areas of tonal values) (one or more directions)
	Encourage students to make quick notes of artists and key terms before directing students to move around demonstration table.	
Top tips	• During a discussion use 'open-ended' questioning, which requires more than a 'yes' or 'no' answer. • Try to encourage as many students as possible to participate by asking them to describe what they can see.	

2) Main lesson activities: Exercise 1 (Materials exploration in pencil tone)

Demonstration	• Draw a grid of boxes that can be quickly shaded in pencil (Part III, Unit 1). Starting with a 2H pencil, demonstrate the use of pressure to increase the tone created with the side of the pencil. Use increasingly soft pencils to show the darker tones created. Discuss the change of tone from light grey with hard pencils to almost black with very soft pencils.
Additional student activity	• Remind students to use the side of the pencil, varying their pressure to change tone, and to work with a range of soft to hard pencils. Some students will need to practise controlling the amount of pressure they apply to make a wide range of tonal values. Students should label the pencil grades used and make notes on what they have observed and learnt.

3) Main lesson activities: Exercise 2 (tonal drawing)

Demonstration	• Use a medium pencil (2B) to draw a series of circles and round shapes. Shade these in to make them look three-dimensional, with light from one direction and a floor shadow. Use an eraser for highlights and tidying edges, and a softer pencil for darker shadows. The shapes can look like balls or rounded pebbles.
Additional student activity	• Remind students to use the motion of the whole arm to draw circular shapes. Give advice on when to use an eraser and/or a darker pencil. Students can use arrows to remind them of their chosen light direction. Label the use of different grades of pencil.
Top tips	• Students often spend more time erasing than drawing! Encourage students to start a new sketch instead of erasing one. • They should mainly use the eraser to draw highlights out of tonal areas.

4) Main lesson activities: Exercise 3 (tonal drawing: Ceramic jars, cups and saucers)

Demonstration	• Draw the outline of a cup or jar from observation. Use tonal shading to block in mid-tones and shadows. Add highlights with an eraser and increase tonal range with a darker pencil. Talk about the direction of light, looking for highlights and possible reflected light.
Additional student activity	• Help distribute still-life objects and encourage students not to draw too small. Discuss proportion and observation of light direction. Use erasers for highlights not for over-correction. Several studies can be made on the same page, annotating problems and understanding.

Top tip	• Seeing tonal values can take some practice for students:
	  o Suggest half-closing their eyes to help show tonal changes.
	  o Camera phone monochrome photographs can help, but students should also work from life.

5) Plenary suggestions

Demonstration	• Gather student drawings together to discuss with the class. Reinforce the use of key terms vocabulary. Refer to the artist drawings from the beginning of the lesson.
Additional student activity	• Explain which drawings demonstrate the use of tonal values and control of pencil shading. Discuss which aspects students found difficult to do. Store work from the lesson safely.

Reflection

When reviewing students' work, ask yourself whether they are showing control of pencil tone in the exercise and whether this is also the case in the still-life drawing? It can take several drawings for students to see tonal values as they will be more familiar with drawing in line. Students could organise their work and make further notes in their sketchbook to consolidate their learning. Students could set up a similar still life at home to draw, as well as taking black and white photographs of it for reference.

Key terms

- **Student's Book key terms:** chiaroscuro, form, shape
- **Additional key terms:** tone

DRAWING LESSON	Line, wash and texture

The following notes give you brief ideas for how to develop a sequence of lessons. The exercises often involve dividing a sheet of paper into a grid so that different material and techniques can be compared.

Classroom resources

- *Classroom arrangement:* No special requirements
- *Materials and equipment:* Cartridge paper, pencils, permanent ink, dipping pens, small watercolour brushes (sizes 3 and 8), water, mixing palettes, white wax crayons or oil pastels.

Research sources

- Use the following artists as a starting point for presenting example work to students:

Line drawing examples:	Henri Matisse	David Hockney	Vincent van Gogh
Wash examples:	Henry Moore	Rembrandt	James Gurney
Texture examples:	Max Ernst	Georges Seurat	Albrecht Durer

LINE LESSON: Mark-making

1) Exercise (materials exploration in pen and ink)

Demonstration	• Show artists' examples followed by the technique for mark-making exploration in line, dot, stipple and splatter with ink in a grid on cartridge paper.
Additional student activity	• Assist students with making a wide variety of marks, controlling ink levels on the pen or brush and the level of hand pressure used in applying ink to the surface.

2) Main lesson activity (line drawing task from photographs of animals)

Demonstration	• Draw in line from a photo using a pen or brush. Draw the same figures but add shading in stipple or cross-hatching.
Additional student activity	• Hand out references, or students can select their own. Faint pencil outlines can be used to add confidence, before drawing in ink.

WASH LESSON: Tonal values and fluid effects

Tonal values and fluid effects with ink and water are explored in this lesson.

3) Exercise (materials exploration in brush and wash)

Demonstration	• Create wash tones from light to dark, add new washes to dry layers to change tone, and show the effect of adding ink to wet paper.
Additional student activity	• Guide students in diluting the ink to make different shades of grey, loading the brush and controlling the flow of ink on the paper. Emphasise that white is the paper colour. Ensure that water and palettes are cleaned when very dirty.

4) Main lesson activity (line and wash task from observed piece of fruit)

Demonstration	• Draw fruit in outline, and use tonal washes to add form and shadow.
Additional student activity	• Check students are drawing on a suitable scale and mixing a range of tones in the palette, and not just on the drawing. They should allow washes to dry before adding a second layer.

TEXTURE LESSON: Pencils and brushes

5) Exercise (materials exploration in pencil, brush, pen and white wax crayon)

Demonstration	• Show different textures that can be made with a pencil tip, rubbing pencil over a textured surface, by dragging brush and stipple, wax resist and wash.
Additional student activity	• Ask students to divide their paper into 20 or more boxes. How many different textures can they create?

6) Main lesson activity (texture drawing task from animal photographs)

Demonstration	• Draw an animal outline. Use appropriate textures and tones to complete the image.
Additional student activity	• Ensure that outlines are large enough. Discuss texture techniques that will suit each animal and encourage test experiments next to the drawings.

Reflection

Students are often experienced in pencil drawing but less confident in other drawing techniques. By exploring a range of approaches, some students will adopt new techniques that add variety to their work. Recording from observation and being able to draw ideas on paper are fundamental to much artistic development.

DRAWING PROJECT IDEAS

The projects here are examples of how to consolidate these drawing skills over a longer period of time. The timescale will depend upon your circumstances and each element of the project may extend over several weeks.

Classroom resources
• *Classroom arrangement:* Still life may work with tables around a central display. Portrait work often requires students to sit opposite one another. • *Materials and equipment:* Drawing boards can be useful for larger, sustained drawings. Select drawing materials as appropriate for the project. Another advantage of a drawing project is that material requirements are minimal.

Research sources
• Suggested starting points for artist examples:

Still life:	Pablo Picasso	Paul Cezanne	Keith Mallett
Surreal portraits:	Giuseppe Arcimboldo	Salvador Dali	Antonio Mora
Interiors:	Henri Matisse	Edward Hopper	Raoul Dufy

PROJECT SUGGESTIONS

1) Still life

1. Discuss introduced examples by artists, as well as the selection of objects and composition.
2. Create individual observational drawings of personal items, focusing on chiaroscuro.
3. Draw a still life arranged by your teacher (for drawings focusing on composition).
4. Draw a still life(s) that you select (for sustained larger-scale drawings).

2) Surreal portraits

1. Introduce examples of surreal portraits combining disparate elements.
2. Draw other students in pencil using tonal values over several drawing sessions.
3. Explore animal references for elements that can be combined with the human face.
4. Select one pencil portrait and alter it using erasers to add animal elements. Finish the drawing using ink and wash over the final composition.

3) Interiors

1. Discuss introduced work by artists, looking at composition and the arrangement of space.
2. Draw individual items of furniture to develop confidence with materials.
3. Draw a corner of a room for homework, or use photographs.
4. Do a panoramic drawing of your classroom use a long thin sheet of paper.
5. Use references from home, do a sustained panoramic drawing of your bedroom.

4) Assessment of projects

When reviewing the project work, consider the following aspects of the four Assessment Objectives:

Assessment Objectives
• **AO1:** Observational drawings of people, places and personal items, ideas for designs and combinations of elements, notes on insights from the response to artists.
• **AO2:** Exploration of drawing techniques showing evidence of use of a range of materials with notes and experiments in deciding which techniques to develop further.
• **AO3:** Develop ideas through a series of investigation, relating work to the work of Van Gogh, and considering aspects of the elements of art.
• **AO4:** Produce a sustained final outcome drawing that realises the intentions in supporting work and shows an understanding of visual language.

PAINTING LESSON	Colour

These lessons introduce the concepts of the colour wheel and colour mixing. Watercolours are a good choice of media to start working with in this area as they are easy to clean up and many students have some familiarity with them already.

Follow-on lessons continue to use watercolour and are developed further using opaque paints, as well as introducing texture.

Classroom resources

- *Classroom arrangement*: Water and paints can be shared between two or three students.
- *Materials and equipment*: Watercolours, watercolour brushes, palettes, water, paper towels, sketchbooks or cartridge (not thin paper that will buckle). Colour images of Van Gogh paintings, or internet access by students on phones or tablets.

Research sources

- These lessons are based around the paintings of Vincent van Gogh. Some good examples of his work to use are:

| *Van Gogh's Chair* | 1888 | *The Bedroom* | 1889 | *Starry Night* | 1889 |
| *Wheatfield with a Reaper* | 1889 | *Sunflowers* | 1888 | | |

LESSON TASKS

1) Starter suggestions

Demonstration	• Discuss **primary** and **secondary** colours, explain their relationship in the **colour wheel**, and show a good example by Van Gogh with a strong use of colour.	
Additional student activity	Ask questions such as:	
	• What are primary colours?	(red, yellow, blue)
	• How do you make purple?	(blue and red)
	• Which primary colours has Van Gogh used?	(discuss the variations that can be seen)
	• Encourage students to make quick notes of colour information, key terms and Van Gogh paintings before directing them to move around the demonstration table.	
Top tip	• Colour mixing is something that students 'think' they know, but it is easily forgotten. Asking trick questions can help to reinforce the basic concept of primary colours, for example: 'Which colours do you mix to make blue?'	

2) Main lesson activities: Exercise 1 (colour mixing and colour wheel demonstration)

Demonstration	• Show how to mix water and colour on the palette, and how to apply the paint from a loaded brush. Demonstrate mixing primary colours on the palette, keeping the block colours clean. In pencil, divide a circle in to six segments and demonstrate painting a colour wheel with mixed secondary colours.

Additional student activity	• Let students experiment with mixing colours and painting test swatches before they attempt the colour wheel exercise. Check that students are wetting the colour blocks first, are not scrubbing too hard with their brushes and are mixing the colours on the palette. Students should experiment with combinations of different primary colours (warm and cool) to make the best examples of secondary colours. Multiple colour wheels and swatches should be labelled with the colours used from the watercolour set.
Top tip	• Students should change water often to ensure that the colours can be mixed correctly. This is especially important for lighter colours such as yellow. Remind students to rinse brushes clean after applying a colour.

3) Main lesson activities: Exercise 2 (Van Gogh painting analysis)

Demonstration	• Show examples of Van Gogh paintings discussing the use primary and secondary colours. Introduce the idea of **complementary colours**.
Additional student activity	• Ask students to identify primary and secondary colours in Van Gogh's paintings. Can they can identify uses of complementary colours? Ask them to choose a favourite example by Van Gogh.
Top tip	• 'Complementary colours' is a new concept for many students. Simple visual examples can help reinforce the idea.

4) Main lesson activities: Exercise 3 (Van Gogh colour mixing exercise)

Demonstration	• Show students how to identify and mix paint colour swatches of all the primary and secondary colours they can see in their chosen Van Gogh painting.
Additional student activity	• Help students to identify colours they may have missed, or suggest alternative colour combinations to mix the colour they can see. Students can try painting complementary colours next to each other. Student work should dry while painting materials are being cleared away.

5) Plenary suggestions

Demonstration	• Ask volunteers to show their work and to identify their reference painting.
Additional student activity	• Discuss with students which colours work well in making the colour wheel. Also talk about problems in mixing the secondary colours and why they chose that specific Van Gogh painting.

Reflection

If students have time, they can try painting a quick colour sketch of their chosen Van Gogh painting using the colours they have identified. By the end of the lesson, students should be familiar with the primary and secondary colours. A few questions should help you to see whether the knowledge has been absorbed:

- How do you make orange?
- What are the secondary colours?
- How do you make red (trick question)?

The colour tests and colour swatches need to be organised and labelled to make them more useful for future reference, and to evidence their learning.

Key terms
• **Student's Book key terms:** complementary colours
• **Additional key terms:** colour wheel, primary, secondary

PAINTING LESSON	Line and colour wash, opaque colour

The following lessons all use the same still life as a basis for observation and colour reference.

Classroom resources

- *Classroom arrangement*: Desks arranged so that all students can see the still life based on Van Gogh's work.
- *Materials and equipment*: Waterproof ink and pens, watercolours and soft brushes, poster paint or acrylics and larger brushes.

Research sources

- Set up a still life inspired by the paintings of Van Gogh using objects such as a chair, old boots, flowers or kitchen pots. The still life should include objects with primary and secondary colours. The objects do not need to look like those in the Van Gogh painting, but should be inspired by it. If possible, display or have the Van Gogh paintings at hand for students also to refer to.

STILL-LIFE LINE AND COLOUR WASH LESSON

1) Exercise (still-life pencil composition and ink drawing)

Demonstration	• Block in the still-life composition in pencil and draw over it using ink and pen, creating different marks for textures.
Additional student activity	• Encourage students to draw the main shapes in pencil, and to add detail in ink using different textures for each object.

2) Main lesson activity (watercolour washes over dry ink)

Demonstration	• Mix the main colours of the still life and paint washes over the dry ink drawing. Complete the painting with additional layers of colour.
Additional student activity	• Try to get students to mix the main colours before starting to paint and allow drying time before additional layers of washes.

OPAQUE COLOUR LESSON

3) Exercise (materials exploration)

Demonstration	• Demonstrate colour mixing and painting using poster or acrylic colour. Emphasise the ability to 'cover' paper and paint 'over' another colour.
Additional student activity	• Guide students in using small amounts of paint and mixing in white to make lighter tones. Students should try painting over dry colours and creating texture with thicker paint.

4) Main lesson activity (Opaque paint colour-wheel exercise)

Demonstration	• Show students how to paint a colour wheel using opaque paints.
Additional student activity	• Examine which primary colours work best for mixing the secondary colours, and how much water to add to make the mixture easier to paint with the brush.

STILL-LIFE PAINTING LESSON

5) Exercise (composition drawn in pencil)

Demonstration	• Return to the still life and make a larger drawing from a different viewpoint.
Additional student activity	• Students need to move to a different viewpoint for this second still life. They can work quickly in pencil and add some shading if they wish; it will all be covered by opaque paint.

6) Main lesson activity (opaque still-life painting)

Demonstration	• Mix and apply main colour areas. Add detail in layers of overpainting.
Additional student activity	• Try to get students to paint in all general areas before adding detail. Encourage them to work over the whole painting. This final outcome may take several sessions.

Reflection

Creating several pieces of work from the same still life makes efficient use of reorganising the classroom and introduces the concept of development of a theme. Students often find watercolour easier to work with but struggle with the lack of white for mixing. When they start to use opaque paints, they can see the value of being able to overpaint mistakes and use white to lighten colours.

Exploration of colour and painting can be developed in many different ways. Transparent or opaque paints will be preferred by different students after experimentation, and developing deeper skills in a chosen painting medium can produce superior results.

Classroom resources
• *Classroom arrangement:* Still life may work well with tables around a central display. Portrait work often requires students to sit opposite each other. Acrylic painting and easels can require more space. • *Materials and equipment:* Watercolours or opaque paints, brushes and painting surfaces.

Research sources
• Suggested starting points for artist examples: *Bedroom:*   *The Bedroom*, 1889   *Bedroom Letter* sketch, 1888 *Emotional portrait:*   *Van Gogh Self-portrait*, 1889   *Self-Portrait with Grey Felt Hat*, 1887 *Night city:*   *Cafe Terrace at Night*, 1888   *Starry Night over the Rhone*, 1888

PROJECT SUGGESTIONS

These projects present very different ways to continue to explore painting through the work of Van Gogh.

1) Bedroom

1. Discuss Van Gogh's *The Bedroom* drawing and painting, including perspective.
2. Produce observational photographs and drawings of your bedroom.
3. Do small studies and compositions for a 'Bedroom' painting.
4. Paint a bedroom composition emphasising colour and/or texture.

2) Emotional portrait

1. Discuss the emotional mood of portraits using colour, facial expression and mark-making.
2. Collect photographs and drawings of portraits with mood and emotion.
3. Do larger ink drawings to explore texture and brush directions.
4. Produce a final outcome sustained portrait incorporating a strong use of colour and texture.

3) Night city

1. Look at the use of light and reflection in Van Gogh's night paintings.
2. Collect night-time references of city scenes, cafes and shops.
3. Do colour studies, drawings and compositions for night scene painting.
4. Produce a final outcome painting.

4) Assessment of projects

When reviewing the project work, consider the following aspects of the four Assessment Objectives:

Assessment Objectives
• **AO1:** Observational photographs and drawings of people and places, ideas for designs and combinations of elements, notes on insights from the response to the work of Van Gogh.   • **AO2:** Exploration of drawing and painting techniques evidenced in colour swatches, trial paintings and test pieces, as well as techniques used for a final outcome.   • **AO3:** Develop ideas through a series of investigation, increasing in complexity and compositional elements. Links are drawn with the work of van Gogh and consider aspects of the elements of art.   • **AO4:** Students have produced a sustained final outcome that realises the intentions in supporting work and shows an understanding of visual language.

UNIT 3: GRAPHIC MEDIA

GRAPHIC MEDIA LESSON	Text and images

This lesson is introduced using text and images. Some basic graphic materials are used in a composition combining images and lettering. Students refer to the work of artist Niki de Saint Phalle. They are encouraged to use their imagination in working with the images provided and using different lettering styles.

Classroom resources

- *Classroom arrangement:* Space to spread out, references and marker pens.
- *Materials and equipment:* A3 cartridge, coloured marker pens, black fine liners, photographs of different zoo animals.

Research sources

- Niki de Saint Phalle produced many graphic images; often in letters to friends. In addition to the images suggested below, you can use an image search to find images you think will work well for your students:

My Love We Won't	1968
Letter to Peter	1994
Vive L'Amour	1990
I Rather Like You a Lot	1970

LESSON TASKS

1) Starter suggestions

Demonstration	• Show examples of graphic design drawings by Niki de Saint Phalle. Point out where she has combined a range of images and writing as part of the design. Also comment on the simple use of colour and the arrangement of objects across the page without a horizon or suggestion of space. Show some of the zoo animal references and introduce the idea of students making their own design about animals, or visiting a zoo.
Additional student activity	• Ask students to describe what they can see in the Saint Phalle images, and what the drawings are about. Students can suggest ideas for their own work or the animals they would include, and why.
Top tip	• Niki de Saint Phalle is more famous as a sculptor. You could show some of these images to give a fuller picture of the artist's work.

2) Main lesson activities: Exercise 1 (pencil drawing from photographic references)

Demonstration	• Explain to students that they are going to design a letter about a visit to a zoo, which includes drawing and writing, using provided photographic references. The page could be a simple description of some of the animals in the zoo or something more imaginative or surreal. The writing should be arranged as part of the composition.
Additional student activity	• Ask students to choose animal references to use and write some notes on their initial ideas. Drawing some thumbnail sketches will help with this. The designs should be in light pencil for working-over at a later stage.
Top tip	• Students do not need to work to the edge of the paper. A generous white border will add impact to the graphic images.

3) Main lesson activities: Exercise 2 (colour with up to four markers)

Demonstration	• Refer to the Saint Phalle images and show how they use only a few bright colours. Point out how white can be left as part of the design. Leaving the background white speeds up the task and adds to the bold graphic effect.
Additional student activity	• Let students choose marker pens and lay flat areas of colours over their design using the pencil drawing as a guide.
Top tip	• Students should apply colour first to prevent the black marker lines from smudging. This also allows for the later adjustment of outlines to clearly surround coloured areas.

4) Main lesson activities: Exercise 3 (outline drawings and writing in fine-liner pen)

Demonstration	• Demonstrate the use of fine liners to define figure designs and go over the writing. Show the effect of using different thicknesses of pens, as well as cross-hatching and other textures.
Additional student activity	• Let students practise using different pens on a test sheet before using them on their design. Encourage students to use some thicker black lines and areas to make their design clear to the viewer.
Top tip	• Small watercolour brushes and drawing pens can also be used for this exercise but can be more difficult to control. The regularity of fibre pen marks is less expressive but can work well for graphic designs.

5) Plenary suggestions

Demonstration	• Display student designs on a table, pointing out novel ideas, and good use of colour or control of line.
Additional student activity	• Students can explain which design they like the most, or the reasons behind their own design.

Reflection
The materials used for this lesson have been limited to speed up the process. Think about other simple graphic materials that could be used:

- Pencil crayons are easy to use and could create blended colour changes.
- Collaged magazine photographs could be cut to shape and stuck down.
- Brightly coloured paper could be used instead of coloured markers.

These additional materials might allow students to make their work more personal and develop their own vision inspired by this starting point.

GRAPHIC MEDIA LESSON	Poster design

Designing posters for advertising, illustration or information is a common task in graphic communication. In this lesson, students design a bold poster balancing a simple image and a key word. Traditional skills in tracing and transferring images can be replaced by light tables or digital processes.

Classroom resources

- *Classroom arrangement:* Space to spread out references and marker pens.
- *Materials and equipment:* A3 cartridge, tracing paper, blue, red and black coloured markers, photographs of different birds and animals (can be black and white but need to be roughly A4 in size).

Research sources

- Shepard Fairey has produced bold graphic images for posters. His website features many examples.

Top tip

- Reference images chosen for this task should have bold shadows and not be complex, as students may take a long time to trace and transfer the image.

LESSON TASKS

1) Starter suggestions

Demonstration	• Show examples of work by Shepard Fairey, pointing out the limited use of colour and strong shadows. Discuss using a simple image and word to convey an idea. Introduce using an animal and a word in a poster to protect the environment.
Additional student activity	• Ask students whether they recognise any of the people in Fairey's work. Then discuss word ideas for their own posters and choices of animals or birds.

2) Main lesson activities: Exercise 1 (pencil design)

Demonstration	• Trace an animal photograph about A4 in size, transfer it onto A3 paper and combine it with the chosen word using clear pencil lines.
Additional student activity	• Make sure that students turn over their tracing paper to transfer the image to paper. The chosen word needs to be drawn in clear block letters.

3) Main lesson activities: Exercise 2 (black and colour added)

Demonstration	• Use black marker for the animal shadows and to define the poster lettering. Consider using positive or negative lettering, which can be black, white or coloured. Shade mid-tone areas using a selected colour such as red or light blue.
Additional student activity	• Encourage students to fill in black areas and not just draw lines. Only one colour can be used for the mid-tones of the poster and the lettering.
Top tip	• Coloured markers should be light in tone so as not join up with the black areas.

Reflection

The final image should have a good balance of black, white and mid tone colour. Suggest that students squint at the image to see the shadow areas more clearly.

GRAPHIC MEDIA LESSON	Line drawing

Line drawing is used in many areas of graphic communication. Vector lines are often used in digital work, but this project relies upon fibre-tip pens and observational drawing skills. Reference photographs are used, but the intention is to produce something that has the liveliness of a line drawing.

Classroom resources

- *Materials and equipment:* A3 cartridge, black fibre-tip pens, multiple copies of photographs of market and street scenes from local area (can be photocopies).

Research sources

- Sameer Kulavoor is a graphic design artist working in India. Some of his work uses photographic references for outline drawings of life in his local area. His work *Kalaghoda Musings* is a good starting point for this lesson.

LESSON TASKS

1) Starter suggestions

Demonstration	• Show some examples of Kulavoor's line-drawing designs, pointing out the overlapping images and changes in thickness of line. Look at photographs of local street scenes that students will recognise and ask them for ideas of which elements they could use in their own line drawings.
Additional student activity	• Ask students to describe what they can see in Kulavoor's drawings, and how they think he made them. Describe the local images full of people and ask students to isolate areas that could be used in a separate design.

2) Main lesson activities: Exercise 1 (pencil design)

Demonstration	• Select areas of people, activity or buildings from the photographs and sketch in pencil on the A3 sheet. Change photographs and work in patches across the page overlapping images in a similar way to Kulavoor's work.
Additional student activity	• Encourage students to work quickly and draw on a big scale, leaving detail to be put in with the ink pens. They should try to get a variety of objects and sizes in their designs.
Top tip	• Accuracy and realism are not too important in this lesson, so avoid tracing paper. Students' drawings will have more life when they have been inked in.

3) Main lesson activities: Exercise 2 (inking process)

Demonstration	• Use medium and thicker black pens to draw in the final designs on top of the pencil sketches, referring back to the original photographic references.
Additional student activity	• Encourage students to include a variety of line widths and patterns or textures where relevant. At some point, remove the references so that students can focus on completing the design as a whole.

Reflection
Students often work very slowly when referring to photographs. Try to encourage students to enjoy letting the lines do much of the work, as distortion and changes of scale will add to the charm of the drawing.

GRAPHIC MEDIA LESSON	Mural designs

Design briefs often involve creating concepts for architecture and building. This can stimulate student imaginations as they are designing for a 'real' space. In this lesson, students refer to the work of Sameer Kulavoor but use buildings from their local environment as the basis for a mural project.

Classroom resources
• *Materials and equipment:* A3 cartridge, black fibre-tip pens, markers, photographs of local buildings.

Research sources
• Sameer Kulavoor designed a mural in New Zealand that would make a good starting point for this lesson. His website features a video and further details.

LESSON TASKS

1) Starter suggestions

Demonstration	• Show the video and discuss Kulavoor's mural. Show images of local buildings.
Additional student activity	• Discuss how Kulavoor uses white in the mural design. Ask how it fits in with the building. Ask which local buildings could be used for a mural design.

2) Main lesson activities: Exercise 1 (pencil drawing of chosen building)

Demonstration	• Draw the chosen building and shade it in pencil for solidity and depth.
Additional student activity	• Encourage students to fill the paper, or go over the edges. Shading should not be very dark. Students can use a ruler but it will slow them down.

3) Main lesson activities: Exercise 2 (design ideas for the mural)

Demonstration	• On a separate piece of paper, sketch objects and people that fit in with the theme chosen for the mural. They can be quite simple and cartoon-like.
Additional student activity	• The theme may be related to the use of the building or the area in which it is located. Consider where the different images will fit into the building drawing.
Top tips	• If students have access to WiFi, they can find visual references quickly on their smartphone or tablet for this type of lesson.

4) Main lesson activities: Exercise 3 (mural design)

Demonstration	• Show students how to pencil the design on the building drawing and complete it using a black pen and coloured markers.
Additional student activity	• Encourage students to vary line thickness, use two extra colours and refer to Kulavoor's mural for ideas on arranging images around the architecture.

Reflection
The result of this lesson is a plan or concept for a mural. The emphasis here is on visual problem solving as students combine their ideas with the limited areas available on the building.

Graphic media projects are often about communication or fulfilling a design brief. A wide range of materials can be used as well as digital resources, which are commonly used in commercial graphic design.

Classroom resources
• *Materials and equipment:* Standard graphic media materials

Research sources

• Suggested starting points for project ideas:
  Film poster: Saul Bass
  Mural: Fernand Leger

PROJECT SUGGESTIONS

These suggestions offer varied approaches to graphic media projects that include artist influences, as well as 'real world' design challenges.

1) Film poster design

1. Look at the Saul Bass poster designs and choose modern films for which to design posters.
2. Sketch ideas, collect resources and develop film title font alternatives.
3. Make a mock-up design using coloured paper, scissors, white paint and black marker pens.
4. Draw, ink and complete the final outcome poster design.

2) Artist car design

1. Look at the BMW Art Car designs done by artists.
2. Choose a car and artist inspiration to research, and collect references.
3. Create alternative design ideas, sketches or colour studies.
4. Use the front and side outlines of the car as the basis for final design ideas on an A2 sheet of paper or board.

3) School canteen mural design

1. Look at the paintings of Leger showing people in groups. Look at photographs of the school canteen.
2. Explore ideas for a canteen mural, and collect images and resources.
3. Make sketches and colour studies for the mural based on the canteen's architecture.
4. Produce final designs of the canteen on scale boards, or produce a scale model of part of the space.

4) Assessment of projects

When reviewing the project work, consider the following aspects of the four Assessment Objectives:

Assessment Objectives
• **AO1:** Students will often need to observe places or objects first-hand as part of their brief. They may also need to record their responses to written or visual works of art that are part of their starting point.
• **AO2:** Exploration of graphic media, and the selection of techniques for a final outcome should be evidenced. Often reproduction and printing are areas that need exploring as part of this process.
• **AO3:** Develop ideas through a series of investigation, relating work to the work of others, and considering aspects of the elements of art. Scale drawings, models and test pieces of design work all contribute to this assessment objective.
• **AO4:** Produce a sustained final outcome design that realises the intentions in supporting work and shows an understanding of visual language. Finished pieces of work and completed design proposals should present a personal and coherent visual statement.

UNIT 4: NON-TRADITIONAL MEDIA

By their nature, non-traditional media lessons cover an endless range of possibilities. These lessons attempt to give some starting points for exploring this rich area of art and design.

NON-TRADITIONAL MEDIA LESSON	Mixed-media portrait

This lesson involves collage and lettering to create a portrait of a classmate. The emphasis is on the combination of media rather than skills in representational painting.

Classroom resources
• *Classroom arrangement:* Paired students should work opposite each other.   • *Materials and equipment:* A2 paper, drawing and painting materials, glue, coloured paper, close-up photographs of subject.

Research sources
• Jean-Michel Basquiat was an American artist. In the 1980s, he was famous for his combination of many different styles and materials in his work.   • Some suggested images are: *Scull*, 1981   *Cabeza*, 1982   *In Italian*, 1983   *Logo*, 1984

LESSON TASKS

1) Starter suggestions

Demonstration	• Show images by Basquiat, pointing out the use of mark-making and writing, as well as different styles and mediums. Outline the task of making a portrait of a classmate using many different styles and media.
Additional student activity	• Ask students to describe what they can see in the paintings. What are the paintings about? How were they made? Ask students to think of different media to use in a portrait work about a classmate.

2) Ideas and planning

Demonstration	• Demonstrate mind-mapping ideas to describe a student, including their names, hobbies, friends and interests. Pair students for this task.
Additional student activity	• Let students work with a partner to list colours, images and written information that could be included in their portraits of each other. Sports, mascots, music and other interests can all be useful.
Top tip	• Different students will use alternative methods to record their ideas. Encourage this practice. Such lists and diagrams can also be used on a larger scale in the final outcome.

3) Main lesson activities: Exercise 1 (large outline drawings)

Demonstration	• Show how an outline of a student can be drawn quickly from life in pencil using the length of an A2 sheet of cartridge paper.
Additional student activity	• Encourage students to pose for each other and block out the proportions of the figure, or upper body and head. Each student needs a clear pencil outline to work with.
Top tip	• No detail is required in this drawing, but students will slow down and draw in great detail if they are not encouraged to work quickly.

4) Main lesson activities: Exercise 2 (collage and painting)

Demonstration	• Show examples that use collage and paint to add colour to sections of clothing and the background of the figure silhouette.
Additional student activity	• Encourage students to cut out and stick down some solid areas of coloured paper to form much of the clothing on the figure. Limit colour selection to two or three colours, which can be repeated in the use of paint. Students can allow paint to splash and drip as part of the process.
Top tip	• Drawing boards are useful for placing the paper at an angle to allow paint to drip and run down the surface. Newspaper can be used to protect tables or floor areas.

5) Main lesson activities: Exercise 3 (drawing and writing)

Demonstration	• While student work is drying, demonstrate how to use graphic materials on your dry example piece (pastels, charcoal, wax crayons and marker pens to colour areas, add texture and written information). Diagrams, lists, song lyrics, family trees could all be part of this portrait piece.
Additional student activity	• Students should refer to their notes to remind them of elements to include in work. Encourage the use of a wide range of drawing materials to complete the image.

6) Plenary suggestions

Demonstration	• Ask some of the pairs to show their final pieces to the class and explain how the work relates to their student subject.
Additional student activity	• Encourage students to describe how each separate material has been used on the piece.
Top tip	• Students can be shy about showing their work. More confident students will be happy to start the process, which may well include some humour and laughter. Then try to encourage shy students to take part in the sharing of work.

Reflection
This lesson could be extended to include photography. Students photograph each other in close-up
and include some of these elements in their collage portraits:
• Photographs of objects and interests of the portrait subject.
• Photographs of family, friends and places involved in the life of the subject.

NON-TRADITIONAL MEDIA LESSON	Future robot collage

This lesson explores collage and photomontage techniques using pre-printed material from books and magazines. Plan ahead for this lesson by asking students to bring in old magazines from home, if your department does not have a collection already.

Classroom resources
• *Materials and equipment:* Colour magazines, newspapers, glue, scissors, fine liners.

Research sources
• Raoul Hausmann was an Austrian artist and writer. His experimental collages are the starting point for this lesson. Some good examples are: *Tatlin at Home*, 1920   *ABCD* (self-portrait), 1923   *The Art Critic*, 1919 • Also show students the mixed-media sculpture *Mechanical Head*, 1919.

Top tip
• Demonstrate safe use of cutting knives, metal rulers and cutting mats.

LESSON TASKS

1) Starter suggestions

Demonstration	• Discuss the collages of Hausmann and the *Mechanical Head* sculpture. Ask what modern technology might be included in a contemporary robot head.
Additional student activity	• Ask students to describe what they can see in the collages. Get them to brainstorm images from magazines that they could use.

2) Main lesson activities: Exercise 1 (planning and collecting resources)

Demonstration	• Show students how to plan ideas for a futuristic robot using sketches and collaged magazine images.
Additional student activity	• Let students select a library of images from magazines. Encourage them to cut elements from magazine images of machines, computers and other adverts.

3) Main lesson activities: Exercise 2 (collage activity)

Demonstration	• Arrange collage elements to make a good robot composition before sticking down the elements. Allow initial ideas to spark searches for extra images.
Additional student activity	• Let students build up their design from layers of collaged magazine material. Encourage imaginative and surreal use of imagery to form individual designs.
Top tip	• Students must use glue carefully to avoid making a mess of their work.

Reflection
A successful collage involves selecting and combining unrelated photographic images to make a new image. Complex images may be too confusing and photographic backgrounds can make the design more difficult to understand. Once students are more confident, photomontage can be a quick way to generate ideas.

NON-TRADITIONAL MEDIA LESSON	Mixed-media still life

Traditional still life is given a modern twist through the use of mixed-media techniques. Acrylic painting is used to add some colour and texture, but relief forms and cardboard texture play an equal part in the final outcome.

Classroom resources

- *Classroom arrangement:* desks arranged around the still-life arrangement
- *Materials and equipment:* A3 or A4 boards for final outcome, charcoal, corrugated cardboard, PVA glue, knives and cutting boards.
- *Still life:* Traditional arrangement of fruit, plates and cloth

Research sources

- Pablo Picasso made several still-life pieces incorporating three-dimensional elements. Some good examples are:

Still Life (painted wood with tassels)	1914
Still life with Chair Caning	1912
Violin (metal)	1915
Goat skull and bottle (bronze)	1951

LESSON TASKS

1) Starter suggestions

Demonstration	• Show some traditional still-life paintings and then the examples from Picasso. Explain how Picasso expanded the boundaries of what could be used to make a still life.
Additional student activity	• Before showing the images, ask 'What is a still life?' Ask students to describe what they can see in the images and why Picasso's still-life paintings were so different.

2) Main lesson activities: Exercise 1 (charcoal drawing)

Demonstration	• Draw the still life in charcoal on the board to be used for the mixed-media work.
Additional student activity	• Encourage students to wipe off charcoal with a paper towel and rework the design until they are happy with the composition.
Top tip	• Encourage students to draw large, bold shapes, allowing the composition to run off the board.

3) Main lesson activities: Exercise 2 (adding relief and 3-D shapes)

Demonstration	• Cut corrugated card to repeat some of the charcoal drawing shapes and stick on the board with PVA glue. Add more layers to build different levels of relief.
Additional student activity	• Encourage students to look at the main shapes in the image, such as a bowl or table top, a large piece of fruit or a vase. They should cut these out of cardboard first.
Top tip	• Tracing paper or paper templates from the drawing can be used to help students cut the correct shapes from the cardboard.

4) Main lesson activities: Exercise 3 (acrylic colour layer)

Demonstration	• Using a dry brush, mix and add some acrylic colour to the relief piece to reflect the colours of the fruit, plates and cloth in the still life.
Additional student activity	• Encourage students to try to mix colours that approximate what they see in the still life. Applying colour with a dry brush will ensure that some cardboard shows through.

Reflection

Students who are less confident in representational drawing can produce successful work if they do not spend too long worrying about their charcoal drawing. Cutting clear shapes and building relief creates a good surface on which to apply some colour.

NON-TRADITIONAL MEDIA LESSON	Geometric portrait

In this lesson, graphic media are used to make a portrait that has a lot of geometric abstraction. Students are not introduced to the artist inspiration until they have drawn the portrait over their geometric grid. When students see the possible combinations of line and colour in Lee's work, they will be keen to use the graphic materials on their own drawing.

Classroom resources

- *Materials and equipment:* Pencil and ruler, pen, markers, metallic pens, pencil crayons.

Research sources

- The work of Korean artist Minjae Lee is used as a starting point for this lesson.
- Students can search for portraits of people they like, or you can supply reference portraits of famous people with good lighting. Monochrome images work well.

LESSON TASKS

1) Main lesson activities: Exercise 1 (geometric drawing)

Demonstration	• Show students how to fill an A3 sheet of paper with repeated geometric shapes in light pencil (look at *Battle ON* before demonstrating the drawing of the geometric pattern to see where you are leading the students).
Additional student activity	• Encourage students to choose a shape first. They can consider diagonal shapes, squares or triangles. The aim is to divide the paper into many similar smaller shapes.

2) Main lesson activities: Exercise 2 (student portrait)

Demonstration	• Use a darker pencil to draw a portrait from a reference photograph on top of the geometric pattern.
Additional student activity	• Encourage students to select their own image from which to draw. This image may be a famous person, as often used by Minjae Lee.

3) Main lesson activities: Exercise 3 (look at the work of Minjae Lee)

Demonstration	• Show examples of Minjae Lee's work. Ask students to comment on the use of colour and pattern.
Additional student activity	• Get students to describe what they can see and to look for geometric patterns in the work. Ask students what they like about the work and how it relates to their own drawings.

4) Main lesson activities: Exercise 4 (colour design using pens, marker pens and metallic pens)

Demonstration	• Show students how to use a range of graphic materials on top of their drawing. Colour some parts of the geometric patterns in monochrome and some in colour, allowing the portrait to be clearly seen.
Additional student activity	• Encourage students to start with blended areas of pencil crayon or marker pen. Once some areas are blocked in with colour, they can define details and shapes in pen and metallic pen.

Reflection

This lesson has been designed to produce an outcome in a single long lesson. It could easily be the starting point for a much longer project that incorporates a wide exploration of materials, as well as photography and digital experiments.

Non-traditional media projects can be a rewarding way to explore a wide range of materials and techniques. They can raise the confidence of students who are less comfortable with traditional drawing and painting.

Classroom resources
• *Materials and equipment:* Wide range of collage materials and modern graphic tools.

Research sources

• Suggested artist starting points for project ideas:
 3-D painting
    • Jane Perkins – Perkins recreates artist's work using found objects; an alternative would be to look at the 'plate' paintings of Julian Schnable.
 Fast-food cityscape
    • Megan Coyle – Coyle makes magazine collage images. If students enjoy using the fast-food imagery, they may also like to look at propaganda artist Ron English.

PROJECT SUGGESTIONS

1) 3-D painting

1. Look at the work of Jane Perkins and discuss objects that you could collect.
2. Choose a work of art or image to remake and collect objects.
3. Draw out the image and stick objects to the composition.
4. Paint over the surface to produce a relief paining full of smaller objects.

Top tip
• Students can find it difficult to collect a lot of objects. Bottle tops, make-up containers, plastic cutlery and packaging can all be used. Alternatively, simple shapes could be cut from cardboard.

2) Fast-food cityscape

1. Look at the work of Megan Coyle. Discuss packaging and fast-food paper waste.
2. Plan ideas for a cityscape collage made of fast-food packaging. Collect packaging.
3. Make a cityscape design in magazine colour using a photographic reference.
4. Draw out a larger design and create a collage of the fast-food packaging.
5. If desired, add additional drawn or painted elements to the final outcome.

Top tip
• Fast-food packaging is only a suggestion. Any form of printed material would work well for this lesson.

3) Assessment guidance

Each of the suggested painting projects has some similar elements and they all enable students to cover aspects of the four Assessment Objectives.

Assessment Objectives
• **AO1:** Recording can be through photography or drawing of objects and places used in the project, as well as recording insights and ideas.
• **AO2:** Explore materials and techniques in collaging or work over found objects.
• **AO3:** Develop ideas that demonstrate critical understanding in the arrangement of found objects and collage packaging material.
• **AO4:** Present a personal and coherent response that recreates an image using found objects or a cityscape that contains printed design information.

UNIT 5: NEW MEDIA

New media covers a diverse range of techniques. Here, two contrasting lesson ideas give an idea of the range of possibilities.

NEW MEDIA	Table-top animation

This lesson is designed to be a basic but fun introduction to stop-motion animation. Working in pairs allows students to learn the processes involved more quickly. Generating a range of animation ideas and beginning to understand the animation process are the important elements of the lesson.

Classroom resources

- *Classroom arrangement:* Working in pairs.
- *Materials and equipment:* Tripod or way to fix position of camera, plasticine.

Research sources

- This lesson can be taught with smartphones, tablets, webcams or many other digital camera systems. You should research and experiment with the equipment you have available for your students. Students will need to use stop-motion software, or be able to insert photographs into video editing software.
- Examples of plasticine animation to stimulate imaginative ideas.

LESSON TASKS

1) Starter suggestions

Demonstration	• Show some examples of stop-motion animation explaining its history.
Additional student activity	• Encourage students to comment on how the films have been made, discuss the stop motion they have seen in films and advertising, and describe any experiments they have made already on their own at home.

2) Introduction

Demonstration	• Show examples from the 'Note-to-self' of students creating their own animation, and set students the task of making a short animation of a plasticine character making its way across a desk that is full of obstacles.
Additional student activity	• Ask students to comment on the videos shown, suggest ideas for what they could animate in their own video and what thoughts they would try to express.
Top tip	• The *Morph* videos show students how limited resources and a simple character can make an enjoyable piece of work. Students often have very ambitious plans that are too difficult to make, which results in a poor educational experience.

3) Main lesson activities: Exercise 1 (planning)

Demonstration	• Show ideas for making a simple plasticine character and ways to animate pencil-cases, pens and paper with the help of reusable adhesive to hold things in place.
Additional student activity	• Students can produce sketches for a simple character, ideas for a desktop landscape and ideas for animating objects.

4) Main lesson activities: Exercise 2 (character construction)

Demonstration	• Show alternative ways to make a very simple character in plasticine. A simple ball will work and any figure designs should be very basic.
Additional student activity	• Set groups of students a short period of time to make their characters out of plasticine.
Top tip	• Students will want to make complex characters and use many different colours of plasticine. Limit the colours available to a maximum of two, with the second colour only being used for eyes or very small details.

5) Main lesson activities: Exercise 3 (set construction)

Demonstration	• Show the students how to turn their desk top into a landscape or an obstacle course.
Additional student activity	• Students use pencil cases, books, stationery and other imaginative ideas to create an environment for their character to travel through.

6) Main lesson activities: Exercise 4 (filming process)

Demonstration	• Show the process for shooting and moving to film the animation of the character and elements of the set. Emphasise the importance of not moving the camera as it will produce an unpleasant jump in the film.
Additional student activity	• Students film their character moving across the desk top, moving around and climbing over obstacles
Top tip	• Using an animation app will allow instant review of the work. Otherwise the frames will need to be made into a film on a computer, which will add an extra stage to the lesson.

7) Plenary suggestions

Demonstration	• Ask groups to show their animation work to the class.
Additional student activity	• Let students explain the idea for their animation as well as the difficulties they had along the way, and discuss the end result. This is often an enjoyable sharing of many of the short films made.

Reflection

Through a process of trial and error, students should become more aware of how far to move their character. At the end of the lesson, students should have an understanding of the main elements of stop-motion: character, set and camera. This introductory lesson can stimulate a strong interest in the animation process, but many of the students will want to improve the quality of their work. There is the opportunity to look in more depth at many aspects of film making to produce more considered work such as:

- scriptwriting and storyboarding   •   character design   •   set design
- more sophisticated characters with an armature   •   adding sound and effects during editing.

Working in pairs is useful for an introduction to animation, but students will need to work independently to submit work for their IGCSE Art & Design course.

NEW MEDIA	Yayoi Kusama costume design

This lesson is designed to engage students with installation art. The lesson should produce imaginative and surreal ideas that could be realised if developed into a full project. Students respond to the work of Yayoi Kusama by designing a costume with a wig that they could wear to camouflage themselves in an environment inspired by Kusama's work.

Classroom resources

- *Materials and equipment:* A3 cartridge, colouring pencils or markers and drawing materials, visual references to selected Kusama installations.

Research sources

- Installation art history
- Yayoi Kusama has an artist's website
- Leon Bakst – costume design for the Diagalev ballet

LESSON TASKS

1) Starter suggestions

Demonstration	Share examples of installation art and Kusama's work. Discuss the task of developing ideas for creating an environment and a camouflage costume. Look at costume design drawings by Leon Bakst for further inspiration.
Additional student activity	Encourage students to describe and respond to installation art examples, to come up with ideas for an environment installation, and to comment on drawing detail and different designs in Bakst's work.

2) Main lesson activities: Exercise 1 (environment ideas)

Demonstration	Draw some repeating organic shapes that might be used to paint an environment, such as bubbles, tentacles or broken rock.
Additional student activity	Help students to come up with ideas that contrast size, shape and texture. Try to ensure that all students have at least two designs to choose from. Choose a design to use for costume.

3) Main lesson activities: Exercise 2 (costume design)

Demonstration	Draw a simple outline of a figure to use as a template for costume design, adding detail in pencil and colour.
Additional student activity	Help students to draw templates with good proportions and fill the costume with designs on a scale that allows for the addition of colour.
Top tip	Adding a cartoon element to these designs can increase student interest without detracting from the learning process.

4) Plenary suggestions

Demonstration	Display work on a table and gather students round.
Additional student activity	Ask students to identify work they like and ideas that are different. Ask students which room in a house they would paint if they were to realise their installation design.

Reflection
This lesson may inspire some students to explore installation art further. If you only have one or two students who want to pursue the idea, you could find a small space in which they could build an installation. Larger groups may require students to create their work as a model or in a virtual environment.

NEW MEDIA PROJECT IDEAS

Students need to be well motivated to develop new media ideas as they often require experimentation with a wide range of equipment, or the construction of a large source of elements for an installation. However, such independent work is often very personal and evidences a lot of learning and achievement.

Classroom resources
• *Classroom arrangement:* Usually requires an individual working space.   • *Materials and equipment:* Wide variety of equipment, dependent on project.

Research sources

• Suggested artist starting points for project ideas:
 Day in the life animation:
   o The film-maker Chris Marker made a science fiction film using only still images and sound.
   o Modern handheld devices can be used to record a visual collage of daily life.
 Family tree installation:
   o Christian Boltanski has made many installations that could be inspiration for this project.

PROJECT SUGGESTIONS

1) Day in the life

Day in the life is a film-making project where students collect a large range of visual sources of information to use to make a short film about their life:

1. View artist video examples and discuss themes for the video such as people, places or emotional states.
2. List ways of recording visual elements for the video, smartphone or camera video and still images, drawings, gif animations, flick books, screenshots or sound recording.
3. Collect different visual elements, including scanning/photographing drawings and documents.
4. Edit all elements to make a moving visual collage.

2) Family tree

1. Look at Boltanski's work, discuss information to collect and display ideas.
2. Plan an installation that involves displaying family tree information and photographs.
3. Collect information.
4. Construct the installation.
5. Review, assess, and make changes and additions.

Reflection

These projects are suggestions to help you think about how to develop new media projects. They are starting points that can be adapted to suit the equipment and space that you have available.

Students familiar with video apps and modern devices may suggest many different ways to make a film collage project. Try to ensure that they (not a computer algorithm) are making all the editing decisions.

Family tree installations could involve a real tree, or a constructed tree, or be reduced in scale to fit on a board or even be presented in video format.

3) Assessment guidance

When reviewing the project work, consider the following aspects of the four Assessment Objectives:

Assessment Objectives
• **AO1:** Recording devices can be used for first-hand observation, which can also include site visits and collecting objects. Ideas and insights will often be recorded in diagrams and notes. • **AO2:** Exploration of image manipulation and video editing needs to be evidenced by students. A variety of techniques may be used in an individual manner and need to be clearly recorded. • **AO3:** Storyboards, trial videos or constructions should show developing ideas through a series of investigation increasing in complexity. Critical understanding should be shown in aesthetic decisions and relationship to the work of other creators. • **AO4:** Students have produced a sustained final outcome that realises the intentions in supporting work and shows an understanding of visual language.

Refer to page 203 in the Student's Book for a full-colour version of this student's work.

PROJECT BRIEF

Organic form and plant shapes are thoroughly explored in this project, with the final outcome being shown bottom right. This work is part of the submission and shows the main elements of the project. The student starts by looking at different plant forms through first-hand observation of roses and flowers. A wide range of media are used, including ink and wash, pencil and crayon on a tonal ground, watercolour and ink drawing. More substantial studies are undertaken in acrylics. Different artists are referred to, and pencil thumbnail studies explore alternative compositions. During the development process, the student explores a wide range of different colour schemes and the final outcome is painted in a more realistic palette.

Assessment
• **AO1:** *Record ideas, observations and insights relevant to intentions as work progresses.* The student makes use of extensive first-hand source material in photography and drawings. Sophisticated drawing skills are demonstrated in several of the studies. Excellent skill is shown in recording observations from a variety of relevant sources showing intentions effectively. During the development process, additional first-hand resources are used in the consideration of composition. • **AO2:** *Explore and select appropriate resources, media, materials, techniques and processes.* A wide range of media are explored, including photography, pencil, ink and wash, ink pen, watercolour and acrylic paint. Techniques experimented with include tonal pencil, stippled ink drawing, blended watercolour and graduated acrylic painting. There is an excellent exploration of media, materials, techniques and processes showing effective selection of relevant resources. • **AO3:** *Develop ideas through investigation, demonstrating critical understanding.* Colour palette choices and composition play an important part in the development of the work. Warm and cool palettes are used to explore ideas for the final outcome with reference to the work of artists; an Edward Hopper painting is used as a basis for developing a warm colour study with a limited palette of earth colours. Careful consideration is made of compositional possibilities in a comprehensive sheet of alternative layouts and design ideas. The student shows an excellent development of ideas through investigation, demonstrating effective critical understanding. • **AO4:** *Present a personal and coherent response that realises intentions and demonstrates an understanding of visual language.* The project is consistent in maintaining a focus on organic forms, but avoids repetition by exploring a range of alternative compositions. The student looks at a variety of artists, media and styles of work. The formal elements of art are considered at different stages of the project. The final outcome itself is a confident acrylic painting. Consideration for light, shade, colour and texture are all present in the outcome, which clearly relates to the early research and developmental work. A high level of observational ability is evident in the supporting studies and the outcome. There is an excellent realisation of intentions demonstrating effective understanding of visual language.

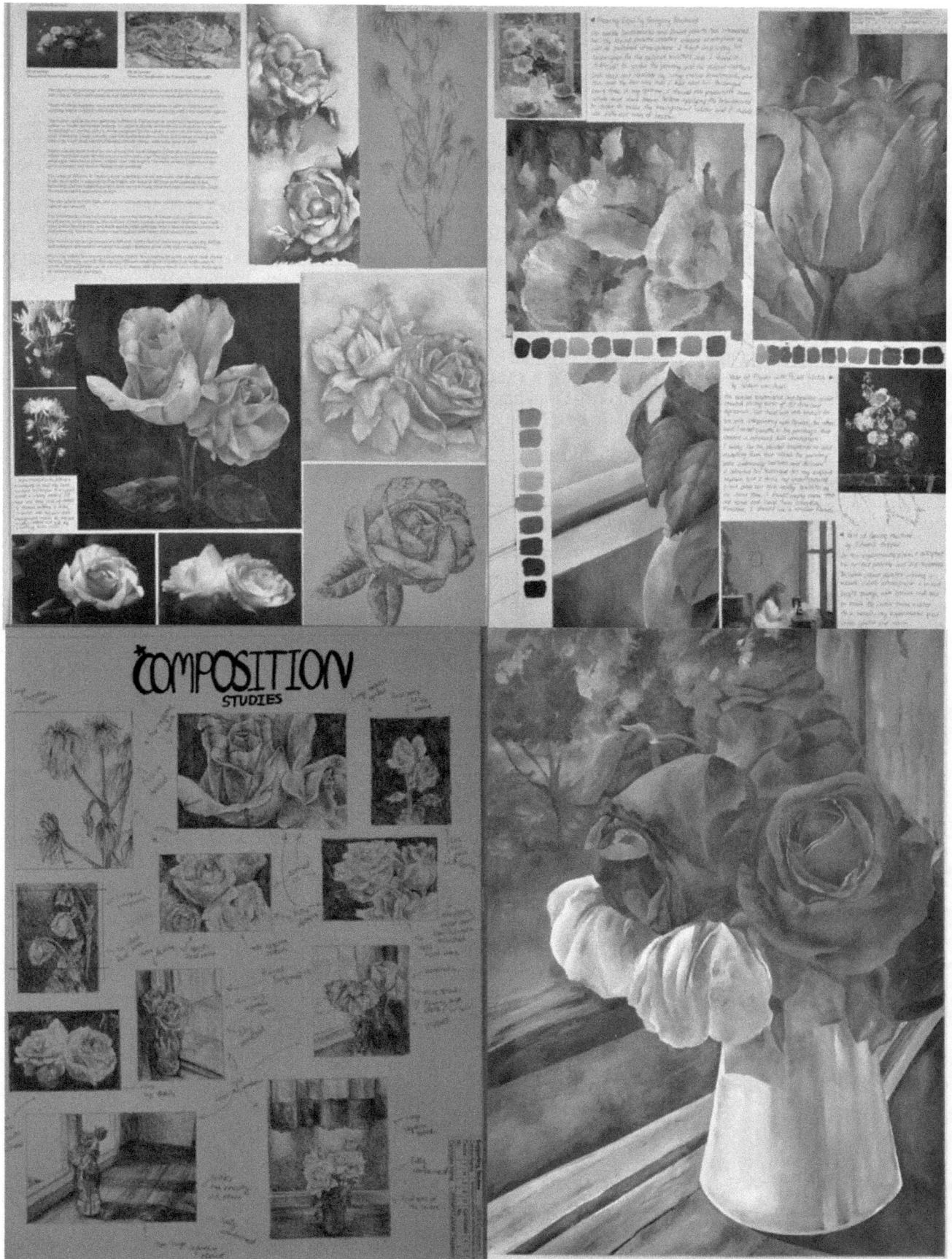

DEVELOPING WORK

There are many possibilities for how to build classroom work into coursework (Chapter 1). Generally, it can be helpful to initially set a creative starting point that a whole class can use to learn new skills and to explore ideas. Lessons may be more prescriptive and teacher-led early on in a project. Using a creative theme or starting point for the coursework also helps to prepare students for the externally set assignment (Chapter 2), where they will have to choose their own starting point from those listed on the IGCSE question paper.

As a project progresses, expect individual students to take a more independent and personal approach to developing their work once they have been taught enough to do this. Less able students will need greater support and input from you.

Once students have some skills and experience of painting techniques and processes, you would expect them to focus on refining their work and ideas with further drawings, colour studies, compositions and refined development pieces. All stages of work should be thoroughly documented, reflected on and analysed to give evidence of a student's intentions. Final painting outcomes larger than A2 will need to be photographed to thoroughly record the work.

Further projects

- Suitable starting points for a painting project:

City life	Movement in a busy place	Italian Futurist artists
Modern icon	Celebrity altar piece	Pop artists and Byzantine icon paintings
Natural forms	Abstraction through observation	Georgia O'Keefe

---

Further research

- **Websites:** Museum of Modern Art, New York; Tate Modern, London and related galleries
- **Journals:** *Modern Painters, Art Forum, The Artist*

Checklist

✓ I have introduced students to the large variety of possible materials, techniques and approaches available for painting within the constraints of what I can offer at my school or college.

✓ I understand how to help students choose a successful area of painting that they can explore.

✓ I know what type of support work is required if my students chose to work in painting.

✓ I understand how to teach students to test out ideas in smaller studies and final outcomes.

✓ I know how to teach students to research and record relevant information for painting.

✓ I have enough knowledge, experience and understanding of painting to successfully teach my students.

INTRODUCTION

Learning objectives

By the end of this unit students should:

- explore a variety of approaches to monoprinting
- recognise materials and techniques needed to make a monoprint and apply them to your own project
- understand a variety of approaches to relief printing
- know how to employ a range of different materials and tools to make a relief print
- understand how to use line, tone, texture and composition in etching
- know how to employ a range of different materials and tools to make and ink up an etching
- understand a variety of approaches to screen printing
- know how to employ a range of different materials and correct tools to make a print.

Classroom resources

- A clear space to work in, different types of printing inks, variety of papers, basic printing materials, lino, card, rollers, plates, cutting tools, cloths, storage space. Printmaking requires planning and resource management for each technique. Students need to clear up properly at the end of a session.

Research sources

- Examples of work and techniques can be found by searching through Pinterest online.
- There is a good overview of different printmaking techniques online at Artsy.

General lesson ideas

- Show the work of inspirational artists using different printmaking techniques. Discuss what the difference is between a screen print and an intaglio print. This helps identify what method of printing will suit students' work, and encourages them to reflect on their choice of a particular printing technique.

Key consideration

- Test practical activities before setting them for your students. This will help your understanding of techniques and identify potential problems. Urge students to work to their strengths and interests within the limits of resources. Check that they have correctly used key terms and technical information.

Reflective log

- What practical skills do I need to develop to help my students achieve?
- How can I use practical and theoretical lessons to help my students to develop their work?
- How can I structure my teaching to fully use the resources and facilities that I have available to me?
- Are there any local exhibitions or resources that my students could visit or use?

UNIT 1: MONOPRINTING

PRINTMAKING	Monoprinting

Monoprinting is one of the most straightforward printing techniques. This lesson explores a variety of approaches. Once your students have mastered the basics, they can start to experiment by using stencils and a number of colours in their own projects. Students can print with quite basic materials or even without access to a press.

Classroom resources

- *Classroom arrangement:* Clear and clean the surface on which you will be working.
- *Materials and equipment:* Printing ink or **oil-based** paint, a '**plate**' to work on such as Plexiglas, acetate or any flat surface on which ink can be rolled out and wiped clean after, roller to roll out the printing ink, **squeegee**, which can be used if you do not have access to a **printing press**, a printing press (hand operated), papers (different weights to experiment with cut to A5), card, scissors, sharpened hard pencils such as 2H, ballpoint pens in different colours, tracing paper, masking tape, cloths to clean plates, white spirit to clean plates and rollers.

Research sources

- Artists to look at who use monoprints in their work:

Tracey Emin – portraits	Lucian Freud – portraits	Edgar Degas – retroussage work
Pablo Picasso – portraits	Gillian Ayres – stencil work	

Top tip

- Ensure that students understand the importance of cleaning rollers and surfaces after they have finished printing.

LESSON TASKS

1) Starter suggestions

Show the work of some of the suggested artists. Look at the subject matter of the portrait.

2) Main lesson activities: Exercise 1

Additional student activity	• Discuss with your group what a monoprint is. Discuss the quality of the **line** of a monoprint. • Look at the quality of the text in Emin's images. As prints are reversed, discuss with students how they could overcome this problem. • Discuss the work of Lucian Freud's **mark-making** and **composition**. Notice the used of **light and shade** in his images. Discuss with students how they think he achieved this effect. • Look at Picasso's monoprint portraits: notice the mark-making and use of pattern in the images. • Discuss the details in all of the work shown, and the strength and quality of the portraits. Discuss with students whether they like this type of printing. It is important that the students express a reason why they dislike (or like) a piece of work. Ask them to identify exactly what they don't like as well as what they do like.

3) Main lesson activities: Exercise 2

Additional student activity	• Get the class to generate a quick drawing of each other. Give them a time limit of 5–10 minutes per drawing. Limit the size of drawing to A5. Make sure that the drawings are linear. Try to get the class to make at least five portrait drawings. Keep the energy of the session going by giving students a countdown, for example: 'You have five minutes to draw the person next to you.' Encourage them the whole time, for example: 'Make sure your drawing is line only' and 'no shading', then 'you have one minute left'.
	• Give the portrait drawing some rules, for example: 'whole figure sitting', then 'profile only', next 'head and shoulders' and then 'look at the pattern of the hair or jumper or textures of clothes'. All the time, make sure that students are considering the composition on the page.
	• Avoid giving the class too much time to worry about the image, as the exercise is about working quickly and generating a number of drawings from which to produce a print.
	• Give students time to decide which drawing they will work with. Then, once they have made a decision, get them to roll out a small square of ink on a printing plate. Make sure that the ink square isn't much bigger than the A5 drawing.
	• Ask students to follow these steps. Carefully lay a piece of paper straight onto the inked-up plate, and tape it at the top to the plate to stop it moving around. Lay the chosen portrait face up onto the paper, with masking tape at the top to keep the drawing in place. Lay a sheet of tracing paper over the top and also tape it to the plate to keep it in place. Now use a ballpoint pen or a sharpened hard pencil to trace the portrait. Once finished, remove the tracing paper and the original drawing. Carefully peel back the paper and the print will show a reversed image of the original drawing.
	• Ask the class to place a fresh sheet of paper onto the inked plate and use a squeegee or their hand to firmly press across the image. Ask them to carefully peel back the paper to reveal a negative image of the print.
Top tip	• Images will be reversed when monoprinting. Remind students to consider this if their print contains text.
	• Ensure that students know they have to work fast. Ink will dry quickly, especially when using a solvent-based one. An oil-based medium will give more time to work.

4) Plenary suggestions

At the end of the session, ask the class to lay out their drawings and prints. Discuss which prints they think are more successful. What made the print work? Was it the composition? The scale? The quality of line? The printing skill? The thickness of ink? The thinness of ink? Ask students to reflect on this and ask them what they felt went well in their own printing.

Encourage students to keep reflective notes during this part of the session while directing them to look at each other's work.

PROJECT SUGGESTIONS

At the end of this session, ask the students to apply this monoprint technique to their own project. The students need to produce a set of prints using this technique and using a variety of papers, scale and colour.

> **Top tip**
> • Encourage students to experiment with printing on different surfaces and types of paper such as old envelopes, book pages, graph paper, tissue or handmade paper.

5) Main lesson activities: Exercise 3

Additional student activity	• Let students create a monoprint with a stencil. Using thin card, ask your class to cut out a number of shapes. Now get them to roll out block printing ink onto a printing plate. Ask them to arrange the cut shapes onto the inked up plate. Get students to ink up the roller with a different colour (darker works best). Ask them to gently roll the cut shapes with the darker colour while they are on the plate. Tell students to not worry if some of the ink transfers onto the plate as this will add to the overall printed effect. Now get them to gently place a sheet of paper onto the plate and press firmly with their hand, running it over the whole sheet. Now get them to gently peel the paper back to reveal the print.
	• With the cut stencils still in place on the plate, ask students to use the roller and gently apply a different colour over the plate. Get them to place a sheet of paper onto the plate and press firmly. Then they can peel it off again to produce a new print. As the stencil card is slightly raised, the image will be visible.
	• Finally, get students to roll the whole plate using a dark colour, and then carefully to peel off the stencils to reveal the original colour. Get them to place a sheet of paper on the plate and use a squeegee to print the image.
Top tips	• Using this method of stencil printing is more effective when using contrasting colours, finishing with the darkest colour to give maximum contrast.
	• Once students have practised this technique, they can start to experiment with textured stencils such as lace or net.

6) Plenary suggestions

Ask students to look at each other's' work. Encourage them to discuss what went well and what didn't work out. Ask them to reflect on ways they could improve their work in the future. It is important that students learn from each other and share good practice. Encourage this in the classroom.

Conclude the session by asking the class to work out a way to print using this technique as part of their individual project. Which colours, shapes and textures could they apply to their own work? Ask students to find at least one contemporary artist who uses stencil monoprinting in their practice. He or she doesn't have to be a well-known artist.

Reflection

Ask students to reflect on what it is they enjoy about how the artist works. It may be the subject matter, the colours they use or the patterns they make.

Ask them to apply how they work to their own project. It is important that they do not copy the work but use the style, technique or subject matter to inform their own project.

Key terms
• **Student's Book key terms:** composition, oil-based, plate, printing press, squeegee
• **Additional key terms:** light and shade, line, mark-making

Assessment Objectives

Each of the suggested exercises has some similar elements and they all enable students to cover aspects of the four Assessment Objectives.

- **AO1:** Record ideas, observations and insights relevant to intentions as work progresses.

  Response to drawing exercises and initial observational primary research selected for print exercises.

- **AO2:** Explore and select appropriate resources, media, materials, techniques and processes.

  Use of processes, tools, appropriate media and materials in printmaking exercises.

- **AO3:** Develop ideas through investigation, demonstrating critical understanding.

  Demonstrate an ability to understand and use printmaking exercises to develop a relevant response and generate a body of work.

- **AO4:** Present a personal and coherent response that realises intentions and demonstrates an understanding of visual language.

  The records of reflection and evaluation of printmaking sessions, feedback and response to the body of work produced in the classroom.

Further research

- The references given are diverse and give students a starting point of artists who use monoprinting.
- You can build on this to give your students examples of practitioners they can relate to.

UNIT 2: RELIEF PRINTING

PRINTMAKING	Relief printing 1

A relief print is produced by cutting into a flat surface made from **wood** or **linoleum** using a **gouge tool**. Ink is applied to the block using a **brayer or roller**. Paper is placed on the block and an image is produced either by using a printing press or by **hand burnishing**. The print is a **negative image** of what is cut away, as only the raised surface is **inked up**. This section will show you a variety of approaches to relief printing and suggest a range of different materials and tools from which to make a relief print.

Classroom resources

- *Classroom arrangement:* Clear and clean the surfaces on which the class will be working.
- *Materials and equipment:* A 'block' to cut into (wood, lino or rubber), cutting tools or gouge tools (a u-gouge for general cutting and a v-gouge for detail), ink pads in various colours, printing press (hand-operated machine for printing; if your centre has no printing press, use the back of a wooden spoon to apply pressure to the print), papers (experiment with different types and colours), masking tape and cloths for cleaning up.

Top tip

- Ensure that students understand the importance of cleaning rollers and surfaces after they have finished printing.

Research sources

- The Museum of Modern Art (MOMA)'s introduction to printmaking provides an overview of the history of relief printing, as well as short tutorial guides to help you with your techniques.

LESSON TASKS

1) Starter suggestions

Discuss what a relief print is with students. Relief printing is produced by cutting into a flat surface made from wood, linoleum, rubber, foam, card or even vegetables. This cutting is done with a gouge tool. Ink is applied to the block and paper is pressed against it either by using a printing press or hand burnishing the paper with the back of a spoon. The print is a negative image of what is cut away, as only the raised surface prints.

Top tip

- Remind students that when cutting into a block, they need to remember that what they cut away will be the paper and what is left uncut will be the print.

2) Main lesson activities: Exercise 1

Additional student activity	• Collect a variety of materials, such as wood, linoleum, rubber, card and vegetables such as carrots and potatoes, which can be cut into to produce a block print.
	• Give students a selection of different types of blocks to cut into using cutting tools with various gauges. The blocks can be various shapes and sizes, but keep them smaller than A5 so they are easy to work with. Now ask students to select a block and a gouge tool. Ask them to cut a spiral. Then ask them to choose a different block and ask them to cut straight lines across the block.
Top tip	• It is important that you let students interpret the questions in their own way, and that they understand there is no right or wrong for this task.

3) Main lesson activities: Exercise 2

Additional student activity	• Ask students to choose a different block and cut some cross-hatching. Continue giving instructions, such as asking them to cut spiral shapes, dots, wavy lines, triangles, circles and zig-zags.
	• When the blocks are all cut, press them into the ink pads and print them onto the different types of paper.
	• Have lots of different types of paper to print on: heavy paper, coloured paper, tissue paper, handmade paper, damp paper and so on.
	• Ask students to write notes and observations on the materials and tools used for each print. This will give students a record of what does and doesn't work well.

4) Plenary suggestions

At the end of the session, ask the class to lay out their prints. Discuss with students which prints in their opinion are more successful. What made the print work? Was it the size of cutting tool? The scale? The quality of line? The printing skill? The thickness of ink? The thinness of ink? The paper it was printed onto?

Reflection
Encourage students to keep reflective notes during this part of the session while directing them to look at each other's' work. It may be that there will only be time to lay the work out and have a walk round. Make sure that this part of the session doesn't become a competition. Even the students who had a disastrous session will have learnt from the experience: acknowledge this and give everyone in the class something positive to take away.

PROJECT SUGGESTIONS
Ask students to collect their prints and make them into a small test book for homework.

PRINTMAKING	Relief printing 2

This session will help students identify images that would be suitable to develop into a relief print. Looking at the strong line and dynamic work of the suggested German Expressionists will enable you to discuss the importance of composition, light and mark-making achieved in relief printing.

Classroom resources

- *Classroom arrangement:* Clear and clean the surface that your class will be working on.
- *Materials and equipment:* Printing ink, a brayer or roller, lino block, cutting tools, printing press or back of a spoon if your school does not have a press, variety of paper to print on (experiment with different colours and types of paper), scissors, sharpened pencil, pen, tracing paper, masking tape and cloths for cleaning up.

Top tip

- Ensure that students understand the importance of cleaning the rollers and surfaces after the printing is complete.

Research sources

- Artists to refer to in your lesson who use relief printing in their work:

  Karl Schmidt-Rotluff – *Woman with Pigtails*, 1923   Käthe Kollwitz – *The Hunger*, 1925

  Ernest Ludwig Kirchner – *Alemania Kämpfe*, 1915   Gerhard Marcks – *Elder with a Spade*, 1955

LESSON TASKS

1) Starter suggestions

Show the students some images from the suggested artists.

2) Main lesson activities: Exercise 1

Additional student activity	• Discuss the strong printed images. Look at the sharp contrast between black and white. Discuss why they would be considered strong graphic images.

3) Main lesson activities: Exercise 2

Additional student activity	• Discuss with students the illustrative quality of the images and how this style of printing could be used in a graphic novel or in story telling, because a relief print can be used to produce a high number of **editions.** Ask students to illustrate a scene from a favourite book or film. They should think of a particularly dramatic scene: a landscape, a character or an action scene. Ask the class to consider a dramatic effect achieved through the use of gouging, cross-hatching, strong lines to give a sense of detail and drama.
	• When the students have decided on their image, get them to draw it on tracing paper which is cut to the same size as the lino block. They should then flip the tracing paper over and tape it onto the lino before carefully tracing the image onto the block using a sharpened pencil or a pen such as a biro.
	• When students start cutting the lino, make sure that they cut away from themselves and use a piece of masking tape to fix the lino to the table to stop it slipping around. Remind students to use lots of mark-making such as dynamic lines, cross-hatching, circles, and to keep their lines strong and consistent.
	• Once they have finished cutting, students can test what they have printed. If something doesn't look right, they can go back and cut some more detail.

4) Plenary suggestions

Ask the students to look at each other's' work. Are the images dynamic? Could they be classed as an illustration? Ask them to reflect on ways they could improve their work in the future. Conclude the session by asking the group to find at least one contemporary artist who uses relief printing in their practice. It doesn't have to be a well-known artist. Ask them to reflect on what it is they enjoy about how the artist works. It may be the subject matter, the colours they use, the patterns they make. Ask them to apply how they work to their individual project.

Reflection
It may be helpful with younger students to show them images which would be difficult to develop into a relief print such as soft-edged blurry photographs compared with strong black and white images.

Key terms

- **Student's Book key terms:** editions
- **Additional key terms:** brayer, gouge tool, hand burnishing, inked up, linoleum, negative image, roller, wood

Assessment Objectives

Each of the suggested exercises has some similar elements and they all enable students to cover aspects of the four Assessment Objectives.

- **AO1:** Record ideas, observations and insights relevant to intentions as work progresses.
  The generation of a test book from initial proofs with observations on relevance of processes. The drawings produced and developed and selected for the printing exercise.
- **AO2:** Explore and select appropriate resources, media, materials, techniques and processes.
  The testing of various printing tools, media and materials to work with while exploring relief printing techniques.
- **AO3:** Develop ideas through investigation, demonstrating critical understanding.
  Demonstrate an ability to understand and use printmaking exercises to develop a relevant response and generate a body of work.
- **AO4:** Present a personal and coherent response that realises intentions and demonstrates an understanding of visual language.

  The records of reflection and evaluation of printmaking sessions, feedback and response to the body of work produced in the classroom.

⌁ Further research

- Ask students to use the artists above as a starting point and look for contemporary local artists who use similar techniques. You can also give your students examples of practitioners they can relate to.

UNIT 3: ETCHING

PRINTMAKING	Etching 1

Etching is a printmaking process where a printing plate made of metal such as zinc or steel is coated in a non-acidic substance like wax. Once this 'coat' has dried, it acts as a **ground** to protect the plate. The etch is created by drawing into the waxy ground and exposing the metal plate. Then the plate is placed in a bath made up of a corrosive liquid that bites into the exposed lines. Once the print is etched, the plate is inked up and put through a press – a form of printing called **intaglio**. **Drypoint** is a technique that involves drawing directly onto a plate with a **scribe** or etching tool. The method is straightforward, as there is no acid process, and students can be more spontaneous. When they have finished drawing, they are ready to ink their plate up and print.

This section will introduce your students to a range of different materials and tools to make and ink up plates to print. It will also address the use of line, tone, texture and composition in intaglio printing.

Classroom resources

- *Classroom arrangement:* Clear and clean the surfaces that your class will be working on.
- *Materials and equipment:* Acetate, etching tool, printing ink, printing paper, blotting paper, newsprint, water tray, masking tape and cloths for cleaning up.

Top tips

- Ensure that the students understand the importance of cleaning rollers and surfaces after they have finished printing.
- Intaglio prints are in reverse, so keep this in mind if your students intend to use text in their work.
- During the drawing-up process, students can check what the drawing will look like in reverse by using a mirror.

Research sources

- Read overview and brief history of drypoint.

LESSON TASKS

1) Starter suggestions

- Discuss with students what an etching is and what drypoint is.
- Explain to the class how they are both techniques in the intaglio family of printing.
- Discuss intaglio printing with the class.
- Explain that a quick and easy way to produce an intaglio print is with drypoint using acetate.
- Start with producing a test sheet so your students can understand how the process works and so that they can refer to the sheet when planning a print.

2) Main lesson activities: Exercise 1

Additional student activity	• Ask students to experiment by producing a variety of marks on a sheet of acetate. Also ask them to vary the pressure when scratching the acetate. They will find that the deeper they score the acetate, the darker that area will print. In contrast, lightly working the tool across the acetate sheet will produce a fainter to more mid-tone mark. • Shading affects can be achieved through hatching, cross-hatching, stippling, dots, scribbles and so on. • When students are ready to print, get them to rub ink into the acetate sheet, ensuring that it is worked into all the grooves. Ask them to carefully rub away the surface ink with a tissue. • Use paper that has been soaked in water and then blotted dry to print on. The slight dampness of the paper will allow the ink to print more easily. Lay the damp paper over the acetate sheet and place a sheet of newsprint over before running it through a printing press. • Carefully peel back the paper to reveal the print.
Top tip	• As the paper is damp, it is a good idea to dry it between two sheets of blotting paper under a number of drawing boards. This will ensure the print dries flat.

3) Plenary suggestions

At the end of the lesson, ask students to write notes on their drypoint test sheets. They can make notes on how hard they pressed, which tools they used, the type of ink they used and so on. They can keep these sheets in their sketchbooks or research files to refer to when working on future prints.

Reflection

Etching is a process for which many centres do not have the required facilities. It may be a good idea to ensure that your students understand the differences between drypoint and etching. The use of tone in an etching using aquatint compared with the use of mark-making in a drypoint to achieve a sense of light and dark should be examined and reflected upon.

It is important that your students do not copy the work of a suggested artist, but rather use the style, technique or subject matter to inform their own project.

PROJECT SUGGESTIONS

This type of intaglio printing is immediate and spontaneous, and it is a good way to sketch straight onto a plate. If any of your students are strong drawers, this may be a technique that they wish to pursue further.

PRINTMAKING	Etching 2

Classroom resources

- *Classroom preparation:* Clear and clean the surface on which your class will be working.
- *Materials and equipment:* Acrylic plate or Plexiglas, etching tool, printing ink, printing paper, blotting paper, newsprint, water tray, masking tape and cloths to clean up with.

Top tip

- Ensure that students understand the importance of cleaning plates and all surfaces after they have finished printing.

Research sources

- Look at the etchings of:

Käthe Kollwitz	*Self Portrait Hand on Forehead*, 1910
Jake and Dinos Chapman	*Exquisite Corpse*, 2000
Edward Hopper	*Night Shadows*, 1921
Arne Bendik Sjur	*Series of drypoint portraits*, 1986

LESSON TASKS

1) Starter suggestions

Look at the examples of drypoints and etchings from the suggested list. Discuss the images and mark making in the prints with the class. Talk about the quality of line and ask students to select a drawing or photograph from their own sketchbook, which they think will work as a print.

Top tip

- You will need to check the images to make sure that they are suitable for the task and ask students individually why they have selected a particular piece to turn into a drypoint print. Students can record this information in their reflective notes.

2) Main lesson activities: Exercise 1

Additional student activity	• Ask students to place their drawing on the desk with a piece of masking tape at the top to hold it in place. Then place the Plexiglas over the drawing, and fix masking tape at the top and the bottom of the plate. It is useful to make a **registration mark** at the top and bottom of the drawing to make sure that the plate and drawing are aligned between printing proofs.
	• When students are ready to print, let them rub ink into the acetate sheet, ensuring that it is worked into all the grooves. Then they should carefully rub away the surface ink with a tissue. They should print on paper that has been soaked in water and then blotted dry. The slight dampness of the paper will allow the ink to print more easily. Ask students to position the damp paper over the acetate sheet and place a sheet of newsprint on top before running it through a printing press. Then they can carefully peel back the paper to reveal the print.
Top tip	• Students can draw on the produced **proofs** when planning what to add to the print.

3) Plenary suggestions

Ask students to look at each other's work. Encourage them to reflect on ways they could improve their work in the future. It is important that students learn from each other and share good practice. Encourage this in the classroom.

Conclude the session by asking the class to work out a way to print using this technique as part of their individual project. Ask students to find at least one contemporary artist who uses etching in their practice. This artist doesn't have to be a well-known artist.

Ask students to reflect on what it is they enjoy about how the artist works. It may be the subject matter, the colours they use or the patterns they make. Ask them to apply how they work to their own project.

Reflection

By the end of this session, students will know how to use techniques to achieve line, tone and texture in an etching. They should also know how to select the correct tools and understand the process of inking up a plate to print and printing intaglio.

Key terms

- **Student's Book key terms:** drypoint, ground, intaglio, proof
- **Additional key terms:** registration mark, scribe

Assessment Objectives

Each of the suggested exercises has some similar elements and they all enable students to cover aspects of the following four Assessment Objectives.

- **AO1**: Record ideas, observations and insights relevant to intentions as work progresses.

  The generation of a drypoint test sheet with observations on mark-making exercises. The drawings produced, developed and selected for the printing exercise.

- **AO2:** Explore and select appropriate resources, media, materials, techniques and processes.

  The testing of various printing tools, media and materials to work with while exploring drypoint and intaglio printing.

- **AO3:** Develop ideas through investigation, demonstrating critical understanding.

  Demonstrate an ability to understand and use printmaking exercises to develop a relevant response and generate a body of work.

- **AO4:** Present a personal and coherent response that realises intentions and demonstrates an understanding of visual language.

  The records of reflection and evaluation of printmaking sessions, feedback and response to the body of work produced in the classroom.

Further research

- Ask students to use the artists above as a starting point and to look for contemporary local artists who use similar techniques. You can also give students examples of practitioners they can relate to.

PRINTMAKING	Screen printing 1

This session focuses on a variety of approaches to screen printing. You can support students in employing a range of different materials and correct tools to make a print.

Classroom resources

- *Classroom arrangement*: Clear and clean the surfaces on which your class will be working.
- *Materials and equipment:* Screen (frame with gauze), squeegee, **heavy gauge waxy paper** (best for cutting stencil), cutting mat, tracing paper, masking tape, screen printing ink, sharp craft knife, spatula for scrapping the screen clean of ink after printing, cleaning solution for screen ink, and soft bristle brush to clean the screen.

Research sources

- Sister Corita Kent, Andy Warhol, Robert Rauschenberg, Roy Lichenstein, Frank Shepherd Fairey, Kara Walker

LESSON TASKS

1) Starter suggestions

Discuss with the students the images you have shown the group. Talk to them about what sort of work would be suitable for screen printing. Touch on the history of the process – where it started and why. Screen printing derived from an early form of stencil printing, which started in Japan. Up to the late 1930s, screen printing was mostly used for commercial purposes, until it eventually became favoured by artists.

2) Main lesson activities: Exercise 1 (What is screen printing?)

Additional student activity	• Screen printing can be as simple or complex as you would like to make it. It is particularly useful for mass production and producing large editions. It is popular with underground movements and sub-cultures because of the simplicity of the process and the ability to produce prints cheaply.
	• Explain that a screen print is made by using a mesh-covered frame or **screen** to push ink through onto a flat surface. The ink is pushed through the screen onto the paper or fabric by a squeegee. Screen printing has the advantage of not reversing the printed image, so it is popular when printing text.
	○ Ask students to choose a simple image and draw it onto a piece of heavy gauge, waxy paper. Geometric shapes, circles or a simple pattern are the easiest to work with.
	○ Get students to use a sharp craft knife, while leaning on a cutting mat, to cut out the drawing to create the stencil.
	○ Tell students to lay the stencil onto the outside of the screen and tape it down. Remind them to put their stencil on top of the paper onto which they will be printing. Then they can place the screen onto the mesh. Suggest to students that if there is space between the edges of the stencil and screen, they should put masking tape on the underside to stop ink leaking onto the print.
	○ Ask students to spoon out a line of ink along the bottom of the screen.
	○ Tell students now to use the squeegee to **flood** the screen, which means giving the mesh plenty of ink to print with. To do this, they need to keep the screen tipped up and not touching the paper onto which they will be

	printing, while using the squeegee away from them to push the ink.
	○ Let students place the screen onto the paper and pull the squeegee down. This will push the ink through the mesh. Students lift the screen up and remove the **first proof**. This proof will be a chance to check over the print to see whether there are any **bleeds** of ink which need to be taped up.
	○ Explain to students that they are now ready to print.
	○ Make sure that they place the screen carefully onto the paper and ensure that they keep applying ink. Tell them to pull the squeegee towards them in a smooth and firm manner. They must not stop midway.
	○ Explain that once they have reached the bottom, they need to lift the screen to push the ink through to the top to flood the mesh. This will stop the screen drying out and blocking.
Top tip	• After cleaning the screens, get your students to hold them up to the light to make sure that there are no blockages with printing ink, as these would render the screen unusable.

3) Plenary suggestions

At the end of the session, ask the class to lay out their prints. Discuss with students which prints in their opinion are more successful. What made the print work? Was it the composition? The scale? The colours? The printing skill? The thickness of ink? The thinness of ink? Ask students to reflect on these questions and find out what they felt went well in their own printing.

Reflection
Ask students to give each other a suggestion on how they think they could develop their print. What does it remind them of? Encourage students to keep reflective notes during this part of the session while directing them to look at each other's work.

PROJECT SUGGESTIONS

These screen-print tests can be used to make some collages. Look at the work of Matisse, who cut out his shapes or Kara Walker, who uses cut-outs of her prints to create installations.

PRINTMAKING	Screen printing 2

Classroom resources

- *Classroom arrangement:* Clear and clean the surfaces on which your class will be working.
- *Materials and equipment:* As for screen printing Lesson 1.

Research sources

- Jordan Andrew Carter

LESSON TASKS

1) Starter suggestions

Look at some of the work of Jordan Andrew Carter. He screen prints over existing photographs in a playful and humorous way. He blocks out elements of the original image and adds, through screen printing, new elements to the picture. His use of colour is bold and gives a striking, pop art feel to his work.

2) Main lesson activities: Exercise 1

Additional student activity	• Ask the class to find photographs of people or places they find interesting. They can prepare for this session by finding old photographs in junk shops or newspaper images to bring to class. If they have photocopies of the pictures, they can experiment by cutting out shapes to print over the original image or by drawing and painting directly onto them. • Ask students to cut out different colours or text and lay them over the images, and then encourage the class to photograph this work so they can keep a record of their ideas. If students do not have access to a camera, it might be a good idea for you to keep a digital record for the art department. You can perhaps start a blog for the work your students produce in your teaching sessions. • Once students have decided what they want to overprint and which colours they will be using, they can prepare their screens by cutting stencils and taping them to the screen.

Top tips

- It is a good idea for students to have a few copies of the original image to practise on before they print over their original photograph.
- Make sure that students are not using precious photographs from home.

3) Plenary suggestions

Ask students to look at each other's work. Ask them to reflect on ways they could improve their work in the future. It is important that students learn from one another and share good practice. Encourage this in the classroom. Conclude the session by asking the class to work out a way to print using this technique as part of their individual project.

Ask the class to find at least one contemporary artist who uses etching in their practice. This artist doesn't have to be well-known.

Ask students to reflect on what it is they enjoy about how the artist works. It may be the subject matter, the colours they use or the patterns they make. Ask them to apply how they work to their own project. It is important that they do not copy the work. Instead they should rather use the style, technique or subject matter to inform their own project.

Reflection

By the end of this session, students should know how to produce a screen print and understand that there are a variety of ways to use this printing technique. They should also know how to select and prepare the correct tools to make a screen print.

Key terms

- **Student's Book key terms:** screen
- **Additional key terms:** bleeds, first proof, flood (the screen), heavy gauge waxy paper

Assessment objectives

Each of the suggested exercises has some similar elements and they all enable students to cover the following aspects of the four Assessment Objectives.

- **AO1:** Record ideas, observations and insights relevant to intentions as work progresses.

  The generation of digital images, worked on photographs and proofs produced during the screen printing process.

- **AO2:** Explore and select appropriate resources, media, materials, techniques and processes.

  The testing of various printing tools, media and materials to work with while exploring screen and stencil printing.

- **AO3:** Develop ideas through investigation, demonstrating critical understanding.

  Demonstrate an ability to understand and use printmaking exercises to develop a relevant response and generate a body of work.

- **AO4:** Present a personal and coherent response that realises intentions and demonstrates an understanding of visual language.

  The records of reflection and evaluation of printmaking sessions, feedback and response to the body of work produced in the classroom.

Further research

- The references given are diverse and give you a starting point of artists who use relief printing in their practice. If appropriate, it may be worth looking for contemporary local artists who use similar techniques. This can be built upon by you to give your students examples of practitioners they can relate to.

UNIT 5: STUDENT CASE STUDY

Refer to page 221 in the Student's Book for a full-colour version of this student's work.

PROJECT BRIEF

Working with an organic form and developing the theme, the student in this case study has experimented with print and colour, and explored the same form. The student has focused on the printing process and use of colour by producing a number of relief prints.

Assessment

- **AO1:** *Record ideas, observations and insights relevant to intentions as work progresses.*

  The student has presented an idea that could be developed, and has demonstrated an intention to explore further (AO1). Where has this image come from? What is the trigger for the whole project? Was it a theme, a gallery visit or an artist's work? What has attracted the student to the organic form in the first place?

- **AO2:** *Explore and select appropriate resources, media, materials, techniques and processes.*

  There is some evidence of exploration of techniques and material selection through testing (AO2). The positive and negative design cut out of the rectangle as well as producing a simple design image could be developed into a stencil to produce a series of simple screen prints. The student should be trying different tones and scale of print. The student should try printing on different colours of paper or materials such as fabric, wood, leaves, tracing paper and so on.

- **AO3:** *Develop ideas through investigation, demonstrating critical understanding.*

  The idea, to some extent, has been developed through an understanding of the printing process and there is evidence of a critical understanding of technique through reflection of the outcomes and in particular to the 'accidents' in the printing process, which are used to develop a whole new set of prints (AO3).

- **AO4:** *Present a personal and coherent response that realises intentions and demonstrates an understanding of visual language.*

  The combination of prints and collages by the student shows a simple body of work using similar tones and colours. However, we would like to see a more playful, brave and dynamic outcome.

  The student has presented a number of prints as an outcome, which demonstrates an understanding of visual language (AO4) and an ability to work with materials and media to a satisfactory standard. Working with a printing mistake (reflecting) demonstrates the ability to exploit a happy accident.

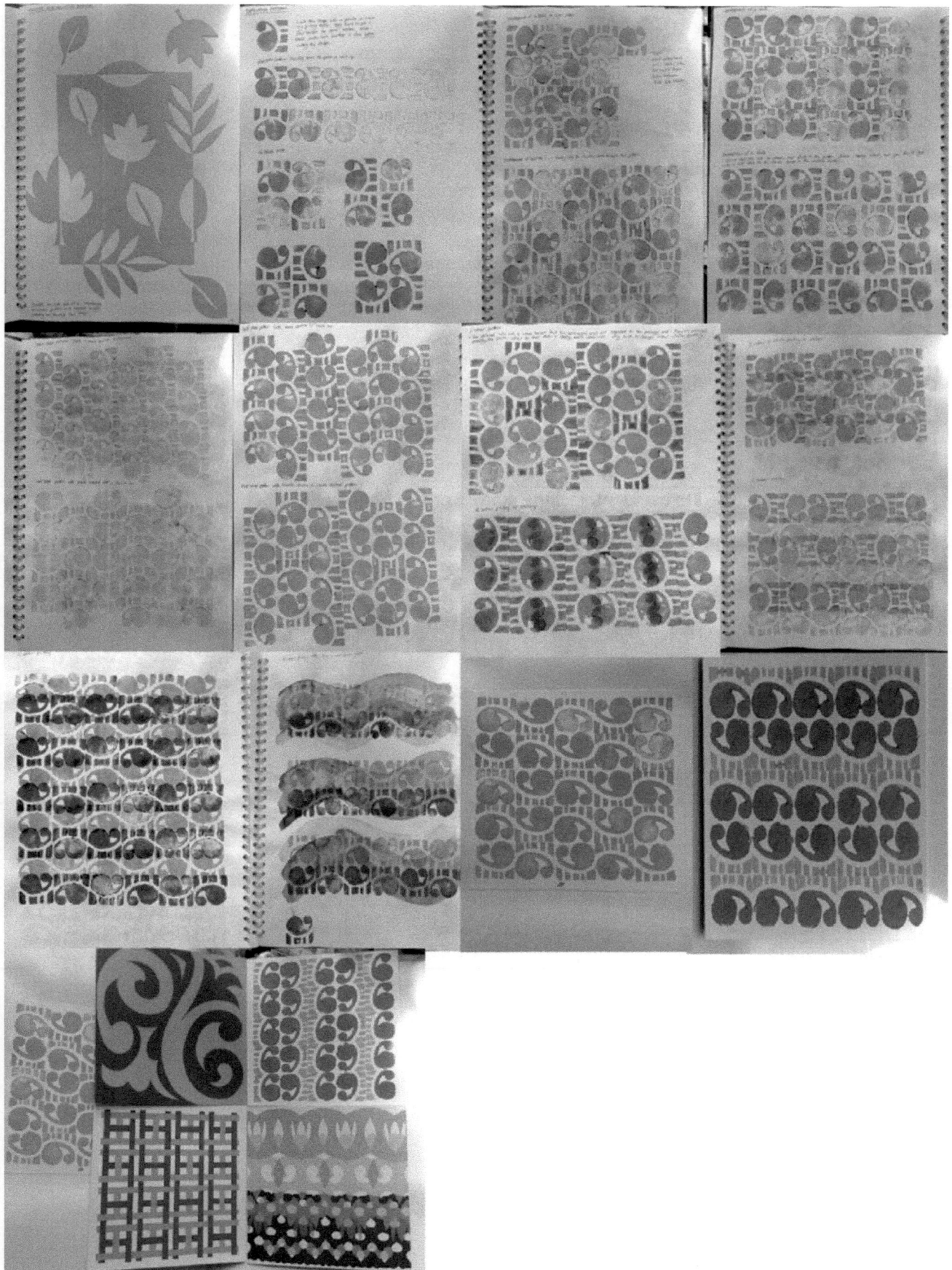

DEVELOPING WORK

The main emphasis throughout this section has been on the technical aspect of printmaking and how to learn new processes. It is important to set up the classroom in advance and test the process to identify any problems before the students are given a demonstration. To begin with, the lessons will be much more prescriptive until students understand and master the processes.

As students progress through the course, you should encourage them to take a more independent approach to developing their work and applying a suitable printing process. The more able students can be encouraged to be more independent and find their own direction. The less able students will need continued support and suggestions about which printmaking process to apply to their projects. Once students begin to develop their printmaking skills, they can then start to incorporate more experimental printmaking techniques and processes to projects.

All stages of the students' work needs to be documented and reflected upon. It is important that they keep a record of their testing in sketchbooks and self-made sample books. As they master the different printmaking techniques, they will be accumulating a rich source of experimentation and reflection as well.

Further projects

Once students have started to use printmaking in their work and generated a set of prints, encourage them to apply a different technique to the same project. This will provide an opportunity to experiment and develop ideas to take their work in a different and often unexpected direction.

Further research

- *Print Workshop: Hand-Printing Techniques and Truly Original Projects* by Christine Schmidt; ISBN 10: 0307586545
- *Modern Printmaking: A Guide to Traditional and Digital Techniques* by Sylvie Covey; ISBN 10: 1607747596

Checklist

✓ I have introduced students to a range of different materials, techniques and tools to make a print.

✓ I have helped my students to recognise the materials and techniques required to make a print and be able to apply them to their own project work.

✓ I have taught my students to use line, tone, texture appropriately in their printmaking.

✓ I have enough knowledge, experience and understanding of printmaking techniques to successfully teach my students.

INTRODUCTION

10.1 Sculptures and ceramics

10.2 Theatre and set design

10.3 Environmental and architectural design

10.4 Product design

10.5 Craft design

10.6 Student case study

Learning objectives

By the end of this unit students should:

- understand the large variety of possible materials, techniques and approaches available for three-dimensional (3-D) work
- understand how they might choose a successful area of 3-D that they can explore
- know what type of support work is required if they chose to work in 3-D
- understand what sculpture and ceramics are and the variety of possible materials, techniques and approaches available for making this type of art
- understand how they might test out ideas in 3-D and in the round
- know how to gather, research and record relevant information for making sculpture and ceramics.

Classroom resources

- Student's Book Chapter 10 Three-dimensional studies, pages 222–249
- Mood boards (digital or handmade) for each unit in Chapter 10, displays of 3-D work, 3-D artefacts to provide stimuli.

General lesson ideas

- Introduce 3-D by showing mood boards for each unit with examples of work by relevant artists.
- Encourage curiosity from students with questions and answers.
- Ask students to write down all types of supporting work for 3-D studies that they can think of without looking at their Student's Book, and then check. They can keep their list in their sketchbooks for reference.

Key considerations

- Consider the visual elements of space, volume, form and scale.
- Consider how AOs are addressed in the various sections.
- Think about which projects or topics are suggested or which could you devise.
- Test practical activities yourself before setting them as tasks for students. This will give you a greater understanding of materials, techniques, potential ideas and possible problems.
- Encourage students to work to their strengths and areas of interest within the limits of resources.
- Check that students have correctly used key terms and technical information.

Reflective log

- What practical skills do I need to develop in order to help my students achieve?
- How can I use practical and theoretical lessons to help my students to develop their work?
- How can I structure my teaching to make the most of the resources and facilities that I have available to me?
- Are there any local exhibitions or resources that my students could visit or use?

Key terms

- **Student's Book key terms:** abstract, CAD, coiling, decorative, functional, kinetic, maquette, mould, pinching, reductive, representational, scale, slab building, slip, symbolic, throwing, wedge

UNIT 1: SCULPTURE AND CERAMICS

SCULPTURE AND CERAMICS	Lesson 1

This series of lesson ideas provides a general introduction to sculpture and ceramics with some suggested themes or approaches. It also includes ideas as to how your students can start to record observations and insights at the beginning of an assignment for inspiration. Many of the tasks can be adapted to suit your own circumstances.

Classroom resources

- Student's Book pages 224–231
- *Materials and equipment:* Collection of existing sculptural and/or ceramic objects (as required by tasks below), your own PowerPoint presentations, mood boards or worksheets about sculpture and ceramics, A2 paper and drawing materials, access to the internet, PowerPoint and CAD.

Research sources

- Starbeck provides a mail order service of 3-D artefacts from around the world.
- Possible further sculptors: Alexander Calder (kinetic), Andy Goldsworthy (outdoor), Auguste Rodin (figurative), Constantin Bráncusi (abstract).
- Possible ceramicists: Hara Kiyoshi, Kate Malone, Beate Kuhn.

LESSON TASKS

1) Starter suggestions

Research (paired activity)	• Ask students to read the definition of the term 'sculpture' 'ceramics' and 'maquette' in the Student's Book. Give students a short time online or with books to find an inspiring, visual example for each term.
Demonstration	• Show students a range of sculptural and ceramics objects, and illustrate what sculpture and ceramics are in their various forms. Alternatively, prepare a PowerPoint presentation.
Brainstorm (group activity)	• Ask students to create a mind-map of all that they know about ceramics. Guide them to include sub-headings from the Student's Book, such as types of clay, techniques and the stages of making an artwork.
Drawing	• Ask students to choose one sculpture or ceramic object from a selection that you have gathered. Ask them to make three to four quick, timed, observational sketches of the object from different angles or viewpoints on the same piece of paper. This should last no more than five minutes to appreciate scale and stimulate an awareness of form, space and volume.
Inspiration	• Use a mood board on a focused area of sculpture such as abstraction, carvings, religious sculpture or figurative sculpture. Talk to your students about them.

2) Main lesson activities

Drawing	• Ask students to draw a selection of existing sculptures or ceramics from primary sources, such as Egyptian artefacts, as a project starting point. Ask them to annotate their drawings with keywords about the designs, techniques and materials.
Research	• Ask students to investigate a sculptor, ceramicist, or style of sculpture that they find inspiring. Ask them to present their findings as a series of sketchbook pages, a PowerPoint presentation or a mood board.
Research materials	• Ask students to research examples of sculpture in one of the following areas: Clay, metal and wire, plaster and stone, plastic, wood, found objects. Ask them to present their findings in a sketchbook, on a sheet or digitally.
Collaborate	• Give a pair or group of students a suitable theme such as kinetic sculpture or outdoor sculpture and allow them to research their theme online or via books, before giving an illustrated talk to the class.
Mini project	• Gather resources about an individual sculptor such as Anthony Gormley, Ai Wei Wei, Barbara Hepworth, Louise Bourgeois, Cornelia Parker or Claes Oldenburg. Ask students to design a sculpture in the style of the artist and present as a handmade A3 sheet of drawings and written annotation or using CAD.
Top tip	• Don't try to cover all aspects of sculpture and ceramics in your scheme of work. Structure your lessons around a theme or focus so that students can learn in greater depth.

3) Plenary suggestions

Display	• Ask students to create a temporary exhibition of their work on the wall to pool ideas. Encourage discussion about the display.
Reflect	• Ask students questions to check their progress and understanding. What have you done? Why have you done this? What have you learnt from this? What went well? What could be improved?
Consolidate	• Ask students to write a summary of their answers to the above questions in their sketchbooks.

Reflection

Collect in student work on a regular basis. Spread out all tasks on a table. Ask yourself what is going well and what further resources or support your students require from you. Identify what aspects of the Assessment Objectives have been addressed.

SUGGESTED ASSESSMENT OF STUDENT'S BOOK ACTIVITIES

Skills activity A	• See Student's Book page 225
	• In order to do this activity well, students will need to work carefully from first-hand observation (AO1). They will need to be thorough and detailed in all types of recording, both written and visual to cover AO1 successfully. They should also show clear analysis in answering the questions about whatever artwork they have chosen to demonstrate their critical understanding (AO3). A class could be taken to a local exhibition to complete this activity or use sculptures that you have collected. Guide students to use key terms accurately and appropriately in their written work. Encourage students to be curious and ask questions.

This section can be used to introduce hands-on, practical 3-D materials, techniques and processes and to develop student confidence in handling a range of media.

Classroom resources

- *Classroom arrangement:* It is easiest for students to work in table groups to share equipment and materials. Wipeable, table surfaces are advisable. Carefully consider health and safety.
- *Materials and equipment:* Digital camera or iPad for taking photographs, a range of 3-D materials and equipment appropriate to the tasks below, appropriate 2D images as inspiration for tasks.

Research sources

- Possible artists: Martin Senn, Isabelle Bonte (for 3-D wirework) and artists as suggested in the tasks below.
- 'How to' demonstrations for 3-D techniques on YouTube.

LESSON TASKS

1) Starter suggestions

Demonstrate	• Present samples that you have made to show what you would like students to do. Demonstrate the stages of making, the possibilities and the challenges of a technique such as slab-building.
Discussion of exemplar work	• Show examples from previous students to explain a particular idea or process that you want your class to try. For example, a range of pottery made using coiling or pinching will help to demonstrate the technique to students.

2) Main lesson activities

In all tasks, encourage innovative use of media. Allow students to record work in progress as a series of photographs and technical notes as appropriate for recording purposes later.

Space, volume, form	• Observing an object such as a hammer or bottle, ask students to make the object in 3-D using wire. This is sometimes called drawing with wire. Students could experiment with various thicknesses of wire to see what works best.
Reductive method	• Give students a block of clay or plaster and carving tools. Ask them to carve into the material to create an imaginative sculpture. Use a theme such as the human form to focus ideas. Show further inspiration from other artists on the same theme, such as Auguste Rodin, Michelangelo and Henry Moore.
Constructive method	• Give students a cardboard box and a craft knife and/or tough-cut scissors. Ask them to cut the box into shapes that can be joined together to form a new design. Card can be folded, bent, slotted, stacked and reassembled by gluing or taping. Show inspiration from other artists such as Naum Gabo's heads or Dale Chihuly (glass sculptor).
Modelling	• Ask students to make a wire figure that can be bent and manipulated into an action pose such as running, dancing or climbing. Cover the wire figure with scrunched tissue paper dipped in glue to form the body. When dry, the figure can be stained or painted. Show inspiration from other sculptors such as Alberto Giacometti.

Working in relief	• Give students a board to work on. Ask students to use paper and card to build out from the board to form a pleasing 3-D composition. Show inspiration from other artists such as Frank Stella or from origami forms.
Skills activity B	• Student's Book page 227 • Students can use this activity to begin to explore ceramic making techniques.
Skills activity C	• Student's Book page 229 • Students can use this activity to develop their understanding of decorative processes on ceramics.

3) Plenary suggestions

Evaluation	• Ask students to present their main activity to the class and talk about the following: The techniques and materials used, and what went well? What they have learnt? What could be improved?
Develop	• Ask students to sketch or list ideas for how their work might develop next, based on the main activity that they have tried.

Reflection
Collect in students' practical work after a main lesson activity is completed. Write down what you think they still need to research in order to better develop their ideas such as more information about a technique or about an artist's work. Give students feedback to help support them in their work during a lesson.

SUGGESTED ASSESSMENT OF STUDENT'S BOOK ACTIVITIES

Skills activity B	• Student's Book page 227 • Students need to show independent insight in their research (AO1) and allow it to inform their understanding and development of their chosen technique (AO3). You would expect to see an understanding of what was or was not successful (AO2). Students should accomplish a refined level of practical skill leading to a varied set of outcomes with potential to take further (AO2 and AO4). Ideas should show confident use of volume, space and form.
Skills activity C	• Student's Book page 229 • Students need to work creatively but also methodically to experiment, test and record their materials, techniques and processes (AO2). Students will need to demonstrate how they can refine ideas informed by their learning to strongly develop their practical work as a skilful set of varied decorative tiles (AO3, leading to AO4). They will need to show confident use of colour, pattern, texture and composition.

This section provides suggestions for students communicating their ideas with relevant supporting drawings, photography and research and how to document the stages involved in making 3-D work. It concludes with some ideas for whole assignments that incorporate all the AOs.

Classroom resources

- *Classroom arrangement:* A large table area is useful to display exemplar material.
- *Materials and equipment:* Digital camera or iPad for taking photographs, a range of 2D materials and equipment appropriate to the tasks below.

Research sources

- Relevant examples of work from www.cambridgeinternational.org/support
- Your own examples of artists' sketches, design work, maquettes and planning.
- Possible Artists: Bill Mack (relief), Johnson Tsang (distortion), Ray Katz (interlocking forms), Debbie Barber (decorative ceramics).

LESSON TASKS

1) Starter suggestions

Demonstration	• Show students a range of sketchbooks, design sheets, digital presentations and any other appropriate methods that demonstrate the gathering, researching and recording of information in a 3-D art project.
Gather ideas	• Facilitate a class discussion to generate ideas for how information might be successfully presented. Consider issues such as scale, colour, layout, text and style.

2) Main lesson activities

Visit	• Arrange a trip to a local exhibition of sculpture or ceramics. Ask students to document and record their trip with visually interesting methods such as a concertina book of drawings.
Appreciate context	• Ask students to research using books and online and then design a timeline to show key pieces of sculpture and ceramics across the centuries and from a variety of cultures.
Design work	• Ask students to sketch alternative ideas for a final outcome once they have a clear direction for their assignment. Encourage them to consider how information will be presented most effectively with relevant annotation and where they might take inspiration from other artists.
Technical notes	• Give students a lesson to write up and present a practical ceramics activity that they have completed with relevant stages of the process and technical notes. Make sure that they include detail such as names of materials used, application of techniques, photos before and after kiln-firing and firing temperatures to show their understanding.
Record final outcomes	• Set up a suitably lit area with a plain background and ask students to photograph their final 3-D ceramic or sculpture. Photographs should be clear and detailed to show off the work to the assessor at its best.

3) Plenary suggestions

Record stages of work	• Ask students to photograph 3-D work at the end of any practical session to show the stages of development in a piece.
Evaluate	• Ask students to choose their most successful 3-D test piece and write up a reflective evaluation of the process using their notes and photographs.
Present relevant insights	• Question students about artists that have influenced their own practical 3-D work. Ask them to create an annotated, visual sheet to record this as homework. Encourage students to explain the following: Who is the artist or designer? Describe their work. Which materials are used? How do you think it has been made? What preparation might have been involved? How long do you think it took to make? How is it relevant to your ideas?

4) Internally set assignments

Starting points can vary: A general theme, an artist, a technique or material, an exhibition, or an issue such as poverty. Here are some examples:	
Sculpture theme: Natural forms	• Observe and draw the structure and form of plants, shells, flowers, seeds and pods. • Research designs inspired by natural forms such as the work of Peter Randall-Page. • Explore ideas by drawing designs and carving in clay, plaster, wax or stone. • Document and record all stages of work. • Conclude with one or more refined sculptures in response to the theme.
Ceramics theme: Bowls	• Observe and draw a range of vessels at an exhibition. Focus on interesting shapes and forms. • Research further designs from secondary sources. Refine your focus to a particular style or approach such as the work of Polly and Garry Uttley. • Explore ideas by sketching designs and pressing or casting clay in moulds. Experiment with decoration. • Document and record all stages of work. • Make one or more final bowl designs.

5) Assessment of projects

When reviewing the project work, consider the following aspects of the four Assessment Objectives:

Assessment Objectives
• **AO1:** Observational drawings of relevant objects, ideas for designs, notes and photographs to document technical making processes and the relevance of the artists that have been researched.
• **AO2:** Exploration of relevant 3-D materials showing evidence of use of a range of media or approaches. 3-D samples that shows growing refinement of practical skills.
• **AO3:** Development of ideas through the inspiration of the relevant artists stated above and any others as appropriate and demonstrating how research has been used to inspire and inform student work.
• **AO4:** Production of a sustained final outcome (sculpture/s or bowl/s) that realises intentions in supporting work and shows an understanding of visual language.

UNIT 2: THEATRE AND SET DESIGN

THEATRE AND SET DESIGN	Lesson 1

This series of lesson ideas provides a general introduction to theatre and set design with some suggested themes or approaches. There are suggestions for how your students can start to record and research ideas for inspiration and how to start to show that they have considered audience, role and function in their research.

Classroom resources

- Student's Book pages 232–234
- *Materials and equipment:* Paper, pens, drawing materials and surfaces, practical presentation materials and equipment such as card, glue, scissors and printer, your own PowerPoint presentations, mood boards or worksheets about theatre and set design (as required by tasks below), collection of masks, headdresses or puppets, access to internet, PowerPoint, CAD

Research sources

- Focusing on a theme or style such as animal masks or Bunraku Japanese puppet theatre is a good idea.
- However, for set design with a good introductory video, try searching Ming Cho Lee on YouTube.

LESSON TASKS

1) Starter suggestions

Brainstorm (group activity)	• Students create a mind-map with set design, props, costume and lighting as the four main branches. For each branch, ask students to write down the key considerations and problems that the designer would need to solve in order to create a successful design. Discuss answers as a class.
Contextualise	• Watch a video of a performance. Ask students to make a note of everything that has been designed and what they found inspiring.
Demonstrate	• Show students a range of set designs, props, costumes, masks and headdresses as a series of images and illustrate the possibilities for theatre design.
Inspiration	• Use a mood board on a focused area such as scenery and set design and talk about a range of approaches with your students.
Audience	• Ask students to list of the types of audience they might expect at the following performances: circus, opera or ballet, Shakespeare play, Carnival in Rio de Janeiro, a musical such as Cats, African Drumming, Samba dance. Ask students what sort of costume, sets or props they might expect to see.

2) Main lesson activities

These activities may take more than one lesson or may be continued as homework.

Drawing	• Students draw some masks, headdresses or puppets first-hand from a selection that you have collected. You can use a theme such as Venetian masks or South-east Asian puppets. Ask them to annotate their drawings with keywords about the role and function of the designs and how this has been achieved in the making process.

Research visit	• Arrange a trip to a professional theatre performance to appreciate the various aspects of theatre and set design. Investigate any possibility of a backstage tour for greater understanding. Ensure that students record evidence of their visit with sketches, photographs and written annotation.
Research materials	• Ask students to research one famous character from a theatre production and focus on how the character has been styled in different versions of the production. They should consider colour, materials used, make-up and costume. Ask them to present their findings in a sketchbook, on a sheet or digitally.
Collaborate	• Give a pair or group of students a suitable theme such as carnival performance or Chinese New Year parade as the starting point for a possible assignment and allow them to research their theme, before giving an illustrated talk to the class. Encourage students to analyse and talk about any significant visual elements in the designs, the materials and techniques used and the response being encouraged in the audience.
Skills activity A	• Student's Book page 233 • Students can use this activity to begin to explore costume design or another aspect of theatre of their choice.

3) Plenary suggestions

Display	• Create an exhibition of student drawing or research. Encourage students to write ideas for the following on sticky notes for each piece of work: How work could be improved? How could work develop next?
Reflect	• Ask students about their main research activity to check their progress and understanding. Use questions such as: What you learnt from this? What was most inspiring? Who are you designing for?
Consolidate	• Ask students to write up a summary of their answers to the above questions in their sketchbooks as homework or classwork.

Reflection
What resources do you have in your area that students could access as inspiration, such as a local theatre? Do they have resources for schools? Does the school drama department have any useful items that you could borrow such as a set of masks for drawing? Does your school drama production provide a suitable theme for student design work?

SUGGESTED ASSESSMENT OF STUDENT'S BOOK ACTIVITIES

Skills activity A	• Student's Book page 233 • Students need to show independent insight in their research (AO1) and allow it to inform their understanding and development of their chosen area of interest (AO3). You would expect to see inspiring examples, thoroughly presented images and annotation (AO1) with carefully chosen techniques and materials to visually enhance the presentation (AO2). Students should accomplish a sophisticated research outcome (AO4), which will help them to develop their ideas further.

This section gives suggestions to teach students how to move a project forward with relevant and appropriate exploration of materials, techniques and processes to develop ideas. It also provides suggestions for whole projects.

Classroom resources

- *Materials and equipment:* Samples made by you, relevant to a task, examples of design planning such as sketchbooks, digital work and models, 2D materials appropriate for design work, 3-D materials appropriate for model making such as card, grey or foam board, camera or iPad for taking photographs.

Research sources

- There are lots of visual examples of theatre set model-making, costume and props online. You can also download free templates for sketching ideas such as costume design.

Top tip

- Consider other sections of the Student's Book and Teacher's Guide that may be relevant. For example, if your students are designing a mask or costume for theatre, it might be helpful to also consider approaches in the textiles or crafts section.

LESSON TASKS

1) Starter suggestions

Demonstrate	• Present relevant samples that you have made, such as papier mâché masks. Demonstrate the stages of making, possibilities and the challenges of the technique.
Demonstrate	• Show students a range of styles as appropriate to your scheme of work for planning designs such as costume sketches in watercolour, ink and pencil, digital designs for stage sets and scale models.

2) Main lesson activities

Design	• Ask students to create a series of design sketches to show their ideas for a character's costume in a performance. They should include colour, written annotation and swatches of materials to be used. Using pencil, pen and ink or watercolour provides a suitable style for this type of work.
Design	• Ask students to design scenery using CAD for a specific performance to show that they have creatively considered scale, form, various viewpoints and function.
Model-making	• Ask students to make a scale model of their set design with consideration of various angles and viewing points as well as the needs of the performers. Guide students with appropriate making materials such as card, grey board, foam board, wooden lollipop sticks or balsa wood.
Development	• Ask students to sketch and make alternative ideas for a final outcome once they have a clear direction for their work. Encourage them to consider effective presentation techniques.
Recording	• Ask students to photograph and/or sketch a theatre set model that they have made as if it were full scale and to explore various lighting, atmosphere and mood through their own photography.
	• Ask students to photograph a final costume outcome while it is being modelled along with suitable make-up to communicate the design in character.

3) Plenary suggestions

Evaluation	• Ask students to present their model-making to the class and talk about the following: Which techniques and materials were used? What went well? What they have learnt? What could be improved?
Develop	• After a research or design activity, ask students to sketch, list ideas or talk about how their work might develop next, based on the activity.

Reflection

Ask students to write down what they still need to research in order to better develop their ideas such as more information about a technique or about a designer's work.

INTERNALLY SET ASSIGNMENTS

•	Starting points can vary: a cultural approach, a specific performance, a general theme, such as carnival headdresses. Here are some examples:	
1.	**General theme: Masks**	• Observe and draw a range of masks from different cultures, performances or time periods. • Research further by refining the focus to a particular brief or theme such as African tribal dance performances. • Explore ideas by drawing designs and testing them out in suitable media such as wood, papier mâché, card or fabric. Experiment with decoration. • Document and record all stages of work. • Conclude with one or more refined, full-sized masks in response to the theme.
2.	**Specific performance theme: Madame Butterfly**	• Observe and draw a range of relevant forms associated with this opera such as butterflies, blossom, Japanese artefacts and architecture. • Research previous opera designs from secondary sources for this production. Refine your focus to a particular aspect such as scenery or costume. • Explore ideas by sketching designs and experimenting with samples or models as appropriate to intentions. • Document and record all stages of work. Students should show how they have solved problems and communicated the performance to the audience. • Make the final costume design or model of the set and photograph/video it.
		• Document and record all stages of work. Students should show how they have solved problems and communicated the performance to the audience. • Make the final costume design or model of the set and photograph/video it.
Top tip		• Writing a design brief can help to focus a student's project.

UNIT 3: ENVIRONMENTAL AND ARCHITECTURAL DESIGN

ENVIRONMENTAL AND ARCHITECTURAL DESIGN	Lesson 1

This series of lesson ideas provides a general introduction to architectural and environmental design with some suggested themes or approaches. It shows how your students can start to record their observations and insights to provide inspiration and how they can start to show their critical understanding with relevant research.

Classroom resources:

- Student's Book pages 235–237
- *Materials and equipment:* Access to internet, PowerPoint, CAD, books, your own PowerPoint presentations, mood boards or worksheets about architectural and environmental design, paper, pens, drawing materials and surfaces, presentation materials and equipment such as card, glue, scissors and printer.

Research sources:

- Possible architects: See mini project in main lesson activities.
- Possible gardens: Jardim Botanico de Curitiba, Brazil, Yuyuan Garden, China, Shalimar Bagh, India, Royal Botanic Gardens, England.

LESSON TASKS

1) Starter suggestions

Research (paired activity)	• Ask students to create a definition for the term 'architecture' 'interior design' 'landscape design' and 'environmental design'. Give students a short time online or with books to find an inspiring, visual example for each term.
Inspiration	• Use a series of mood boards or digital images to give a broad introduction to architectural form, interior design and designed outdoor spaces. Ask students to identify the key features of this kind of 3-D work.
Role, function, audience	• Students describe the design styles and features that you might expect in the following locations or spaces: A high-end jewellery store, a vintage market, a Chinese gate in the city, a five-star hotel foyer, a teenager's bedroom, a children's nursery school, an expensive restaurant.

2) Main lesson activities

Appreciate context	• Ask students to research using books and online and then design a timeline to show key pieces of architecture and environmental design from across the centuries. This task can focus on one particular culture or many.
Research visit	• Arrange a trip to an interesting building, park or space. Ask students to observe how people interact with the space and consider how the space works in its wider context or location. Ensure that students record evidence of their visit such as sketches, photographs, video or written notes referring to the role and function of the space.

Collaborative research	• Ask students to research one style of architecture or landscape design such as traditional Japanese buildings and gardens. Students should refer to relevant visual elements and also consider the materials, techniques and function of the spaces and what has inspired the style. Ask students to present their findings in a sketchbook, on a sheet or digitally.
Collaborate	• Give a pair or group of students a suitable focus such as buildings made from glass, eating spaces or sustainable environmental issues and allow them to research their theme. Ask students to analyse any significant visual elements in the designs, the materials and techniques used and the role and function of the design.
Skills activity B	• Student's Book page 237 • Students can use the first part of this activity to gain a deeper understanding of one architect's style and approach. They could choose a different architect or style and complete the same activity more than once. (The second part of the activity will also provide students with an understanding of how Hadid has tested out ideas to consider scale and space).
Mini project	• Gather resources about an individual architect such as Frank Lloyd Wright, Antoni Gaudi, Richard Rogers, Frank Gehry, Le Corbusier or Alvor Aalto. Ask students to design a building or space in the style of the architect and present as an A3 sheet of drawings and written annotation, or using CAD.

3) Plenary suggestions

Display	• Create an exhibition of student drawing or research. Encourage students to write ideas for each piece of work: How work could be improved? How could work develop next?
Reflect	• Ask students about their main research activity to check their progress and understanding. Use questions such as: What have you learnt from this? What was most inspiring? Who are you designing for? Where do you see your work developing next?
Consolidate	• Ask students to write up a summary of their answers to the above questions in their sketchbooks as homework or classwork.

Reflection

Consider how environmental and architectural design might link to Design and Technology. Are there resources that you can share such as materials, equipment, examples of technical drawing and CAD?

SUGGESTED ASSESSMENT OF STUDENT'S BOOK ACTIVITIES

Skills activity B	• Student's Book page 237 • Students need to show their observations and insights in their research (AO1) and allow it to inform their understanding. You would expect to see carefully presented images and annotation with skilfully chosen techniques and materials to visually enhance the presentation (AO1 & AO2).

This section gives suggestions to teach students how to move a project forward with relevant and appropriate exploration of the key visual elements, methods of recording and appropriate techniques and processes to develop ideas. It will also demonstrate ways in which you can teach students to present a personal and coherent response to environmental and architectural design with suggestions for whole projects.

Classroom resources
• *Materials and equipment:* Samples made by you, relevant to the tasks, examples of design planning such as sketchbooks, digital and models, 2D materials appropriate for design work and drawing, 3-D materials appropriate for model-making such as card, grey board or foam board, digital camera for taking photographs, CAD.

Research sources
• **Possible architects:** See mini project in main lesson activities.
• **Possible gardens:** Jardim Botanico de Curitiba, Brazil, Yuyuan Garden, China, Shalimar Bagh, India, Royal Botanic Gardens, England
• **Sustainable architecture by:** Ken Yeang, Jean Nouvel, Rolf Disch

LESSON TASKS

1) Starter suggestions

Demonstrate	• Present relevant samples that you have made, such as scale models of buildings, interiors or spaces. Demonstrate the stages of making, the possibilities and the challenges.
Demonstrate	• Show and discuss with students a range of approaches for planning designs such as thumbnail sketches, accurate scale drawings, digital designs and scale models.

2) Main lesson activities

	• In all tasks, encourage students to solve problems related to scale, location, function and audience.
	• Most tasks will take longer than one lesson.
Skills activity A	• Student's Book page 236 • Students can begin to explore how to communicate scale by placing a design in a site-specific location.
Drawing	• Ask students to draw some architectural spaces from primary sources. Use locations around your school and extend this task as homework. Focus the drawing tasks with titles for each such as looking up, looking down, looking through, looking into. This will help students to consider space, perspective, angles, viewpoints and depth.
Scale drawing	• Ask students to use CAD or hand-drawn methods to practise scale drawing in 3-D. This could be based on an existing object, a feature such as a doorway or from an existing handmade model.
Interior design	• Ask students to create a mood board to show an idea for a new domestic interior such as a living room. This should include drawing/s of the space, swatches of materials and finishes to be used and written annotation.

Model-making	• Ask students to design and make a scale model of a pavilion to be located in a local park and to explain how they see the design being used and by whom.
Recording	• Ask students to photograph their model as if it were full scale and create a photomontage to show it in a new location.
Recording	• Ask students to create a 3-D CAD version of a space that they have designed and explore how to animate to move through the space onscreen.

3) Plenary suggestions:

Evaluation	• Ask students to present their model-making to the class and talk about the following: What techniques and materials were used? What went well? What they have learnt? What could be improved?
Develop	• Following a research or design activity, ask students to sketch, list ideas or talk about how their work might develop next, based on the activity.
Reflect	• Ask students to write down what they still need to research in order to better develop their ideas such as more information about a technique or about a designer's work.

SUGGESTED ASSESSMENT OF STUDENT'S BOOK ACTIVITIES

Skills activity A	• Student's Book pages 236 • Students need to show clear recording skills (AO1) of their chosen location with photography or video. Their sketched ideas on top of the printed photos should be skilfully recorded (AO1) and show the development of ideas demonstrating understanding of location and scale (AO3). You would expect to see a creative and coherent response in the ideas shown (AO4).

INTERNALLY SET ASSIGNMENTS

Starting points can vary such as an interior design brief, a specific location such as an area for re-development, a material or technique such as buildings made from wood, a cultural theme such as an oriental garden or a general theme.

1) General theme: Sheds, pods and huts

1. Observe and draw a range of sheds, pods and huts.
2. Research examples from secondary sources, such as mud huts, beach huts, tree houses and cabins.
3. Explore ideas for an ideal shed, hut or pod for a specific client by sketching ideas and experimenting with scale models and drawings.
4. Present a final design as a model, drawings or using CAD showing what has influenced the design and clear use of relevant visual language.

2) Specific location theme: Redevelopment of the entrance to a local public building

1. Observe, photograph and draw the existing building and its surroundings.
2. Make notes about how the entrance is used.
3. Research other public buildings from secondary sources with interesting entrances for inspiration.
4. Explore ideas to redesign the entrance. Draw designs by hand or digitally and experiment with scale models and drawings.
5. Document and record all stages of work.
6. Present the final design as a model, drawings and photomontage.

UNIT 4: PRODUCT DESIGN

PRODUCT DESIGN	Lesson 1

This series of lesson ideas provides a general introduction to product design with some suggested themes or approaches. It shows how your students can start to record their observations and insights to provide inspiration and how to start to show their critical understanding with relevant research.

Classroom resources

- Student's Book pages 238–241
- *Materials and equipment:* Access to internet, PowerPoint, CAD, books (as required by tasks below), your own PowerPoint presentations, mood boards or worksheets, paper, pens, drawing materials and surfaces, presentation materials and equipment such as card, glue, scissors and printer.

Research resources

- Possible product designers: Phillipe Starck, James Dyson, Eileen Gray, Luigi Colani, Kenichiro Ashida, Jonathan Ive, Hella Jongerius, Alessi, Ettore Sottsass, Terence Conran.

LESSON TASKS

1) Starter suggestions

Research	• Ask students to present and discuss a collage created as homework showing both functional and decorative product designs, Guide students to identify the materials and processes used to make each product and the target audience for each.
Inspiration	• Use a series of mood boards or digital images to give a broad introduction to product design. Ask students to identify which products are manufactured and which are handmade.
Appreciate problem-solving	• Show students examples of a product in various forms across time or cultures such as a drinking vessel (cup). This will help students to see how a problem has been solved through design alternatives across a range of contexts.

2) Main lesson activities

These activities may take more than one lesson or may be continued as homework.

Appreciate context	• Ask students to research using books and online and then design a timeline to show key pieces of product design from across the centuries. This task can focus on one particular culture or many.
Research visit	• Arrange a trip to a relevant factory or workplace. Ask students to observe the various stages of designing and making a product from the initial brief to the finished item. Ensure that students record evidence of their visit using sketches, photographs, video or written notes referring to the materials, processes, costs and target market as appropriate.
Collaborative research	• Ask students to choose one material such as wood, metal, glass or plastic and find as many different products as possible made from this material. Support students to present their findings in a suitable format and ask them to explain any making processes, important design elements and aesthetics.

Collaborate	• Give a pair or group of students a suitable focus such as lighting products, eating utensils or mobile phone cases and allow them to research their theme. Ask students to analyse any significant visual elements in the designs, the materials and techniques used and the role and function of the design.
Skills activity A	• Student's Book page 239 • Students can use this activity as a starting point for their own project by choosing a product that they could redesign later.
Skills activity B	• Student's Book page 241 • This activity is useful once a student knows what type of product they want to design to focus their research or to help them choose a type of product that they could redesign later.

3) Plenary suggestions

Pool ideas	• Create an exhibition of student research. Encourage students to write ideas for each piece of work: How could work be improved? How could work develop next?
Questioning to assess progress	• Ask students about their main research activity to check their progress and understanding. Use questions such as: What have you learnt from this? What was most inspiring? Who could you design for? Where do you see your work developing next?
Consolidate	• Ask students to write up a summary of their answers to the above questions in their sketchbooks as homework or classwork.

Reflection

Consider how product design might link to Design and Technology. Are there resources that you can share such as materials, equipment, examples of technical drawing, CAD? Are there any local manufacturers or products that could inform the work of your students? How might you give them access to this source of inspiration?

SUGGESTED ASSESSMENT OF STUDENT'S BOOK ACTIVITIES:

Skills activity A	• Student's Book page 239 • Students need to show skilful observations and insights in answering the questions (AO1) and allow this to inform their understanding. The list of questions can help them to formulate a design brief later to structure their own practical work.
Skills activity B	• Student's Book page 241 • Students need to select and use appropriate resources to present this activity skilfully (AO2). • Students need to show skilful observations and insights in answering the questions (AO1) and allow it to inform their understanding. The list of questions may help them to formulate a design brief later to structure their own practical work.

This section gives suggestions to teach students how to move a project forward with further analysis, experimentation and development of ideas. It will also demonstrate ways in which you can teach students to present a personal and coherent response to product design with suggestions for whole projects.

Classroom resources

- *Materials and equipment:* Examples of design planning such as sketchbooks, digital work and models, existing products to draw and analyse, 3-D materials appropriate for testing and experimenting such as wood, metal or plastics, 3-D materials appropriate for model-making such as card, grey board or foam board, digital camera for taking photographs, CAD, copies of the IGCSE assessment criteria.

LESSON TASKS

1) Starter suggestions

Identify a problem	• Set a product design brief for students to follow or help them to create their own.
Demonstrate	• Discuss with students a range of approaches for planning product designs such as thumbnail sketches, accurate scale drawings, digital designs and scale models.

2) Main lesson activities

In all tasks, encourage students to solve problems related to a product fulfilling a decorative or functional role. Remind them to show alternative design solutions and an understanding of how a product will be made.

Most tasks will take longer than one lesson.

Top tip

- Always demonstrate how to use machinery and equipment safely such as band saws, laser cutters, drills and carving tools.

Drawing	• Ask students to draw some existing products from primary sources that are similar in role to those that are going to be designed by the student. Make sure that students add thorough written analysis about the products they have drawn.
Experiment	• Encourage students to investigate what a material can and cannot do to appreciate its potential. Ask students to document their findings.
Recording ideas	• Ask students to use CAD or hand-drawn methods to visualise their ideas for a product and to show it from a range of viewpoints.
Model-making to record and develop ideas	• Ask students to make a series of rough models to show alternative design ideas in 3-D and then evaluate each design to see what works best.
Recording skills to analyse ideas	• Ask students to photograph their models and add analysis about the pros and cons of each design.
Realise intentions	• Ask students to create a final product design refined from previous work or ideas. The final design might be a scale model and series of final drawings or an actual final piece depending on the materials and processes involved. Encourage students to use a high level of finish in the quality of the work.
Consolidate	• Give students a copy of the assessment criteria and evaluate their project against the criteria highlighting any strengths and weaknesses to be addressed.

3) Plenary suggestions

Evaluation	• Ask students to present their model-making to the class and talk about the following: Which techniques and materials were used? What went well? What they have learnt? What could be improved?
Develop	• Following a research or design activity, ask students to sketch, list ideas or talk about how their work might develop next, based on the activity.

Reflection

Ask students to write down what they still need to research in order to better develop their ideas such as more information about a technique or about a designer's work.

INTERNALLY SET ASSIGNMENTS

Starting points can vary such as a design brief, a problem to solve or developing a new design for an existing product. Here is an example:

Design brief	• A local company would like to commission a new range of containers to hold office stationery. This should include a pencil holder/desk tidy and a letter rack with three sections. The products can be made from any suitable material to be sold as a mid-price product and aimed at the domestic office.
Possible approaches	• Draw or photograph existing office containers and analyse their designs using the skills activity questions from the Student's Book as a guide. • Research similar examples from secondary sources, such as catalogues, brochures and magazines. Extend the research to other types of container that may provide inspiration. • Explore ideas to fulfil the brief by sketching, experimenting with scale models and drawings and testing out suitable materials. • Refine the best idea/s showing clear use of visual language, technical skill and problem-solving. • Present a final design as a prototype model with any relevant scale drawings.

UNIT 5: CRAFT DESIGN

CRAFT DESIGN	Lesson 1

Teaching craft design should cover a wide range of techniques, skills and materials but the amount available to you will depend on your particular situation and your students may eventually focus on a specific area. This series of lesson ideas provides a general introduction to craft design with some suggested themes or approaches. It shows how your students can start to record their observations and insights to provide inspiration and how to start to show their critical understanding with relevant research.

Classroom resources

- Student's Book pages 242–247
- *Materials and equipment:* Access to internet, PowerPoint, CAD, books (as required by tasks below), your own PowerPoint presentations, mood boards or worksheets, a range of craft objects across time and cultures, paper, pens, drawing materials and surfaces, presentation materials and equipment such as card, glue, scissors and printer.

Research sources

- Possible makers:

  Jewellery – Marjorie Schick
  Wirework – Martin Senn
  Papier Mache – Saulo Moreno
  Mosaic – Sonia King
  Puppetry and Local craft – there are many cultural sources and traditions around the world.

LESSON TASKS

1) Starter suggestions

Discuss research	• Ask students to present and discuss a visual brainstorm of images created as homework showing a range of crafts. Guide students to identify the materials and processes used to make each item and to explain why they chose to include it in their brainstorm. Ask what interested them about each image.
Provide inspiration	• Use a series of mood boards or digital images to give a broad introduction to craft design. Ask students to identify which crafts are functional, decorative or both.
Appreciate possibilities	• Show students examples of crafts in various forms across time or cultures. Facilitate a class discussion about where the examples originate from, how they are made and the materials used.

2) Main lesson activities

These activities may take more than one lesson or may be continued as homework.

Primary research	• Arrange a trip to a craft studio or workplace or invite a local craftsperson to do a demonstration in school. Ask students to observe the various stages of designing and making. Ensure that students record evidence of their visit such as sketches, photographs, video or written notes referring to the relevant materials, processes, skills and techniques. Alternatively, arrange a trip to a museum or gallery to see craft first-hand.

Research	• Ask students to choose one area of craft such as jewellery or puppetry and to find examples made from a range of materials such as plastic, wood and clay. Support students to present their findings in a suitable format such as on an A2 sheet or as a PowerPoint presentation. Ask them to explain any making processes, important design elements and aesthetics.
Collaborate	• Give a pair or group of students a suitable focus such as African jewellery, South-east Asian puppets, papier mâché crafts or Indian metalwork and allow them to research their theme. Ask students to analyse any significant visual elements in the designs, the materials and techniques used and the role and function of the designs.
Skills activity A	• Student's Book page 243 • This activity is useful to help a student decide what type of craft they want to focus on. Encourage students to include a wide range of techniques, skills and materials even if they are only looking at one aspect of craft such as local craft.
Skills activity B	• Student's Book page 246 • This activity allows a student to go deeper into one area of craft. A different craftsperson could be chosen for the same task, depending on the interests of the student.

3) Plenary suggestions

Questioning	• Discuss with pupils what techniques or skills they need to learn or refine in order to develop their craft ideas. Make sure that it is feasible with the materials that you have available to use.
Skills activity C	• Student's Book page 247 • Present this activity to students as a homework task. You may want to provide a list of possible places that they can visit to help them to complete the work.
Collaborate	• Ask students to present and share research findings with the rest of the class to pool ideas and knowledge of craft. Encourage curiosity and questioning by the listeners.

SUGGESTED ASSESSMENT OF STUDENT'S BOOK ACTIVITIES

Skills activities A, B and C	• Student's Book pages 243, 246 and 247 • In all three skills activities from the Student's Book, students need to select and use appropriate resources and present skilfully (AO2). Students need to show skilful observations and insights in their annotation (AO1) and allow it to inform their understanding. They should acknowledge the sources of their research and make clear where they have used primary or secondary sources. • Having provided a general introduction to craft design, all the activities above can precede students writing a more specific and focused design brief. The student may wish to write their own, but you should support them to check that it is possible to meet all the assessment criteria of the course through their proposed brief.

CRAFT DESIGN	Lesson 2

This section gives suggestions to teach students how to move a project forward with further analysis, experimentation and development of ideas once students have a clear design brief. It will also demonstrate ways in which you can teach students to present a personal and coherent response for craft design using a design brief.

Classroom resources:
• *Materials and equipment:* Examples of a craft design brief that you have prepared, existing craft objects to draw and analyse, 2D materials for presenting supporting studies such as pens. pencils, glue, scissors, A2 paper, 3-D materials appropriate for testing, experimenting and making a final craft item, digital camera for taking photographs, copies of the IGCSE assessment criteria.

LESSON TASKS

1) Starter suggestions

Identify a problem	• Set a craft design brief for students to follow or help a student to create their own.
Top tip	• Make a list of craft materials that you have available for students before they finalise a design brief so that the brief is realistic.
Demonstrate and inspire	• Show and discuss a range of functional and decorative craft objects (actual or images) relevant to each student's intentions. Challenge students to research further independently with a focus on their specific design brief.

2) Main lesson activities

In all tasks, encourage students to solve problems related to a craft design fulfilling a decorative and/or functional role. Remind students to show alternative design solutions and an understanding of materials and techniques in their chosen area of craft.

Drawing	• Ask students to make relevant first-hand, observational drawings to support their craft design brief. This can be drawings of existing craft objects in order to analyse them or another relevant source such as drawings of natural forms to support a design brief of nature-inspired jewellery.
Experiment	• Encourage students to investigate relevant materials and techniques by making samples to develop their craft skills and to appreciate their potential. Ask students to record and document their findings with photographs, sketches and annotation.
Recording ideas	• Ask students to refine ideas and document how they have solved any design problems in trying to fulfil their brief. Students can focus on alternative decorative ideas and/or alternative ways that their idea can function.
Recording skills to analyse ideas	• Ask students to photograph their work in progress and add analysis about the pros and cons of each design idea.
Realise intentions	Ask students to create a final craft piece/s refined from previous work and ideas. Encourage students to use a high level of finish in the quality of the work.
Consolidate	• Give students a copy of the assessment criteria and evaluate their project against the criteria highlighting any strengths and any weaknesses to be addressed.

3) Plenary suggestions

Develop	• Following a design activity, ask students to sketch, list ideas or talk about how their work might develop next. Help them to create a timesheet to guide the progress of their work.
Reflect	• Ask students to write down what they still need to research in order to better develop their ideas such as more information about a technique or about a designer's work.
Evaluation	• Ask students to present their final craft piece/s appropriately. Encourage them to evaluate their work against the requirements of their original design brief.

Reflection
What local crafts and resources could I encourage my students to use? Do any of my students have existing craft knowledge and skills from outside school that they could make use of?

INTERNALLY SET ASSIGNMENTS

Inspiration for a craft design brief can come from a variety of sources such as a cultural style, a material or a technique but should involve an element of problem-solving. Here is an example:

Design brief	• Design and make a contemporary item of jewellery from the material of your choice for a special celebration. The design should reflect traditional jewellery design from the country where you live. This could be through the use of similar motifs, patterns, symbols or colours but made in a new material or using a traditional making technique but with contemporary styling.
Possible approaches	• Draw or photograph existing jewellery designs by visiting a local exhibition or maker's studio. Evaluate and analyse how they are made and where inspiration has come from for the designs. • Research similar examples from secondary sources, such as catalogues, books, the internet and magazines. Extend the research to other contemporary design that may provide inspiration. • Explore ideas to fulfil the brief by sketching, experimenting with techniques and testing out suitable materials. • Photograph experiments on a model to investigate how they sit on the body. • Refine the best idea/s showing clear use of visual language, technical skill and problem-solving. • Present a final design/s as a finished item.

UNIT 6: STUDENT CASE STUDY

See page 249 in the Student's Book for a full-colour version of this student's work.

PROJECT BRIEF

This project explores organic forms from the natural world. It looks at 'Objects in Space'. The student starts by looking at a range of items such as bones, skulls and shells and later focuses on fruit and vegetable forms. During the development process, the student explores various techniques for making both abstract and decorative 3-D work. The final outcome (bottom right) is a glazed ceramic piece inspired by organic forms.

Assessment

- **AO1:** *Record ideas, observations and insights relevant to intentions as work progresses*

  Carefully chosen drawing techniques such as contour drawing are used effectively. Sophisticated photographic references demonstrate the student's understanding of form and space in many of the studies. Written analysis documents the ideas, reflections and evaluation of the student in a highly effective manner as work progresses. Excellent technical notes show understanding of ceramic techniques and processes.

- **AO2:** *Explore and select appropriate resources, media, materials, techniques and processes*

  The student considers media appropriate to 3-D such as wire construction but settles on a more in-depth exploration of clay. Techniques include making thumb pots, slab building and carving into clay followed by exploration of how to apply surface decoration using glaze. The student chooses materials effectively and refines their techniques and processes as work progresses.

- **AO3:** *Develop ideas through investigation, demonstrating critical understanding*

  The student confidently references a range of sculptors such as Henry Moore and Peter Randall-Page, and contemporary makers such as Kate Malone and Jacques Vesery. Ideas are confidently developed informed by growing critical understanding of both other artists' work and specialist clay techniques and processes. Initial 3-D ideas tend to be more obvious models of organic forms but this is followed by more sophisticated development and appreciation of both abstraction and decorative pattern.

- **AO4:** *Present a personal and coherent response that realises intentions and demonstrates an understanding of visual language*

  The project is coherent in maintaining a focus on organic forms but a progressive and creative journey is presented. The student looks at a variety of 3-D art, media and styles of work. The final outcome is a strong ceramic piece combining various forms together to make a successful vessel that has both sculptural and decorative qualities. There is a strong realisation of intentions demonstrating excellent understanding of visual language appropriate to 3-D studies.

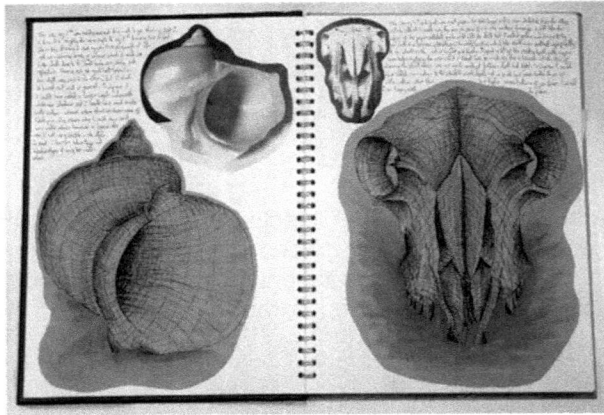

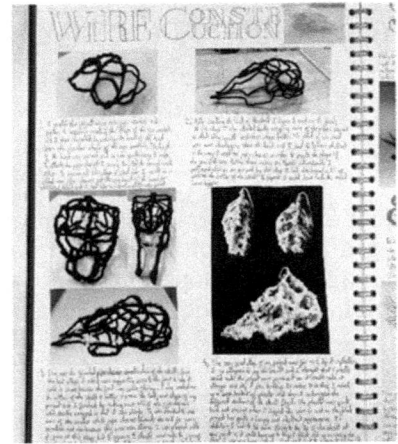

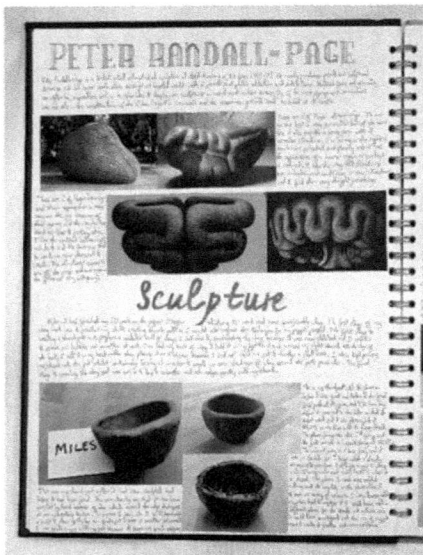

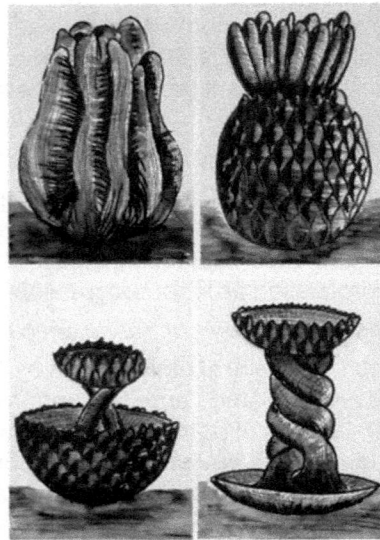

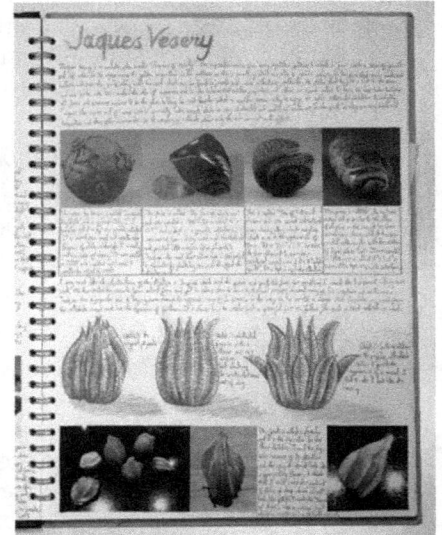

DEVELOPING WORK

There are many possibilities for how to build classroom work into coursework (Chapter 1). Generally, it can be helpful to initially set a creative starting point that a whole class can use to learn new skills and to explore ideas. Lessons may be more prescriptive and teacher-led early on in a project. Using a creative theme or starting point for the coursework also helps to prepare students for the externally set assignment (Chapter 2), where they will have to choose their own starting point from those listed on the IGCSE test paper.

As a project progresses, expect individual students to take a more independent and personal approach to developing their work once they have been taught enough to do this. Less able students will need greater support and input from you.

Once students have some skills and experience of 3-D techniques and processes, expect them to focus on refining their work and ideas with further experiments, samples, maquettes or test pieces. All stages of work should be thoroughly documented, reflected upon and analysed to give evidence of a student's intentions. Final 3-D outcomes will need to be photographed to thoroughly record the work.

Further projects

- Suitable starting points for a 3-D project:

  Art in a Box – look at work by Joseph Cornell and Louise Nevelson.
  Art from Books – look at work by Alexander Korzer-Robinson and Su Blackwell.
  Wirework – look at work by David Oliveira and Julia Griffiths Jones.

Further research

- Contemporary Ceramics Centre
- **Journals:** *Ceramic Review, Crafts Magazine, Architectural Review*

Checklist

- ✓ I have introduced students to the large variety of possible materials, techniques and approaches available for 3-D work within the constraints of what I can offer at my school or college.
- ✓ I understand how to help students choose a successful area of 3-D that they can explore.
- ✓ I know what type of support work is required if my students chose to work in 3-D.
- ✓ I understand how to teach students to test out ideas in 3-D and in the round.
- ✓ I know how to teach students to gather, research and record relevant information for making 3-D work.
- ✓ I have enough knowledge, experience and understanding of 3-D studies to successfully teach my students.

Chapter 11
Photography, digital and lens-based media

INTRODUCTION

Learning objectives
By the end of this unit students should:
• have an understanding of the manual use of a digital SLR camera
• have confidence in using the camera in manual mode to achieve a particular photograph
• have an awareness of composition and how to apply techniques effectively
• be able to use natural light effectively
• be able to use artificial lighting effectively
• be able to edit photographs effectively
• be able to document the making process thoroughly and reflectively
• have an understanding of the components that make a film
• be able to deconstruct a film
• be able to storyboard a film
• have an understanding of different camera shots and how they can be applied
• have an understanding of editing techniques and how they can be applied
• be able to project manage the making of a film
• be able to document the making of a film and reflect on the processes involved effectively.

Classroom resources
• Digital SLR cameras with video and sound capabilities or dedicated video cameras.
• Computers with editing software installed, Adobe Photoshop recommended.
• Student's Book, still imagery section, pages 252–260; moving imagery section, pages 261–267.
• Reflectors.
• Artificial lighting, LED recommended.
• Access to quality print labs.
• Appropriate displays or projectors to view films as a group.

Research resources
• The TES online resource
• Magnum Photos website
• Victoria and Albert Museum website

Top tip

- It is highly unlikely that you will know all the software packages in detail or have the time to undertake lengthy training. Students will have a wide variety of specific editing questions and be interested in developing their skills in a wide variety of ways. Familiarising yourself with providers of high-quality training resources, for example Adobe Education Exchange, will provide students with solutions to specific problems and ensure that the quality of the tuition is at a reliable standard.

General lesson ideas

- Engage students in discussion at the start of each lesson to assess what they already understand and pitch the lesson at the right level. Always exemplify techniques with recognised photographers' work. This will enable students to conduct thorough research in response to what they have been shown. Ensure that students document their learning thoroughly and analytically. Their reflections should showcase their work and reflect all of their hard work appropriately.
- Students will excel with lots of practice. Organise some 'away days' with equipment so students can experiment with the kit and practise their skills. Watch films regularly and discuss them from the viewpoint of a filmmaker. This will help students to understand the principles of filmmaking and also inspire them.

Top tip

- Students will often want to create projects that far exceed their current skill levels and time allowances. Encourage students to reflect continually throughout their projects and set milestones of peer reviews and exhibitions. These milestones and reflection points will highlight to students the need to modify their own projects and take ownership of the changes.

Key considerations

- Make sure that you know the basics of the software packages. A lot of the basic tools and techniques are similar across software packages and knowing these will be an advantage. Get to know the equipment in detail, making sure that you know how to use it safely and that it is safety tested regularly. Ensure that students work safely when they work independently on their projects. A code of conduct is useful for students to follow.
- Make sure that you are familiar with the basics of both the theory and the practical elements of filmmaking. How can you create an immersive project that meets the requirements of the AOs and is exciting for students? How can you use the wider community as inspiration and as a resource in your moving image projects?

Reflective log

- How can I develop projects that meet the requirements of the AOs and enable my students to explore their own interests? How can I find photographers that inspire and engage my students? How can I undertake training to stay up to date with technical developments?
- How can I share best practice with other schools and develop my own course? How did the students document their making? Are there any new methods I could include that would engage my students? How can I use film across the school curriculum to document learning and get my students making media in other areas? Are there any partnerships I can form with local cinemas?

Key terms

- **Student's Book key terms:** aperture, codes, composition, conventions, ISO, reflectors, shutter speed, storyboard.
- **Additional key terms:** deconstruct, editing, exposure, film, lighting, printing, script, sequences, shot list, sound, white balance

UNIT 1: STILL IMAGERY: MANUAL OPERATION OF A DSLR OR SLR CAMERA

TECHNICAL LESSON 1	Exposure: Aperture, shutter speed, ISO

This is perhaps one of the hardest lessons for students to comprehend. Regular practice with their cameras and the teaching aids will help students understand the settings on their cameras and how they change the picture. By the end of this session, students should have a basic understanding of aperture, shutter speed and ISO.

Classroom resources

- *Classroom arrangement:* Access to a projector or TV screen initially before moving outside where there is room to move and take photographs in the environment. It can be beneficial to revisit the theory and practical elements of this lesson regularly and during different lighting situations, for example, early morning and at twilight, as this will force students to react to their lighting conditions and use the camera's functions fully.
- *Materials and equipment:* Prepared slides or a short video explaining exposure and how aperture, shutter speed and ISO affect the photograph. DSLR cameras' ratio – one camera to a maximum of three students. Computers capable of editing photographs. Adobe Photoshop is recommended as an industry standard.

Research sources

- There are many online resources that explain aspects of still imagery. Good suggested sites include Lynda, TES online and the Canon Explains Exposure website.

LESSON TASKS

1) Starter suggestions

Ask open questions to find out what students know already about exposure, aperture, shutter speed and ISO. You may want to record these answers on a whiteboard or video for students to refer back to or use as evidence of their learning.

2) Main lesson activities

Teacher	• Using visual aids such as slides, video, example photographs and DSLR cameras, explain the use of a camera in manual mode to expose a photograph. You may need to break this down into smaller sections such as focus on shutter speed or focus on aperture, as it can be difficult to comprehend.
Teacher	• Set mini tasks in the classroom to check understanding. It can be helpful to start with choosing a shutter speed to suit a situation and then adjusting aperture and ISO to achieve the correct exposure. Start by giving students a shutter speed to use, and then ask them what aperture they need to achieve a correct exposure in the classroom. Working in small groups will help students to learn as they can discuss their decisions and grow their confidence. • When students show some understanding of how shutter speed, aperture and ISO work, you can set some challenges for the groups to complete.

	Ask students to carry out these tasks:
Additional student activity	<ul><li>Take three photographs that freeze motion and have a correct exposure.</li><li>Take three photographs that show motion and have a correct exposure.</li><li>Take three photographs that have a shallow depth of field.</li><li>Take three photographs that have a large depth of field.</li><li>Take three photographs that require a high ISO.</li><li>Download and save images to an appropriate storage space. Cloud-based storage is recommended to safeguard against loss of students' work.</li></ul>

3) Plenary suggestions

Additional student activity	<ul><li>Let students work in small groups, and present their best photographs from the main activity to the rest of the class. Students should discuss why the chosen photographs are the best and why they think they are successful, what they found difficult and what didn't go as planned. Students should identify where they need to improve for their next photoshoot. These presentations can be filmed and used as evidence of learning. Students should write an evaluation of the activity alongside their imagery.</li></ul>
Additional student activity	<ul><li>Ask students to go to the Canon Outside of Auto website. Students can practise their use of shutter speed, aperture and ISO in the virtual environment and test their skills without needing access to a DSLR camera. This can be set as a home study task.</li></ul>

TECHNICAL LESSON 2	Composition

Learning objectives

- By the end of this lesson, students should have an understanding of basic composition techniques and be able to apply them to their own work effectively.

Classroom resources

- *Classroom arrangement:* Access to a projector or TV screen initially before moving outside where there is room to move and take photographs in the environment. Show other photographers' work to exemplify how applying compositional techniques contributes to the success of the images. Encouraging students to 'deconstruct' images in the classroom setting and compare thoughts on what the photographer intended to do will help their analytical work progress beyond descriptions.
- *Materials and equipment:* Prepared slides or a short video exemplifying compositional rules and how photographers have applied them to their own work. DSLR cameras ratio one camera to a maximum of three students. Computers capable of editing photographs. Adobe Photoshop is recommended as an industry standard.

Research Sources

- For insights behind the image
  - Magnum photo website
  - YouTube

LESSON TASKS

1) Starter suggestions

	• Students should be seated so they can clearly see the example images and diagrams. • Paper L-shaped crops can be useful to test compositional theories and see the effect on example imagery.
Teacher	• Start with a question session to establish prior knowledge. Ask open questions to find out what students know already about composition and how it is used in a photographic context. You may want to record these answers on a whiteboard or video for students to refer back to or use as evidence of their learning.
Teacher and students	• Introduce different composition rules and discuss their use within the example photographs. There may be more than one compositional rule in use in each example image. Encourage students to deconstruct the images shown and share their opinions. There are often different interpretations of a photographer's intentions. Try to expand students' vocabulary and encourage them to justify their opinions. Students should make notes or record the discussions to aid their learning.

2) Main lesson activities

Additional student activity 1	• *Composition treasure hunt:* Ask students to take photographs based on some of the compositional rules introduced during the session. Students may be given a set time to complete the activity based on the time available during the school day. This could be as little as an hour or a longer project that can be explored in more depth. Students should download the images, save them safely, produce an annotated contact sheet and select examples from their shoot to print.
Additional student activity 2	• *Presentation of the images taken during the composition treasure hunt:* Ask students to present their most successful images along with a written evaluation. The evaluation should contain the student's intention, a contact sheet of all of the shots taken, an explanation of why this particular shot was chosen and a rationale for any editing that has taken place in post-production. This could include cropping, straightening or dodging/burning to emphasise elements of the image. Students should also write about what they would like to improve upon on their next photography assignment.
Additional student activity 3	• *Homage to recognised photographers:* Recreating another photographer's photograph and imitating their style can be a great help in developing students' practical skills and their attention to detail. Select a range of famous photographs of varying styles and technical difficulty. Then let students form small groups and select one of the photographs to recreate. Attention should be given to the lighting, composition, position of models/objects and background. Props and clothing can be improvised in the classroom setting. This fun activity will greatly aid students' ability to conduct a photographic shoot and test their analytical skills through the success of their recreations. As an extension, students can conduct their own extended projects 'in the style of' their chosen photographer. Research tasks can be linked to an extended project to inform the students' own work.
Top tip	• Students should take every opportunity to conduct meaningful research. Research questions could relate to their chosen photographer's ideas, equipment use and editing techniques. Encourage the regular use of research to inform students' work at every stage of a project. Students should relate their findings to their own work and explain how they are applying them (or not) to their own practice.

TECHNICAL LESSON 3	Lighting

Learning objectives

- By the end of this session, students should have a basic understanding of lighting and how it can change the image. Students will be experimenting with natural and artificial light, reflectors and white balance. Students should be encouraged to practise regularly and develop their skills.

Classroom resources

- *Classroom arrangement:* You may wish to conduct part of the lesson in a classroom environment with access to a projector or TV screen, and for the practical section, move outside or into a studio where there is more room to take photographs and, control the lighting. It can be beneficial to show other photographers' work to exemplify how using lighting can change an image. Students should be encouraged to experiment with lighting equipment to explore their own ideas and practise their camera skills.
- *Materials and equipment:* Prepared slides or a short video to exemplify the use of lighting. DSLR cameras ratio – one camera to a maximum of three students. Photography reflectors or equivalent, one per group. A window offering natural light. LED artificial light or equivalent continuous lighting. A room where natural light can be eliminated, such as a studio or a classroom with blackout blinds. Classrooms should be equipped with computers capable of editing photographs. Adobe Photoshop is recommended as an industry standard.

Research sources

- Subscription training and teaching resources for photography and media.
- Lighting diagram creator – students can use this to illustrate their use of lighting on a photographic shoot.
- A guide to using natural light.
- Creative lighting examples using natural and artificial lights.
- Teaching resource from the National Portrait Gallery: Portraiture from the Victorians to the Present Day.
- High-quality examples of other photographers' work.

LESSON TASKS: Natural lighting

1) Starter suggestions

Natural lighting	
Teacher	• Start with a question session to establish prior knowledge. Ask open questions to find out what students know already about natural lighting and how it is used in a photographic context. You may want to record these answers on a whiteboard or video for students to refer back to or use as evidence of their learning.
Teacher and students	• Look at a selection of photographers who shoot using natural light with students. Discuss how the photographer has used the light available to create the image. Watching behind-the-scenes videos of photographers at work will give students insight into the decision-making process. Steve McCurry is a photojournalist who uses natural light. There are many resources available on YouTube where he discusses how he shoots and his thought processes in the moment.
Further resources	• Technical demonstration using reflectors • Steve McCurry official website

2) Main lesson activities

Teacher	• Demonstrate how to shoot using natural light. You may wish to move to different locations to demonstrate how light changes. A window, a shaded spot outside and full sun would illustrate lighting examples students may face when they are working. You may also demonstrate how to use a reflector with natural light.
Additional student activity 1	• *Experiment with natural light shooting portraits:* Let students work in groups or as individuals for this activity. They should shoot portraits using natural light and reflectors. They should explore natural light in different locations and experiment with the use of reflectors. Then they should download and save images appropriately, produce a contact sheet to show all of the images taken, annotate the contact shoot to highlight the best and worst shots and produce a written evaluation of the activity. Their evaluation should reference images from the contact sheet and students should indicate what they need to improve on for next time.
Additional student activity 2	• *Experiment with natural light shooting still-life set ups:* Objects such as fruit and vegetables, small metal objects and glassware can be photographed individually on tabletops. Backgrounds can be used or areas of the classroom with suitable walls or windows can be used to photograph against. Students may need to use a tripod to steady their shots. Students should be looking to explore the shapes and surfaces of the objects with available light and reflectors. Care should be taken with shiny objects reflecting the photographer or equipment.

💡 **Further research**
• Photographers who can be exemplified for their varied uses of light include: Uta Barth, Tokihiro Sato, Lu Guang, Ansel Adams, Edward Weston, Dean Chamberlain, Wright Morris, Gregory Crewdson, Seydu Keita, Manita Goh, Bill Brandt.

LESSON TASKS: Artificial light

1) Starter suggestions

Teacher	• Ask open questions to find out what students know already about artificial lighting and how it is used in a photographic context. You may want to record these answers on a whiteboard or video for students to refer back to or use as evidence of their learning.
Teacher	• Introduce the equipment that you are going to use and complete a safety induction with students. Some lights become very hot, cables and stands can become trip hazards, and flash or strobe lighting can induce epileptic seizures. All equipment should have passed an electrical safety test before being used in a classroom.
Teacher	• Demonstrate the use of artificial light in a studio environment. Portraits lit with one light are a good starting point for students to explore. Reflectors will be useful to have in case students wish to use them to soften shadows.

2) Main lesson activities

Additional student activity 1	• Students should complete a portrait shoot using artificial lighting. They should try to shoot the same model with various lighting arrangements to alter the mood of the photograph. Students should download and save their imagery, produce an annotated contact sheet, select and edit their chosen photographs, and evaluate their work. Students should take care to evaluate and analyse the work completed rather than to describe what happened.
Additional student activity 2	• Students should complete a lighting exercise to test their control of light. They should photograph a white object against a white background and a black object against a black background. They can use natural or artificial light for this exercise. Remind students to take care to control colour casts during the shoot, as well as the exposure of the photographs. Students should download and save their images, produce and annotate contact sheets, and present examples of their black-on-black and white-on-white images to the class. An evaluation of the activity should accompany the work.

3) Plenary suggestions

Students	• Students should share their work from Additional student activity 1 with the class and discuss their observations, any issues and their views on the work.

⚙ Further research

- Photographers who can be exemplified for their varied uses of light include:
  - Uta Barth
  - Edward Weston
  - Seydu Keita
  - Tokihiro Sato
  - Dean Chamberlain
  - Manita Goh
  - Lu Guang
  - Wright Morris
  - Bill Brandt
  - Ansel Adams
  - Gregory Crewdson
  - Ori Gersht

UNIT 2: STILL IMAGERY: POST-PRODUCTION

TECHNICAL LESSON 4	Editing and printing

Learning objectives

- Students should acquire basic editing skills and know how to get a digital file ready to print. Students may have access to a print lab to print their work, they should be able to provide the print lab with a correctly sized and saved file ready to print.

Classroom resources

- Computers with editing software installed; Adobe Photoshop is industry standard. Files ready to edit and resize. A projector or large screen to mirror the display of the teacher to show the editing process. A print facility, possibly located outside of school capable of producing quality digital prints.

Research sources

- Online training courses
- Adobe Education Exchange

LESSON TASKS

Teacher	• Facilitate a group discussion on digital editing with the student group. Ask questions: What do students know already? What examples have they come across already? Why do photographers edit photographs? What ethics might arise with digital editing? This discussion may indicate subject matter to explore for further lessons.
Teacher	• On a large screen, demonstrate some of the basic editing processes. Cropping, straightening, correcting white balance, converting to black and white, removing blemishes and dust, brightness and contrast, sharpening and clarity and resizing to print should be covered to equip students with basic skills. Students may have particular questions around specific editing requirements for specific photographs. It is likely that there are many different ways of achieving the desired outcome. Resources like lynda.com are invaluable as a teaching tool for students to explore and develop their own methods.
Students	• If classroom resources allow, students can complete the editing of the demonstration photograph while the demonstration is being completed. You can show a technique for students to complete and the teacher can see how the students are managing the new skills and facilitate the learning.
Additional student activity	• Ask students to complete an edit on a provided photograph. Students can practise their basic editing skills on a demonstration photograph. They should take screenshots of their progress and describe what tools they are using, as well as why they are choosing to use them. They should also write an evaluation to compare the original photograph with their edit. The final edit should be printed at the print lab to test their resizing skills.
Top tip	• Students should always include screenshots of their editing process and evaluate their progress.

UNIT 3: MOVING IMAGERY

MOVING IMAGERY LESSON 1	Deconstructing films

Learning objectives

- By the end of this lesson, students will have an understanding of how to deconstruct a film.
- It is important for students to have an awareness of how films are constructed and how they convey meaning to their chosen audiences. A film-maker will harness the power of the story, the camera, the sound and the editing to create the desired feeling and understanding in the audience. A basic understanding of these building blocks of film-making will help students to create their own moving images and communicate more effectively to their chosen audiences.

Classroom resources

- *Classroom arrangement:* The classroom should be set up in order to screen a film. If your school has a theatre space, this would be an appropriate space to use for this lesson. Select a film to deconstruct that is accessible to students. A 30–40 minute film or section of a longer film is appropriate to use for this exercise.
- *Materials and resources:* Sketchbooks or journals to write notes, whiteboard, large TV or projector, appropriate film to deconstruct.

Research sources

- There are numerous good online guides and videos exemplifying the use of camera shots and angles, as well as editing and the grammar of TV and film. Youtube has several suitable videos, but please check suitability for your lesson and students first.

Top tip

- Students can find it very difficult initially to 'step back' from watching the film as a member of an audience and analyse the film. Initially, you will need to take a lead and exemplify the process, as well as prompt students to take notes regularly.

LESSON GUIDANCE

Story and script	• What is happening in the story? What are the characters doing in the scene? What is being said and how? For example, some students are arriving at school on a bus; they are just back from summer holiday and they are catching up with each other. Everyone seems very happy except for one student sitting alone.
Camera angles and shots	• What camera shots are being utilised in the scene? How have they been used to tell the story? What feelings do they convey to the audience? Are there any codes and conventions being used with the choice of camera shots?
Sound	• What music is being played over the top of the footage? What sound effects are being used? Does the sound match the shots? What feelings does the sound convey to the audience? Are there any codes and conventions being used with the choice of sound? For example, scary music just before a monster jumps out to frighten someone.
Lighting	• Is the light in the scene natural light or artificial light? Is the lighting adding to the mood of the shot? What codes and conventions are being used with the lighting?
Editing and sequences	• What editing choices have been used in the scene? How fast or slow are the edits? What does that convey to the audience? How have the cuts been sequenced to help tell the story? How does one scene transition into another?

LESSON TASKS

1) Starter suggestions

Teacher	• Introduce the purpose of the lesson and the format of the lesson.
Teacher	• Ensure that all students have drawn a grid (A3 page is suggested) with the discussion points along the top and scenes 1, 2, 3 and so on down the page.

2) Main lesson activities

Teacher	• Exemplify the process. Watch a short section of the chosen film, which could be the opening scene. Watch it through once and then rewind the film. When watching it the second time, discuss what you can observe with the story, camera angles and shots, lighting, sound, and editing and sequencing. Students may observe other aspects of the scene, so encourage discussion and note-taking in the grids.
Teacher	• Facilitate the deconstruction of the film. Use your judgement when to pause and rewind the film. Ensure that students remain focused on deconstructing the film and do not slip into watching the film as an audience. Encourage them to take notes at all times. Ask open questions if you feel students have missed a key element of the film, for example, a significant edit or camera shot.
Students	• Let students watch the film in sections, and encourage them to contribute to the discussion and share their observations with the class. Students may need to watch a scene a few times to understand all of the elements at work. Remind them repeatedly to take notes during the session, as it is easy to slip into watching the film or become immersed in the discussion.
Top tip	• As this skill takes plenty of practice, deconstructing films regularly will help to develop students' theoretical and practical skills.

3) Plenary suggestions

Additional student activity 1	• Students need to produce a written analysis of the film based on their notes taken during the deconstruction of the film. They may include screenshots of the film to exemplify their points.
Additional student activity 2	• Students need to remake a scene from the film, which will help them put theory into practice. Students should aim to produce a film of no longer than three minutes in length. They should produce a storyboard that illustrates each scene along with a list of chosen camera shots.

PROJECT 1	Planning and shooting a film

By the end of this session, students should have an understanding of how to plan a film and why it is crucial to the success of the project. You may have a particular group theme for your project or you may wish to let students choose their own. This project could be extended over a number of weeks or it could span a couple of sessions depending on the time you have available.

Top tip

- Students very often rush into making a film and neglect to evidence their thoughts, plans, problem-solving and creative decisions. This has a direct impact on their potential marks and they often do not realise the grades they deserve. Getting into good habits early will ensure that documentation and analysing work becomes a natural part of the process.

PART ONE: Planning the film

Classroom resources

- *Classroom arrangement:* A regular classroom setup with internet access will be suitable for this activity. Sketchbooks or large pieces of paper and a variety of pens will help students to explore their initial ideas.
- *Materials and equipment:* Large sheets of paper, selection of pens, sketchbooks and internet-enabled devices.

Research sources

- Suitable research sites for this topic include the Into film website and Storyboard That online.

Top tip

- Students often have very ambitious ideas. Therefore, they will need to plan their films in relation to their time available and realistically against their current skill levels. It is unlikely that a student will be able to produce a 30-minute feature film as a first production. Setting a maximum film length of three to five minutes running time is a realistic film length for a project that will last several weeks.

LESSON TASKS

1) Stages of planning a film

Initial ideas	• Students can record their initial ideas in many ways. Mind-maps exploring themes or feelings can be a good way to start. These can be a jumble of words or sketches that document unresolved or patchy ideas. The mind-map should be followed by a written piece of work that describes what the student is thinking or feeling about their early ideas. Mind-maps can contain some fantastic ideas but, by their nature, they are very difficult to interpret. • Students could conduct some research at this stage. Students should include relevant information about the subject they are researching, screenshots and imagery to illustrate their work and describe why they are looking at the chosen material and how it may or may not impact on their own work. More able students may be able to compare and contrast different sources of information. For example, a student may be interested in producing a documentary about their local community and conducting research into two different documentary filmmakers. Students can then compare and contrast the two styles they have researched before deciding which direction they are going to go in next.
Top tip	• Continually remind students that they are writing for an audience and not just themselves. Swapping books with fellow students and gaining some peer-to-peer feedback will help students to see where they can improve and what 'holes' there may be in their own documentation.

2) Storyboarding

Planning a film through the use of a storyboard is a useful way for students to develop and organise their ideas before conducting a shoot.

> **Top tip**
>
> • There are many different ways of creating a storyboard. Whichever method you select to use with your students, they should include the locations being used, characters needed in each scene, shot list, any sound requirements and any props needed. This will ensure that each element of the film is captured while out on the shoot and that the planned film is captured.

Additional student activity 1	• Students could storyboard a ten-minute section of an existing film to practise how to storyboard. This can be easier to do as a first attempt as students are not trying to resolve their own ideas to place in a storyboard.
Additional student activity 2	• Students could use their initial mind-maps and researched ideas to produce a storyboard. The storyboard should detail the characters, location, shot list and sound requirements for each scene.
Top tip	• Depending on your school's film-making resources, you may want to create a 'equipment booking sheet' for students to book time with cameras and editing equipment.

PROJECT 2	Shooting a film

Safety is very important and a safety briefing should be held with all students before shooting can take place. It is advisable to cover working on location, interaction with strangers, working near water and at heights, working alone and students' responsibilities for keeping everyone on their sets safe.

Top tip

- You may wish to take your student group out on location to conduct some practice shoots before allowing them to film unsupervised. This way you can check how they are working and if you feel they are ready to work safely with the film equipment.

LESSON TASKS

Additional student activity	• Students must document their making process in order to gain the maximum amount of marks for their work. A making diary can be a good way to record this work. A making diary could be a written account of the making process or it could be a vlog. Students should make sure that they refer back to earlier stages in their projects and also make plans for their next steps. For example, the first shoot may have been a disaster because of technical difficulties, so they plan to conduct the next shoot in order to overcome the problems faced. The next diary entry should evaluate the second shoot in relation to the test shoot and initial ideas. Regular documentation and reflection will ensure a well-developed portfolio of work.
Top tips	• If students elect to record their progress via a vlog, they should plan what they are going to say in advance of filming. Vlogs should be short and to the point. • Behind-the-scenes shots of students filming can be a great aid to their evaluations.

PROJECT 3	Post-production

Depending on your school's chosen editing software, you will need to conduct some basic tutorials showing how to import footage, apply edits, alter and import sounds, sequence clips, adjust colour balance and export and save films. Training videos can be found to help support specifics with your editing software.

Top tip

- As with the planning and shooting stages of film-making, the editing process is an integral part of the process and should be documented thoroughly. Screenshots of the editing process can act as a talking point and before and after shots can open further discussion into analytical writing and evaluation.

LESSON TASKS

Additional student activity 1	• It is important to share work and test films with an audience. It is only when films are screened that the film-maker can see if their film makes sense to their audience and is having the desired effect. For example, if a student had planned to make a comedy, and nobody in their audience is laughing, they will probably need to look again at their piece. • Student groups should present a 'rough cut' of their film to the class. Having this deadline will also help students to work within time constraints and can be useful in the lead up to final projects and submissions. Brief students before the session so they can adequately prepare and to establish an understanding of constructive criticism. Students should take notes as they watch each other's films and provide feedback to the film-makers with where they can improve.
Additional student activity 2	• Screening final films to the wider school or community can be a fantastic way for students to see their work in context and to boost their confidence.
Additional student activity 3	• A final evaluation of the shoot is a key element in the making process. It is not so much an end point as a starting point for the project that follows. An evaluation should develop beyond a description of events and analyse the making process. As this can be a difficult process for students, you may need to ask prompt questions to tease out more informed responses, such as: 'What did you plan to film?'; 'What inspired you to make this film (possible links to primary or secondary research)?'; 'Was it a success? Why?'; 'What problems did you need to overcome during the making process?'; 'What have you learnt through making this film?'; 'What skills do you think you need to develop for next time?' or 'What are you most proud of?'
Top tip	• The end of a project can be an opportune moment to assess student's skills and developmental requirements. This may show what needs to be revisited or what projects to set next. • It is very difficult to teach editing software beyond the basics. Having a good knowledge of where to find reliable tutorials to support students' needs will be very helpful.

Further research

- There are many online resources that explain aspects of moving imagery. Good suggested sites include Lynda, Into Film online, and support pages from Apple and Adobe.

UNIT 4: STUDENT CASE STUDY

See the Student's Book, page 269 for a full-colour version of this student work.

PROJECT BRIEF

This is an extract from a larger body of work. This section of the project shows the student's early investigation into layering imagery. They have used research as a starting point for this project. The research has been used as a provocation to start making. The student is experimenting with researched techniques and found imagery to explore their early ideas and techniques. The student has documented their journey through screenshots, experimental pieces, research and reflection.

Assessment

- **AO1:** *Record ideas, observations and insights relevant to intentions as work progresses.*

  The student has used a variety of artists to inform the development of their early experimental work. The student demonstrates some insights into their intentions; however, the student describes the steps involved in creating the work rather than analysing the effectiveness of the experiments in relation to their intentions. Comparing the work against specific intentions would help the student assess the success of their work and give them more insight into the decision-making process.

- **AO2:** *Explore and select appropriate resources, media, materials, techniques and processes.*

  The student has chosen to experiment with found images and editing software to create their initial experiments. This is an appropriate response for an early experiment. Further experiments utilising other media, found objects and materials would be an appropriate next step.

- **AO3:** *Develop ideas through investigation, demonstrating critical understanding.*

  The student has developed their ideas through demonstrating their understanding of researched artists' work and experimenting in response. Demonstrating a more consistent critical understanding in relation to their own work would give the student further insights into their investigation.

- **AO4:** *Present a personal and coherent response that realises intentions and demonstrates an understanding of visual language.*

  The student has produced a personal and coherent response to the researched artists' work. The initial experiment explores the researched artists' use of layering found objects and editing software has been selected to make the piece. Expanded written work explaining the decision-making process involved in selecting and editing the photographs could have further demonstrated the student's understanding of visual language. The student could have explored and compared a wider variety of methods of layering and editing, discussed the success of the image's composition and related their work back to their intentions as next steps.

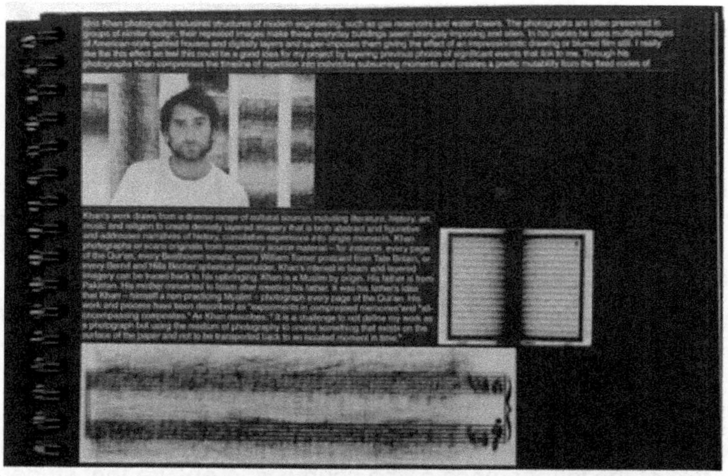

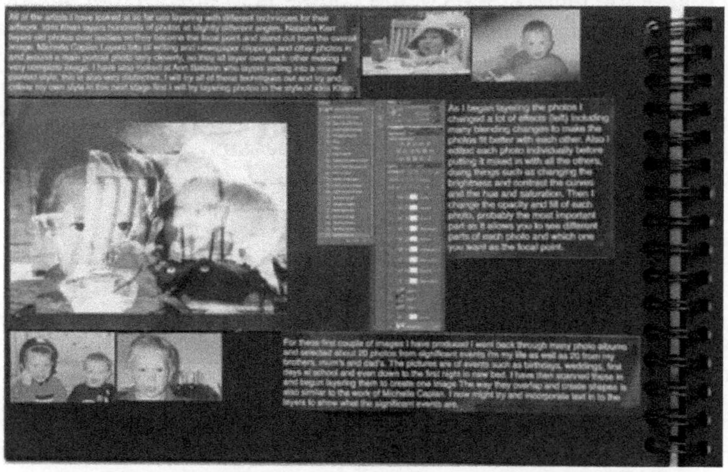

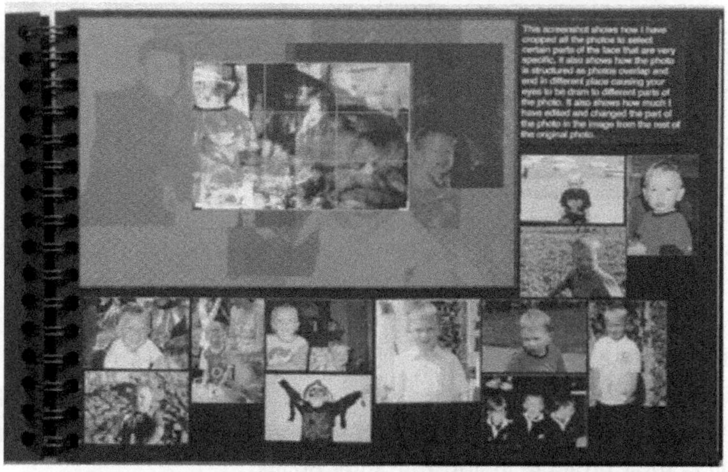

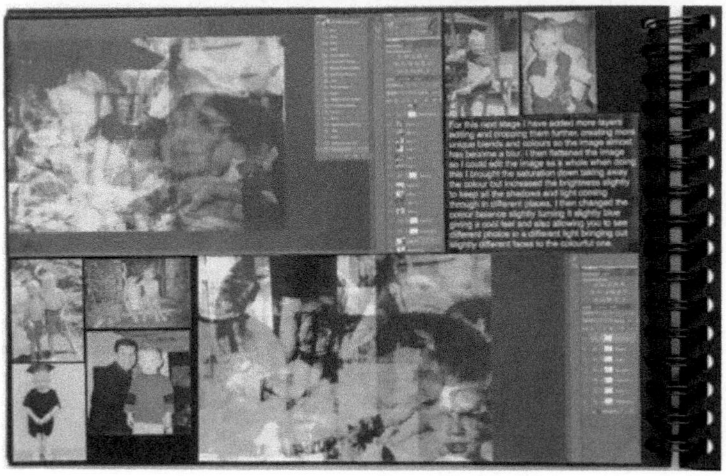

DEVELOPING WORK

There are many technical elements to learn in this section. It is important to develop students' confidence when using the equipment and revisit technical sessions regularly. The more practice students have, the less they will need to focus on making the equipment work and the more time they can spend refining the quality of their pieces and realising their intentions.

It can be easy to neglect evidencing work. Ensure that students document their progress at every stage of their project. Written plans, descriptions of shoots, behind-the-scenes photographs and videos, contact sheets, screenshots of editing processes and experimental pieces, as well as final outcomes all show the students' understanding and engagement with their projects.

As students become more independent with their projects, your role will shift from a demonstrator to a facilitator. Your primary role at the latter stages of the course is to ensure that students are managing their projects effectively. Students should make sure that they are developing, recording, exploring, developing and presenting throughout their projects and documenting this process thoroughly and effectively. You may wish to include 'mini deadlines' to help students structure their projects, such as a mid-way presentation to the class to share ideas and receive peer feedback. This type of exercise will prompt students to reflect on their progress and may open areas of their work to further development. You may wish to scaffold independent projects with a project design cycle. This will enable students to navigate their projects and implement the next steps appropriately.

Further projects
It is very empowering for students to work on live briefs. Talk to the wider community to see whether there are any photography or moving image projects that could be undertaken by your students. Students tend to produce higher-quality work when a real-life scenario is being undertaken.

☀ Further research
• There are many online resources in this field, and suitable web searches are suggested for further research. Good suggested sites include Lynda, Magnum Photos, and support pages from Canon and Adobe.

Checklist
✓ I have taught students the basic technical skills to enable them to use photography and film equipment and techniques successfully and confidently.
✓ I know where to direct students to quality tutorials and demonstrations if they have a technical question to which I cannot provide support.
✓ I have a good knowledge of key photographers and moving image-makers to inspire my students.
✓ I am confident I can help my students to document and project manage their work, and to ensure that they manage to realise their projects in line with their ability.

Chapter 12 — Graphic communication

INTRODUCTION

Learning objectives
By the end of this unit students should:
• understand what graphic communication is and the range of contexts in which it is used
• know how graphic communication uses the visual language of art and design to communicate meaning
• understand and know about the range of practical media, materials and techniques associated with graphic communication.

Classroom resources
• The practical skills used in graphic communication can be varied and often use combinations of image-making techniques. Students could use a range of media such as traditional graphic media, (e.g. pigment, paint, acrylics, watercolour, gouache and airbrush), drawing media (e.g. pencils, charcoal, pastel, wax crayon, pen and ink, marker pens and other mark-making implements), mixed media (e.g. collage and photo-montage), printmaking processes (e.g. screen printing, woodcut, lino print, monoprint, collograph, etching), access to photocopying, computer technology (e.g. for desktop publishing, digital photography, image manipulation and illustration).

General lesson ideas
• Adapting lesson plans elsewhere in this book in, for example, painting and related media, drawing, photography or printmaking may be useful in supporting practical and technical skills development within a scheme of work.
• Any project or scheme of work will benefit from planning common starting points that will allow students to develop their own specialist interests relating to graphic design with lettering, illustration, advertising and packaging or games design as their skills and knowledge develop. The lesson suggestions for each graphic communication sub-topic could be adapted to work across the full range of interests.

Key considerations
• Consider the visual elements of space, volume, form and scale.
• Examine how the AOs are addressed in the various sections.
• Think about which projects or topics are suggested or which you could devise.
• Test practical activities yourself before setting them as tasks for students. This will give you a greater understanding of materials, techniques, potential ideas and possible problems.
• Encourage students to work to their strengths and areas of interest within the limits of resources.
• Check that students have correctly used key terms and technical information.

Reflective log
• What practical skills do I need to develop in order to help my students achieve? How can I use practical and theoretical lessons to help my students to develop their work? How can I structure my teaching to make the most of the resources and facilities that I have available to me? Are there any local exhibitions or resources that my students could visit or use?

UNIT 1: GRAPHIC DESIGN WITH LETTERING

Students will learn about typography and its relationships with images. Activities can be done in any medium, including photography and computer-manipulated imagery, but for students' final outcome you should ensure that the majority of images are from their first-hand studies from primary research.

Key terms

- **Student's Book key terms:** graphic design, pictogram, typefaces
- **Additional key terms:** fonts, typography

LESSON IDEA	Type as meaning

Classroom resources

- *Materials and equipment*: A4 or A3 cartridge paper, a range of coloured collage papers and thin card, scissors, craft knife, glue, rulers, a range of drawing media including HB, B and H grade pencils, tracing paper, layout paper, graph paper; access to a dictionary, thesaurus and a photocopier.
- *Digital resources:* Camera, scanner, image manipulation and drawing software, digital printing.
- *Prepared handout materials:* A4 sheets of words, (for example motion, decay, growth, shadow, jump, hidden, broken, squeezed, and so on), presented in a 72-point lower case example of simple font, for example Arial.
- Photocopies of an A4 page with six squares 8 × 8 cm drawn out.

Research sources

- Early 20th-century European avant-garde design:

  Henrik Werkman   Kurt Schwitters (*the Scarecrow*)
  Guillaume Apollinaire (concrete poetry)   Futurist publishing (Zang Tum Tum)

- Recent and contemporary typographic design:

Wim Crowel	Paula Scher	Sang-Soo Ahn	Shun Sasaki
David Carson	Hamish Muir	Oded Ezer	
Stefan Sagmeister	Neville Brody	Alida Sayer	
Tibor Kalman	Mehendra Patel	Non-format	

LESSON TASKS

1) Starter suggestions

1.1 Use the font tools on a computer or examples in printed books and magazines to introduce the following terms:

- Upper and lower case
- Serif and sans serif
- Roman and italic
- Condensed and extended.

1.2 Let students experiment with the font formatting tools on a computer, for example:

- **bold,** *italic,* <u>underline</u>
- small and large (change the font size)
- light and bold
- ornate and simple
- organic and machined
- positive (black letter on a white background)
- negative (white letter on a black background)
- a range of fonts, such as: Arial, **Bauhaus**, Comic Sans, Courier, *Lucida handwriting*, Times New Roman.

1.3 Get students to choose five fonts that they really like, which are in strong contrast to each other. They should select the same size and style, and use each font to write the following phrase:

'The quick brown fox jumped over the lazy dog.'

1.4 Discuss the differences that appear when the phrase is written in each font.

- Which font does each student like best and why?
- How does it compare to the others?
- Which character could it suggest, for example, if it could speak what accent would it have? Is it timid or brave? Childish or sophisticated?

Top tip

- 'The quick brown fox jumped over the lazy dog' uses every letter in the standard Roman alphabet. It is traditionally used for presenting font samples for this reason.

---

2) Main lesson activities

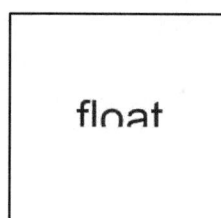

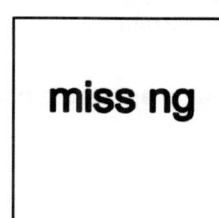

2.1 Use the examples above as a starting point for presenting the idea that making simple changes to the way a word is placed and written can be used to reinforce or illustrate meaning in graphic design projects. Ask students to draw some of their own ideas in response.

2.2 Write the following words on your board, or ask students to note them down: *decay, fade, motion, growth*. Ask students to look up the meaning of the words in a dictionary or thesaurus.

2.3 In 8 cm squares on the prepared photocopied sheets or plain paper, students use the list of words as a starting point for presenting each word in ways that convey or 'illustrate' its meaning.

The aim is for the type to express to the viewer what the word means. Ideas should be developed by considering:

- how tracing and drawing from printed letters can develop ideas
- the scale of each letter in relation to the others, and the edges of the square in which the word is composed
- how line quality, distortions and alterations can be manipulated
- which media are most appropriate, for example drawing with ballpoint pen, charcoal or pencil all looks different on paper, while experimental use of wet materials will give very different results to that of dry media.

Other experiments to try include:

- cutting-up, collaging, folding, bending and tearing the printed words, and redrawing the outcomes
- using a photocopier or scanner to repeat, enlarge or reduce the type provided, as well as moving the word in its original form around on the glass as it is scanned on a photocopier or scanner
- using digital photography to manipulate the text, for example by using thin card to cut out the word shadow so that it can be lit with a desk lamp and photographed, as well as further developing this by using filters and distortion tools in digital drawing software, and so on.
- working with tonal contrasts in grey-scale only to begin, and introducing colour only where appropriate to create a stronger message.

Top tip

- Contrast and form are two of the most powerful communication tools you can use when working with any form of lettering.
- This work may take more than one lesson. Present the outcomes by asking students to choose the best solution for each word, supported by a reflective evaluation of their project work.

3) Plenary suggestions

This lesson takes an approach that is very grounded in the traditions of European languages and related typographic techniques and ideas. If some members of your class are not native speakers of these languages, a discussion on how the ideas set out here might work or fail in other contexts would be beneficial, for example:

- How do written forms of languages based on phonetics (sound and pronunciation) compare with those based on symbols and icons?
- How would the sentence 'the quick brown fox jumps over the lazy dog' be written in Mandarin or Japanese?
- Do the Mandarin forms of the words *motion, decay, growth,* and so on already have an iconographic or illustrative element in the way they are written?

Following from this discussion, consider exploring the fact that many countries have strong traditions of calligraphy as a highly respected art form. You could discuss this in contrast to modern typographic forms.

LESSON IDEA	Pictograms

Classroom resources

- Classroom arrangement, materials and equipment and digital resources as listed above.

Research sources

- Oti Aicher's graphic identities for the 1972 Munich Olympics, online.
- Otto Neurath and Gerd Arntz's ground-breaking work on the use of pictograms, online.
- Search online for an overview of designs for the Olympic games since the 1960s to the present.
- Paul Rand website.

LESSON TASKS

1) Starter suggestions

Using a prepared presentation or handouts, introduce the topic of pictograms for the Olympic Games. How many sports can students identify?

Top tip

- Pictograms like these are often designed using a grid to ensure that the designs work well.

2) Main lesson activities

- Ask students to use tracing paper and trace five of their favourite Olympic pictogram designs. Next they should lay the tracings onto graph paper. Discuss in class how each design is mapped to the grid underneath.
- Consider the school and its curriculum as a topic. Allocate three to five curriculum subjects or departments to each student. Brainstorm what is important to communicate about each one including ideas about the grouping of subjects, for example similar subjects such as sciences, the arts, humanities and so on, or all the subjects on the same floor and so on.
- Introduce a brief for students to design pictograms for the school departments that meet the communication aims already identified.
- Consider developing ideas by:
  - o letting students work first with a freehand pencil (Hb or H grade) or a fine liner drawing to establish ideas
  - o allowing time for the class to help each other with reference images, for example by posing for drawings or photographs acting out a key activity, holding symbolic objects or wearing specialist clothing such as a lab coat, apron or safety goggles, and so on
  - o introducing the use of a simple grid so that all pictograms occupy the same space and have a good sense of composition
  - o introducing colour (e.g. magic markers, felt-tipped pens, coloured pencils) as a further development.

3) Plenary suggestions

The potential power of pictograms is that they can be universally understood without needing to read or understand a specific language. Lead a review of the work produced and discuss:

- the design ideas that work best for a multilingual environment and why
- whether there any local symbols that may not be understood in a wider context and how could these be addressed
- the potential role of colour in reinforcing the communication of pictograms, for example to denote groupings or different levels of information
- the ways in which the designs consider different cultural meanings for the colours used
- the way in which careful consideration of colour and tone can help users with visual impairments such as colour blindness.

Top tip

- If you have a sympathetic head teacher, ask them to play the role of a client so that students can present their ideas in a work-based setting meaningful to their learning.

PROJECT SUGGESTIONS

- If available, produce final designs using a digital drawing programme such as Adobe Photoshop.
- If the resources are available, develop the final work as, for example, screen prints or laser-cut 3-D pictograms on a larger scale suitable for use as signage in the school.
- A digital drawing programme such as Adobe Photoshop or Illustrator could also be used to provide visual mock-ups of how the pictograms could be used as signage across the school campus.

Assessment Objectives

- **AO1:** Evidence to include observations relevant to the stated aims of the brief, for example observational drawing, reference photography, film or video. Ideas (roughs) for designs supported by notes and test pieces or screenshots to document idea development and making processes, and the relevance of the graphic designers that have been researched.

- **AO2:** Exploration of relevant conventional and experimental approaches to the use of a range of media to create lettering, typography and symbols that communicate content and ideas through their own visual forms. Supporting studies consisting of roughs and test pieces or screenshots that show growing refinement of practical skills.

  AO3: Development of ideas through the inspiration of the relevant graphic designers stated above and any others as appropriate, and demonstrating how research has been used to inspire and inform student work.

- **AO4:** Production or selection of outcomes that best solve the communication problem set by the brief. Supporting work to include evidence of ongoing evaluation that demonstrates how an understanding of visual language has been used to enhance the communication.

UNIT 2: ILLUSTRATION

These lessons look at how the creation of imagery can enhance and allow different interpretations of text. Lesson activities focus on illustrations for a range of publications, including magazines, books, posters and leaflets, blogs and websites, and the focus is on producing visual imagery that communicates the role and context of text to a specific audience.

Illustration is about communicating ideas and stories visually, usually through using a combination of images and words. The practical skills used can be very varied and often use combinations of image-making techniques. For this reason, adapting lesson plans elsewhere in this book, for example in painting and related media or printmaking, may be useful in supporting practical skills development within a scheme of work.

LESSON IDEA	Photomontage

Classroom resources

- *Materials and equipment*: A4 or A3 cartridge paper, a range of coloured collage and tissue papers, scissors, craft knife, glue, a range of drawing media, tracing paper, access to a photocopier and coloured photocopy paper; access to printmaking techniques, for example monoprinting, lino printing or screen printing would also be useful.
- *Useful digital resources:* Camera, scanner, image manipulation and drawing software, and access to digital printing.

Research sources

- Artists who use found images to create photomontage and collage include:

  Max Ernst (collages from engraved books)
  John Heartfield, Raoul Hausmann, Hannah Hoch (Dada)
  Roman Cieślewicz
  Richard Hamilton, Eduardo Paolozzi, Robert Rauchenberg (Pop Art)
  Peter Kennard
  David Mach (collages)
  Janet Woolley
  Sarah Perkins

Key terms

- **Student's Book key terms:** collage, photomontage
- **Additional key terms:** found image

LESSON TASKS

Homework	• Before the first lesson, set a topic for research that will stimulate in-class debate, for example:
	  o Too much time using the internet and social media is bad for health.
	  o Is plastic surgery a good thing?
	  o Are teenage mental health problems on the rise?
	  o Can men and women ever be equal?
	  o Air travel is killing the planet

Top tips	• The use of a suitable recent newspaper article as a trigger for this activity could be beneficial in terms of cross-curricula work linked to, for example, English comprehension, geography, economics, sociology, or personal and social education. • Ask students to collect the following materials needed for the lesson: a range of old magazines, newspapers, printed books and other sources of existing images that can be cut up for use in photomontage exercises.

1) Starter suggestions

In class, ask students to share their research and discuss their thoughts on the topic. The aim of this activity is to generate messages in response to the topic that will be communicated visually, that is, each student needs to find something to say through their image-making.

2) Main lesson activities

Students develop photomontages of found images and collage materials to create compositions that convey their ideas generated at the start of the lesson.

- They should work on A4 or A3 paper, using the entire page but considering the use of empty space or large areas of colour or texture as part of the design.
- If possible, they should record developmental work using a digital camera or scanner, so that elements can be repeatedly moved around and reconfigured.
- By the end of the lesson, they should commit to their best idea and stick the image elements down into a completed photomontage.

3) Plenary suggestions

Review the completed work together with students to identify what has worked well in terms of communicating the intended message:

- What is working well and what can be improved?
- Which image elements are missing and what is still needed to aid the story telling?
- How well are colour, tone and composition used to help with the overall messaging of the image?
- Draw up a list of actions to be taken. This might include sourcing more found images or taking some photographs.

PROJECT SUGGESTION: Project 1: Photomontage for editorial illustration

1. This project aims to:
   - consider the use of found images for reference and for their own sake as part of an artwork
   - develop students' appreciation of how image composition can be manipulated to aid story telling
   - introduce the manipulation and editing of found imagery as a tool for creating original illustrations in a wide range of graphic media.
2. Depending on the resources and time available, subsequent lessons featuring teacher demonstration of each technique where needed should encourage students to develop their images as illustrations in a wide variety of ways, for example:
   - Students can use a fine liner pen to carefully trace their photomontages to create a line drawing of their composition. Photocopies of the tracing can be developed through applied experimentation with a range of drawing media to develop multiple versions of the illustration.
   - They can explore different colour schemes or tonal arrangements and use different marks (for example dots, cross-hatching and texture). They can also do this using digital image manipulation software such as Adobe Photoshop if available.
   - They can explore layers using photocopies of the edited images on transparent acetate, or using scanned images in digital image manipulation software, and use these to further develop the images in their own right, or as preparation for further development in photo-silkscreen printing.
   - Students can also use the tracing as a starting point for creating monoprints or lino prints. They could introduce further collaged elements at the printing stage by placing cuttings from magazines under the printed image (chine-collé). Finished prints could be scanned and digitally adjusted and recoloured and so on.
   - They can use a work journal, sketchbook or blog to record their reflective thinking and progress against any actions identified to improve the image.
   - Students should select one outcome image to present as mock-up page for a print-based magazine article. They should be encouraged to think about graphic design decisions for how best to use layout, typography and colour in combination with the image to communicate effectively.

LESSON IDEA	Food illustration

This project uses observational drawing as a starting point for making illustrations suitable for a cookery book. As part of a broader graphic communication scheme of work, the images generated might also be used in subsequent packaging and advertising projects.

Classroom resources

- *Classroom arrangement*: Use an arrangement that will allow students to set up food and cooking ingredient-related still-life set ups using, for example, fruit, vegetables, fresh and packaged ingredients, a dinner table setting, or objects suggestive of a kitchen setting. Desk lamps or other equipment to allow for control of lighting would also be useful.
- *Materials and equipment*: As above.

Research sources

- Encourage students to explore the stylistic possibilities of image-making by finding examples of illustrators' work that use simplification, abstraction, realism and so on in the image design, for example:

  Gillian Blease
  Emma Dibben
  Kavel Rafferty
  Lindsey Spinks
  Lauren Radley
  Christopher Wormell

LESSON TASKS

1) Starter suggestions

In small groups, ask students to set up their own still-life grouping with the objects provided. Encourage them to think about positioning and lighting to suggest a simple story relating to preparing or enjoying food.

2) Main lesson activities

Demonstrate the appropriate techniques to students and then let them undertake a series of full page A3 observational drawings of their still life group using a range of media, such as:

- oil crayon
- chalk pastel
- pencil crayon
- watercolour
- fine liner pens, magic makers or felt-tipped pens
- collage using a range of coloured paper
- mixed media (combinations of the above)
- digital drawing software using a tablet (if available).

3) Plenary suggestions

Lead a discussion on the expressive qualities of each material in terms of its potential for manipulation of:
- colour mixing, colour strength and colour theory (for example, the use of complimentary pairs)
- mark-making and qualities of line, outline, variation of pressure in application, use of sharp/smooth pencils, use of different brushes and so on
- tone and the description of form, shape and so on.
How could placing emphasis on any of the formal qualities discussed create atmosphere and enhance the appeal of the foodstuff depicted in the drawings?

PROJECT SUGGESTION: Project 2: Food illustration for a cookery book or magazine cookery page

Depending on the resources and time available, the lessons that follow should encourage students to develop their images in a variety of ways, including:

- using their own photography
- scraperboard or printmaking
- digital manipulation where available.

The brief is to produce outcomes suitable for use to illustrate a cookery book or a magazine cookery page.

Reflection

Make sure that you have demonstrated to students how the creation of imagery can enhance and allow different interpretations of a text to be presented to a range of audiences specified in a brief. Encourage experimentation with a wide variety of possible materials, techniques and approaches for image-making. Remember to provide opportunities for students to gather, research and record relevant information for developing illustrations for inclusion in a number of publications such as magazines, books, posters and leaflets, blogs and websites.

Assessment of projects

When reviewing the project work, consider the following aspects of the four Assessment Objectives:

Assessment Objectives
• **AO1:** Evidence includes observations relevant to the stated aims of the brief, for example: observational drawing, reference photography, film or video, interviews, annotated texts, (for example student's responses to a newspaper article or short story), or collected data. Ideas (roughs) for designs are supported by notes and test pieces or screenshots to document idea development and making processes, and the relevance of the artists and designers that have been researched.
• **AO2:** Exploration of relevant image-making materials shows evidence of use of a range of media or approaches. Supporting studies consist of roughs and test pieces or screenshots that show growing refinement of practical skills.
• **AO3:** Development of ideas through the inspiration of the relevant artists and designers stated above, and any others as appropriate, demonstrates how research has been used to inspire and inform student work.
• **AO4:** The production or selection of an outcome meets the intentions of the communication brief. Supporting work includes evidence of ongoing evaluation in relation to the brief, and demonstrates how an understanding of visual language has been used to enhance the communication of the intended story or message.

UNIT 3: ADVERTISING AND PACKAGING LESSON

Students should have an understanding of how graphic communication can sell a product or service, promote brand images and communicate information through, for example, posters, fliers, logos, corporate identities, symbols or signs. Print media, packaging and web-based outcomes and campaigns should be explored.

LESSON IDEA	Branding and promoting culture

Classroom resources

- *Materials and equipment*: A range of drawing and painting media, cartridge, tracing and layout paper, a range of coloured collage and tissue papers, scissors, craft knives, glue. Access to printmaking media would also be useful.
- *Digital resources:* Camera, scanner, image manipulation, drawing and page layout software, and access to digital printing.

Research sources

- At the end of the lesson, for homework, ask students to research poster design from online sources such as the following:

   The Poster Museum, New York
   The London Transport Museum (London Underground posters)
   Internet key word searches, e.g:
   - Early 20th-century Russian film and Soviet sporting posters
   - Theatre (Europe, UK, US, India and so on) or Chinese opera posters)
   - Early 20th-century sporting posters
   - Museum posters and websites

LESSON TASKS

Site visit (or homework)	• If possible, start this project with a visit to a local cultural organisation such as:
	• a museum • an arts centre • a performance venue (dance, music, theatre) • a sports venue or event.
	Plan the visit to enable students to collect first-hand information by:
	• making drawings and photographs of the objects on display, the architecture, the performances and events (if possible), and so on • collecting any printed publicity materials available, for example, posters, fliers, guides, and so on • finding out all the key information someone would need to plan their visit • recording any branding or logos used by the location.
	• After the visit, a review of the location/event's website should consider how well designed it is in terms of communicating an exciting visitor experience.
Top tip	• If you cannot plan a site visit but your school has a co-operative music, drama or sports department or club, consider working with it to provide your students with a first-hand experience of a live brief to promote an upcoming performance or event.

1) Starter suggestion

In class, ask students to share their research material and discuss the venue researched as a client for a promotional campaign:

- Who are the core target visitors and audiences?
- What experiences are on offer and what are the benefits of visiting this venue?
- What is the unique selling point of the venue?
- How good is the publicity material currently in use? What could be improved?

The aim here is to develop a brief for branding and promoting the venue or one of its events to new audiences, starting with a poster design.

2) Main lesson activities

Working to the brief devised earlier, students need to select and edit images that will feature in their poster design. Working with a combination of their drawings and photographs, encourage them to develop strong, simplified images that will have impact when viewed from a distance. Demonstrate appropriate media and techniques, such as the following:

- Work over a tracing or photocopy of a drawing or photo using magic markers and paper collage to simplify the image into up to five flat tones or colours.
- In a digital drawing programme such as Adobe Photoshop, work over a scan of a drawing or photo using selection tools or masks to achieve a similar effect to bullet 1 above and also introduce image adjustment tools such as the posterisation tool if available.
- Use printmaking techniques such as relief printing in three colours to simplify and develop an image.
- Introduce or reinforce the techniques relating to photomontage in the lessons in *Unit 2 Illustration*.

3) Plenary suggestions

Pin the work in progress on a wall and, from across the room, review the images with students:

- Which images have the most impact and which lack striking contrasts when viewed from a distance?
- How can empty, coloured or textured space, and editing, improve image composition and impact?
- How could the colour scheme and tonal contrasts be improved?

PROJECT SUGGESTIONS

This project encourages students to promote an experience (rather than a product). Development work could focus on poster design and the power of a well-chosen single image and limited text by:

- analysing and experimenting with the stylistic lessons learnt from research into the history of posters leading to further development of image-based work (photography or illustration) using any appropriate media
- developing outcomes using printmaking techniques such as screen printing
- introducing text and exploring layout designs that incorporate sensitively chosen typography, as well as assessing the composition of the overall design and the key role that colour, tone and contrast, as well as the use of space, play in shaping this
- developing outcomes using digital drawing and layout tools such as Adobe Photoshop, Illustrator and InDesign.

Extension project work could include:

- redesigning the logo and branding of the focus organisation or venue
- incorporating the logo and branding into designs for printed materials such as fliers, guides, maps to support visitor experience, and branding for products on sale
- designing the branding for a website or a smartphone app (students taking this route should be encouraged to produce design proposals for screens such as the home screen, a Visit us screen and so on, rather than getting too involved in designing an architecture for the whole site).

LESSON IDEA	Food packaging and promotion

Classroom resources

- *Classroom arrangement*: Use an arrangement that will allow students to set up still-life arrangements of food, ingredients and objects associated with preparing, eating or drinking the packaged products explored in the skills (homework) activity. Desk lamps or other equipment to allow for control of lighting would also be useful.
- *Materials and equipment*: A4 or A3 cartridge paper, a range of coloured collage and tissue papers, scissors, craft knife, glue, a range of drawing media, tracing paper, access to a photocopier and coloured photocopy paper; access to printmaking techniques, for example monoprinting, lino printing or screen printing would also be useful.
- *Useful digital resources:* Camera, scanner, image manipulation and drawing software, and access to digital printing.

Research sources

- The list of illustrators given in *Unit 2 Illustration, Project 2* could be extended to include a wider range of image-making strategies observed in packaging design and related advertising images. This could include work that is strong on decorative typographic treatments, the use of photography, or the creation of food-related cartoon characters, for example:

  Mr Peanut
  Tony the Tiger
  The Pillsbury Doughboy
  Amul Girl
  Bertie Bassett (Bassett's Liquorice Allsorts, now owned by Cadbury)
  Juan Molinet (an Argentinian illustrator): Fake vintage Japanese ad characters

LESSON TASKS

Homework research	• Ask students to undertake *Skills activity B* on page 282 in the Student's Book, or use the activity as a starting point in class for this lesson and project.

1) Starter suggestions

In class, ask students to work in pairs or small groups to share their homework research and discuss what they have learnt about how designers apply visual language to realise packaging briefs.

2) Main lesson activities:

Refer to *Unit 2 Illustration*: Project 2 Food illustration (see page 204 in this Teacher's Guide).

As described in the lesson suggestion, and after your demonstrations of the appropriate techniques, students undertake a series of full-page A3 observational drawings of their still-life group objects in a range of drawing media. If appropriate, the class could also focus on still-life photography and lighting. Either way, the aim is for students to generate images suitable for use in redesigning packaging for their product.

3) Plenary suggestions

Review the practical work using similar questions to those used in *Unit 2 Illustration: Project 2 Food illustration*, but lead the discussion to focus on the change in context for the images, for example:

- Which images would stand out well in a shop window or on a shelf inside the store and why?
- Do different media and techniques lend themselves to particular audiences such as children, the health-conscious consumer or the luxury market? If so, how and why? Which markets and products might suit a photographic treatment and which are better served using illustrations?
- What kind of lettering, typography and layout would work best with each approach to image-making and why?

PROJECT SUGGESTIONS

From the starting points suggested, students should develop a brief for packaging designs that communicate a key idea about the product's selling point, such as taste, quality or values (for example, organic, sustainable, vegan).

To achieve this, students will need to develop their use of combinations of typography and images, and their use of formal elements such as colour, shape and pattern to communicate effectively.

Development work could include:

- further exploration of image-making, as suggested in *Unit 2 Illustration: Project 2 Food illustration*
- further exploration of packaging nets and layouts, as suggested on page 281 in the Student's book, which could include card 3-D prototypes and mock ups if possible
- exploration of digital typographic and layout tools
- design proposals for a range of products for the same brand, for example flavours or blends of tea, different types of cookies and so on
- design proposals for advertising featuring the packaged product, for example instore posters, window displays, ambient and outdoor advertising, screen layouts for a web-based advertising campaign, and so on.

Reflection

Make sure that you have demonstrated how graphic communication can sell a product or service, promote brand images and communicate information through, for example, posters, fliers, logos, corporate identities, symbols or signs. Provide opportunities for students to explore a variety of possible materials, media, techniques and approaches associated with print media, packaging and web-based outcomes and campaigns used to promote branded consumer products.

Assessment of projects

When reviewing the project work, consider the following aspects of the four Assessment Objectives:

Assessment Objectives
• **AO1:** Evidence includes observations relevant to the stated aims of the brief, for example observational drawing and photography, as well as the student's responses to audience (consumer) feedback or market research. Ideas (roughs) for designs are supported by notes and test pieces or screenshots to document idea development and making processes, and the relevance of the artists, designers and examples of existing advertising and product packaging that have been researched.
• **AO2:** Exploration of relevant image-making, design and layout materials, media, processes and techniques shows evidence of use of a range of approaches. Supporting studies consist of roughs and test pieces or screenshots that show growing refinement of practical skills and application of visual language.
• **AO3:** Development of ideas through the inspiration of the relevant artists, designers and examples of existing advertising and product packaging stated above and any others as appropriate demonstrates how research has been used to inspire and inform student work.
• **AO4:** The production or selection of an outcome meets the intentions of the communication brief. Supporting work includes evidence of ongoing evaluation in relation to the brief, and demonstrates how an understanding of visual language has been used to enhance the communication of the intended message to the audience identified in the brief.

UNIT 4: GAME DESIGN

Students should be able to combine drawing and software skills to create concept artwork, environments, game play, storyboards or character development related to a theme or brief. Supporting work for digitally produced artwork should include evidence of the development of ideas and understanding techniques and processes. Prototype platform games and RPG games concepts can be produced, and should have age-appropriate content.

LESSON IDEA	Mini-me character development

Classroom resources

- *Materials and equipment*: A4 or A3 cartridge paper, a range of coloured collage and tissue papers, scissors, craft knives, glue, staplers, tape (for example masking tape or electrical tape), a range of drawing media, and a range of 3-D modelling materials, for example wire, plasticine or modelling clay.
- *Digital resources:* Camera, scanner, image manipulation and drawing software (including 3-D modelling software if available), and access to digital printing.

Research sources

- Students will probably have identified their favourite computer game characters already and this is worth sharing in class discussion. However, to develop their creative thinking, introduce artists and designers from other art and design disciplines who have created interesting characters, sometimes using unconventional combinations of materials, such as:

    James Jarvis (Amos Toys)
    E-boy
    Alexander Girard
    Alan Aldridge: *Butterfly Ball*
    John Tenniel: *Alice in Wonderland* and *Alice Through the Looking Glass*
    Tim Burton's animated films: (for example, *James and the Giant Peach*)
    Guillermo del Toro: *Pan's Labyrinth*
    Pixar's *Toy Story* (the toys next door are particularly relevant)
    Pixar's animated desk lamp logo

Key terms

- **Additional key terms:** Avatar

LESSON TASKS

	• Before the first lesson, ask students to collect:
Homework	• five long thin shapes or objects • five ovoid/spherical shapes or objects • five chunky shapes or objects • five interesting fragments • five things that say something about themselves (interests, background, history, aspirations and so on).
Top tip	• Collecting techniques could include finding real objects to bring in, drawing from observation, casting from real objects, (for example using plasticene or modelling clay), cutting out from photographic images or paper, textiles and so on, and scanning or photocopying real objects.

1) Starter suggestions

In class (in pairs or small groups), ask students to share their homework collection and discuss the objects that say something about themselves. Expand the discussion to include ideas about their personalities and the possible characters and alter egos they might take on in the world of a computer game. By the end of the introductory section, each student needs to have a starting point for designing their character using some or all of the materials collected.

2) Main lesson activities

Demonstrate appropriate making techniques for joining materials together to construct a 3-D character model that reflects an aspect of the personal brief generated at the start of the lesson. This could be:

- an alter-ego
- an avatar or 'second life' personality
- a caricature or self-portrait
- an imaginary friend.

3) Plenary suggestions

Review the outcomes of the lesson together to consider what makes the characters work particularly well in terms of communicating the key traits:

- Is he, she or it worn out? Lopsided? Perfect or imperfect? Old or new? Fixed, repaired or transformed? And so on.
- Consider pose and body language: Is the character bold, shy, unflinching, gentle, awkward, dreamy or fierce? And so on.

At the end of the lesson, set up a simple photo booth using plain white background and a desk lamp to take carefully lit reference photographs of the work from several viewpoints.

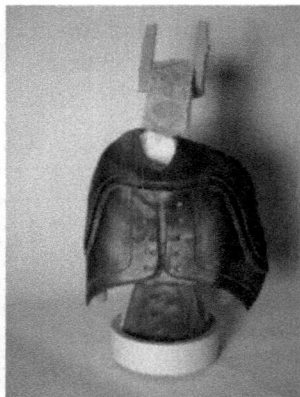

> **Top tip**
> - The photomontage lesson suggestions in *Unit 2 Illustration* may also be adapted to suit this project.

LESSON IDEA	Learning is a game

Classroom resources

- *Materials and equipment*: A4 or A3 cartridge paper, a range of drawing media. If you can, also borrow sets of flash cards that might be used in the language department or elsewhere in the school.
- *Digital resources:* Scanner, image manipulation and drawing software and access to digital printing.

Key terms

- **Additional key terms:** flash cards, rote learning

Homework research

- Before the first lesson, ask students to research or review the basics of language they either do not know or are learning at school, that is, to find out what the words are that are learnt first in the language chosen?
- As part of their research, they should visit some language learning websites.

LESSON TASKS

1) Starter suggestions

In class (in pairs or small groups), ask students to share their homework research and discuss their own experiences of learning a new language (this might include the sign language used by the hard of hearing, Morse code or semaphore, music and so on). Expand the discussion to include knowledge that can be strengthened by the use of visual aids and also repetition and rote learning, for example, learning the names of capital cities or flags around the world. By the end of the introductory section, each student needs to have a starting point for designing elements of a computer game based on flash cards.

Top tip

- If any of your students have a range of mother-tongues, use them as resident experts in this lesson.

2) Main lesson activities

The aim of this lesson is to introduce and reinforce the ideas that all games need to have clear aims and goals for the game player.

- Begin by asking students to set a learning aim from their research, for example to learn five new nouns and verbs to use in simple sentence structure, or to learn the names of the main rivers in their home country and so on.
- Using peer discussion and brainstorming, students should begin to map out the sequences of steps a player will need to take to reach their learning goal.

3) Plenary suggestions

Before the end of the lesson, review the simple game structure created and, as a class, discuss how to make the ideas visually appealing to engage the player, for example:

- Is a character acting as a teacher or guide needed?
- Which icons or symbols need to be designed to denote the key content ideas, for example: What could you use as a visual signifier for 'Mumbai; or 'to eat', and so on?
- What rewards and incentives can the game play offer to keep players motivated?
- What value could creating an online community of players add to users' learning and their enjoyment of the game?
- Is sound needed? If so, in what form?

At the end of the lesson, lead a discussion on how computer games are not just for entertainment but can also be used to learn. You could also ask students to review their game structure with some user testing for homework.

PROJECT SUGGESTIONS

As students will be working on their ideas for a game within the graphic communication (art and design) context, project development should focus on the visual and creative elements of designing the game.

As resources and time allow, their project could be developed by:

- using drawing (freehand and digital) to further develop the images or icons needed to present the game play effectively
- using drawing (freehand and digital) to create environments in which the game can be played; depending on the brief, this might use maps and levels
- undertaking development work suggested by lesson ideas in *Unit 1 Graphic design with lettering*, which may benefit students working with text and typography
- producing a set of finished proposed screen layouts that demonstrate the visuals that users would experience at key stages in the game; in this respect, developing ideas about storyboards (see the Student's Book) could be beneficial.

Reflection
Show students how to combine drawing and software skills to create concept artwork, environments, game play, storyboards or character development related to a theme or brief. In doing so, encourage experimentation with a variety of freehand and digital drawing and modelling techniques and approaches for image-making. Make sure that you provide opportunities for students to gather, research and record relevant information for developing for platform games and RPG games concepts.

Assessment of projects

When reviewing the project work, consider the following aspects of the four Assessment Objectives:

Assessment Objectives
• **AO1:** Evidence includes observations relevant to the stated aims of a games design brief focused on concept artwork, environments, game play, storyboards or character development, for example, drawing, reference photography, film or video, and user (peer) feedback. Ideas (roughs) for designs are supported by notes and test pieces or screenshots to document idea development, and the relevance of a range of computer games that have been researched.
• **AO2:** Exploration of relevant image-making techniques shows evidence of use of a range of media or approaches, including creative digital work. Supporting studies consist of roughs, tests or screenshots that show growing refinement of practical skills.
• **AO3:** Development of ideas through the inspiration of the computer games designers stated above and any others as appropriate demonstrates how research has been used to inspire and inform student work.
• **AO4:** The production or selection of an outcome (a prototype or visual proposals) meets the intentions of the brief. Supporting work includes evidence of ongoing evaluation in relation to the brief, and demonstrates how an understanding of visual language has been used to enhance the communication of the game play intended.

UNIT 5: STUDENT CASE STUDY

A student case study is provided on pages 288–289 of the Student's Book. This additional case study is provided for further guidance on assessment.

PROJECT BRIEF: TO DEVELOP AN ALTERNATIVE POSTER FOR THE STUDENT'S FAVOURITE FILM, *CINDERELLA*

The student starts by focusing on a contemporary version of the story: Replacing the glass slipper with an Adidas trainer, placing the action against urban settings, including a graffiti-covered wall. First-hand reference photographs of classmates are also used throughout to develop approaches to story telling through images.

Most of the work is created using digital photography, typography, drawing and layout tools. Chalk pastels and acrylics have also been used. The work is informed by examples of three contemporary graphic designers, and alternative combinations of image and typography are explored in a number of approaches to image-making and layouts (compositions).

Assessment
• **AO1:** The student makes use of appropriate first-hand source material with digital photography. This is used well to develop digital drawings focused on silhouette, simplified drawing of key story-telling and stylised portraiture. Good digital drawing skills are demonstrated and care is taken to document all subtle alterations to the designs, including experimentation with typography.
• **AO2:** A range of digital media are explored, and some use of chalk pastels and acrylic paint. Hand-drawn lettering and some strong technical skills are used effectively. However, more consideration could perhaps have been given to the communication potential of colour and tone.
• **AO3:** Composition plays an important part and careful consideration is given to the possibilities of combining different typography and image treatments. The student shows critical understanding in the decisions made throughout. The designers used to inspire project work are relevant to the way the student chooses to develop their practical responses. However, there is no evidence of focused study on poster design and, as a result, opportunities to use visual language to create communication impact in this format have at times been partially overlooked. The outcome perhaps is more suited to a smaller-scale format similar to the magazine spreads and book covers studied for inspiration.
• **AO4:** Documentation of development work is thorough and reflective. The final outcome is a confident solution, with strength in resolving the illustration element of the design, resulting from clear synthesis of influences and practical experimentation. A greater focus on the function of posters and how this format is used to communicate with specific target audiences may have led to a more impactful and convincing overall design.

INITIAL IDEA

EXPERIMENTAL

Cinderella

214

DEVELOPING WORK

Throughout this section, there has been repeated reference to writing and responding to communication briefs. This is because graphic communicators are often very concerned with maximising the potential for communication between a client (for example, a writer, a business or an organisation) and specific targeted audiences. Your scheme of work should therefore encourage learning about how to set out very clear communication goals that identify the impact that the designed work should have.

For young students developing an interest in this field, the brief can be a useful tool for measuring the progress of a design. It does this by directing reflective thinking beyond merely describing processes or expressing preferences towards a questioning approach to the creative decisions made about every aspect of the work in order to meet the brief.

For this reason, including activities such as group discussion work, brainstorming, pitching ideas and peer feedback, as well as teacher-led critiques, are worthwhile when devising your scheme of work.

Further projects

As already stated, any project or scheme of work will benefit from planning common starting points that allow students to develop their own specialist interests relating to the units in this chapter, as their skills and knowledge develop. The suggestions made above are intended to provide an adaptable structure without limiting the thematic content. As research in this area is often very outward looking, try developing projects that build on themes suggested by, for example, current events or your local context.

Further research

- *Graphic Design Rules: 365 Essential Design Dos and Don'ts* (ISBN: 978-0711233461)
- *Illustration (Portfolio Series)* (ISBN: 978-1856697101)

Top tip

- A well-considered outcome in this field, particularly if produced using digital tools, can look deceptively effortless alongside a work in, for example, painting, sculpture or textiles where application of skills or craft can be more easily identified. For this reason, it is good practice to encourage consistent and regular use of a journal or blog that records the time and thought put into every stage of refining every detail of a design outcome.

Checklist

- ✓ I have helped students to understand what graphic communication is and to be aware of the range of contexts in which it is used.
- ✓ I have helped students to know how graphic communication uses the visual language of art and design to communicate meaning.
- ✓ I have helped students to understand and know about the range of practical media, materials and techniques associated with graphic communication.

INTRODUCTION

13.1 Printing and dyeing

13.2 Constructed textiles

13.3 Fashion

13.4 Student case study

Learning objectives
By the end of this unit students should: • understand different properties of paints and dyes • understand distinctions between printed and dyed textiles • be able to create a simple print block • explore the use of technology in the textiles industry and the relationship between textiles and fashion • understand the difference between natural and synthetic yarns • understand different methods of constructing textiles • know how to create a simple woven textile • understand the process of textile design and garment construction for the fashion industry • know how to create a mood board to present your research and design ideas • know how to choose the right fabrics and construction techniques.

Classroom resources
• Student's Book Chapter 13 Textile design, pages 290–305. • Mood boards and displays of previous work for each unit in Chapter 13; fabrics, materials and dyes.

Research sources
• Anokhi Museum of Printing, India • Museum of Printed Textiles of Mulhouse • Kyoto Shibori Museum • Traditional Japanese constructed textiles at the Amuse Museum • Centre for Traditional Textiles, Peru • Fashion Institute of Technology, New York • Costume Institute, Metropolitan Museum of Art • Fashion and Textiles Museum, London • Fashion Museum, UK

Top tip

• Find out whether you can build up a bank of fabrics for free. Many local businesses, shops and residents may recycle fabrics for which they have no use, but which could be used in lessons.

General lesson ideas

- Encourage exploration of everyday fabrics and materials. Encourage curiosity with questions and answers. Ask students to write down all types of supporting work that they can think of without looking at their Student's Book, and then check. They can keep this list in their sketchbooks for reference.

Key considerations

- Which projects or topics are suggested or could you devise? Test practical activities yourself before setting them as tasks for students. Encourage students to work to their strengths and areas of interest within the limits of resources.

Reflective log

- Which practical skills do I need to develop to help my students achieve?
- How can I use practical and theoretical lessons to help my students to develop their work?
- How can I structure my teaching to make the most of the resources and facilities that I have available to me?
- Are there any local exhibitions or resources that my students could visit or use?

Key terms

- **Student's Book key terms:** bias, block, carding, catwalk, collection, colourfast, concept, darts, drape, emulsion, fibres, free-motion stitching, fusible webbing, grain, gutta, handle, haute couture, loom, lustre, mood board, mordant, motif, nylon, pigment, pile, pret-à-porter, selvedge, silhouette, spinning, squeegee, stand, stencil, synthetic, tjanting, tjap, toile, vat, viscose, yarn, yurt
- **Additional key terms:** rends, seams, stitching

UNIT 1: PRINTING AND DYEING

LESSON 1	Printing

Students will be encouraged to plan, carry out and comment on a block print, screen print, discharge print and flock print. Activities and further research establishes and explores the links between new technologies in textiles and their applications in fashion.

Classroom resources

- *Classroom arrangement:* You may wish to create a central space for the demonstration of printing and dyeing techniques, and to clear a space for drying dyed or printed fabrics.
- *Materials and equipment:* Student's Book, pages 290–293; a range of fabrics, dyes and paints, carving knives, measuring jugs, plastic bowls, sheets of paper, squeegees (or scrapers), as well as pre-carved printing blocks and suitable substances for printing, such as wood, potatoes, erasers and so on. A screen-printing frame (if you don't have this, you can make one from mesh, a wooden frame and a stapler).

Research sources

- Anokhi Museum of Printing, India
- Museum of Printed Textiles of Mulhouse

LESSON TASKS

1) Starter suggestions

Demonstrate	• Show a range of materials that have been both printed and dyed, and ask students to comment on them. What is similar? What is different? How do you think they were made?

2) Main lesson activities

Additional student activity 1	• Block Printing: Provide students with a range of materials with which to make blocks, and a variety of fabrics on which to print. Discuss geometric and repeating patterns, as well as random prints onto fabrics. Do Skills activity A on page 291 in the Student's Book – making block prints. Students can explore different patterns, including repeating patterns, geometric patterns, random patterns and prints inspired by local or foreign designs. Discuss the outcomes as a class.
Additional student activity 2	• Screen printing: Provide screen printing frames or ask students to make their own by stretching mesh tightly across an empty picture frame. Staple the mesh tight at the edges and tape over the sides so that paint does not spread around the sides. • Ask students to design their patterns on sheets of paper and cut them out. Then they can lay their patterns over their chosen fabric and carefully scrape the paint through the screen over their pattern. Again, students can explore a range of patterns, fabrics and paints, and you should encourage them to experiment. You can also ask them to replicate the pattern they made in the print blocking activity, and comment on the different outcomes and processes.
Top tip	• Don't let the print get dry or it will be hard to remove. Ensure that the screens are cleaned thoroughly with cold water and left to dry before being reused.

Additional student activity 3	• Discharge printing: If you have a suitable cleanser (some household cleaners containing bleach work well), students can reuse their screen to remove colour from fabrics to create a discharge pattern.
Additional student activity 4	• Flock printing: If resources are available, encourage students to carry out flock printing using a variety of fabrics and colours. Ensure that they experiment using the different elements of art and experiment using a variety of inspirations.
Project work	• Although flock printing dates back to ancient China and the Middle Ages in Europe, it now has a wide variety of modern uses. Set students a research activity to explore modern uses and new methods of flock printing. Students could put together a brief portfolio exploring this technique and highlighting what inspires them.

3) Plenary suggestions

Discussion	• After exploring and carrying out several painting techniques, students should discuss the differences and uses of each one. Why might discharge printing be more suitable for a project than screen printing? Was one method easier, or more suitable for a certain approach – for example, is one method more accurate, or easier to replicate? Students should make notes in their notebook.
Display	• Ask all students to create a temporary exhibition of their work on the wall to pool ideas. Encourage discussion about the display.
Consolidate	• Ask students to write up a summary of their answers to the above questions in their sketchbooks as homework or classwork.

Reflection

Ask students questions about their main activity to check their progress and understanding: What have you done? Why have you done this? What have you learnt from this? What went well? What could be improved?

Collect in student work on a regular basis. Spread out all tasks on a table. Ask yourself what is going well and what further resources or support your students require from you. Identify which aspects of the Assessment Objectives have been addressed.

LESSON 2	Dyeing

Classroom resources

- *Classroom arrangement:* You may want to create a central space for the demonstration of dyeing techniques. You may also want to clear a space for drying and displaying dyed fabrics.
- *Materials and equipment:* Student's Book, pages 290–293; a range of fabrics and dyes, wax, tools for batik (tjantings and tjaps if possible), measuring jugs, plastic bowls, sheets of paper, an iron, gutta or water-soluble resist and applicators, frames for stretching silk.

Research resources

- Kyoto Shibori Museum
- Dharma Trading Company online

LESSON TASKS

1) Starter suggestions

Demonstrate	• Show students examples of batik, dip dyeing, tie dyeing, silk painting and shibori, and ask them to comment on the differences, as well as the colours, patterns and textures. What are the differences between these materials and the painted ones students have worked with previously? Ask students how they think each example was made. Revisit the difference between painted and dyed materials.
Top tip	• Research any local dyeing factories or artists near to your school and ask whether they would be happy for you to visit. Visiting a smaller producer, as well as an industrial dyer, is a good way to show students both traditional and modern methods, as well as local uses for dyeing.

2) Main lesson activities

Additional student activity 1	• Batik: Set up the class to allow the boiling of water and melting of wax to take place safely. Let students select materials to dye from your class collection and ask them to spend some time planning out the design and colours that they would like to create. When they are ready, first demonstrate the process yourself and then let students create their own batik fabrics. Move around the room to ensure that they are working safely.
Additional student activity 2	• Research: Although batik (wax-resistant dyeing) is an old process traditionally from Indonesia, the process has spread across South-east Asia, as well as West Africa. Modern batik has also adapted, with designers employing a wide variety of techniques, including etching, screen printing and stencilling, and using unusual materials to dye. Ask students to research local batik processes, as well as global, modern processes. Bring the class together to discuss their findings.
Top tip	• Ensure classroom safety by overseeing the ironing and boiling processes, and ensuring that walking spaces are clear. Discuss safe practices in the classroom with students.
Additional student activity 3	• Silk painting: First, demonstrate the silk-painting technique using a simple design and the gutta or water-soluble resist to which you have access. Show students how to die the silk initially, dry it, iron it and stretch it over a frame. Make sure that students are aware of and follow safe practices while steaming or ironing. Set students single word start points for their projects, or let them choose their own before starting. Students should create their silk-painted work to fulfil this starting point.

Top tip	• If you do not have frames available, you will need to make them. Remember to retain them as part of your classroom resources.
Additional student activity 4	• Tie-dye and dip dyeing: See Skills activity C on page 292 in the Student's Book for tie-dye. These activities are easy to set up and better done by students on their own, to encourage them to explore and play with patterns and techniques. Provide dyes, bowls and fabrics, and ensure safe classroom layout and practice.

3) Plenary suggestions

Discussion	• Display a selection of student work in the classroom, from a single method or a range of methods for printing textiles, and ask students to talk about their work. Give students time to explain their own work to the class, and then discuss where the work could go next, or what students might do differently.
Research	• Ask students to look at more modern methods of dyeing used in the fashion industry. You could encourage them to visit local stores to look at clothes, or do an online search of recent fashion items that use methods such as spraying and digital printing. Students could select an item of clothing or a collection that they like and discuss how it was made and their reaction to it, either in their notebooks or in class.

INTERNALLY SET ASSIGNMENT

Now that students have been exposed to a range of printing and dyeing techniques, and have considered both traditional and modern methods, ask them to select one and complete a piece of work that deals with a specific theme or topic. Students should plan, research, carry out and assess their work. They should also be given time to make alterations, (for example to technique or style), before presenting a final outcome.

Reflection
Ask students questions about their main activity to check their progress and understanding. What have you done? Why have you done this? What have you learnt from this? What went well? What could be improved? Collect in students' work on a regular basis. Spread out all tasks on a table. Ask yourself what is going well and what further resources or support your students require from you. What resources could you retain or modify for future use? Identify which aspects of the Assessment Objectives have been addressed.

UNIT 2: CONSTRUCTED TEXTILES

These lessons will help students to understand the difference between natural and synthetic yarns, and to explore the many different fibres used in the textile industry. They will also explore the various types of weaving looms available and the different weaving structures.

These lessons will also take the student from thinking about woven fabrics to exploring several other ways of creating or decorating fabric, such as bonding, knitting, crocheting, looping, knotting, felting and fusing.

LESSON 1	Identifying fabrics

Classroom resources

- *Classroom arrangement:* You may want to create a central space for demonstrations or shared resources.
- *Materials and equipment:* Student's Book pages 294–297; a range of fabrics, yarns, fibres such as silk cocoons, sheep's wool, goat's hair, cotton balls; a collection of care labels from a range of garments or other textiles. Students should be encouraged to contribute to the selection of these from home to achieve as wide a variety as possible. A2 paper or card, pencils, glue, scissors.

Research resources

- There are numerous online guides for this topic and suitable searches could be carried out as long as the suitability of the topic and content are assessed prior to the lesson. Suitable sites include:
  - Textile affairs online
  - Textile exchange online
  - Binhaitimes.
- Wikipedia is also a good source of information in this field.

LESSON TASKS

1) Starter suggestions

Discussion	• Divide students into four groups to identify which fibres or yarns are used to make fabrics. The groups can use these headings – natural/plant, natural/animal, synthetic/man-made or synthetic/chemical. They can record the information on A2 paper, which can then be used as a classroom display. The groups can be rotated until all fibres are identified.
Plenary	• Display as many fabrics as you can to consolidate students' learning. Pass the materials around for students to see and feel.
Top tips	• Expand the activity by letting students illustrate their answers on the display with fabric samples, fibres, images and so on. Provide a selection of sample fabrics and fibres to start the discussion. • Demonstrate a burn test on different fabrics, making sure that you follow health and safety guidelines. Students can record the results on a chart, which can also be used as a classroom display.

2) Main lesson activities

Additional student activity 1	• In preparation for Skills Activity A on page 294 of the Student's Book, show students a selection of wash-care labels from a range of garments and textiles. Ask questions such as: Why are some fabrics hand wash only? Why do some fabrics need to be washed at low/high temperatures? Why does some fabric construction need to be dried flat? How do you think the fabric was made (ice woven, knitted, felted and so on)?
Skills activity B	• Student's Book, page 295: Skills activity B. As this is part of the student assessment, all students should participate in this activity. If you feel it is appropriate, they can record their responses in their sketchbooks or make group wall charts. Discuss the outcomes with students and as a class.

LESSON 2	Create a woven sample

Classroom resources

- *Classroom arrangement:* Normal class arrangement will be fine, though you may want to create a central space for demonstrations or shared resources.
- *Material and equipment:* A4 cardboard, warp thread, variety of yarns for wefts, illustrations of different weaving looms, and samples of different weaves.

Research resources

- There are numerous online guides for this topic and suitable searches could be carried out as long as the suitability of the topic and content are assessed prior to the lesson. Suitable sites include:
  - ○ Textiles 4 U wikispaces
  - ○ George Weil arts and crafts online
  - ○ The weaving loom
  - ○ Linton tweeds.

LESSON TASKS

1) Main lesson activity

Student activity 1	• Students research a range of weaving looms used in small or domestic settings, such as box, speed, lap and so on. They should consider the types of yarns that can be used with these looms. Discuss with students the many applications of weaving, for example clothing, art installation, sails, footwear, carpets, upholstery, parachutes and so on.
Student activity 2	• Display images of contemporary and creative weaving, and ask students to identify the range of materials used. Have a selection of unusual materials to support this information, such as video tape, string, dental floss, twigs, ribbon and so on. Ask students to record their thoughts about creative and artistic weaving in their notebooks.
Plenary questions	• Show the students images of industrial weaving looms and ask them questions such as: Which countries have large textile industries? Why are these important? How do they differ from smaller or domestic situations?
Skills activity C	• Student's Book, page 295: Students create a plain weaving sample using a simple 'loom' by wrapping warp threads around an A4 piece of cardboard and weaving weft threads through these. Students can vary the range of threads or yarns they use and they should record their thoughts about the construction of the sample in their notebooks.

LESSON 3	Investigate other methods of creating fabrics

Classroom resources

- *Classroom arrangement:* You may want a central space for demonstrations and shared resources.
- *Materials and equipment:* Fabrics, threads, needles, scissors, crochet hooks, knitting needles, iron, ironing board, felting equipment (wool tops, water, bowl, detergent, plastic sheet), fusible film (Bondaweb™ or Wonder-under™), craft/art magazines for research, silicone paper (baking parchment).

Research resources

- Love to knit online
- Instructables for beginners guide to crochet
- Martha Stewart online
- Search 'crafts tutsplus'
- Fusing fabric with Margaret Beal

LESSON TASKS

1) Starter suggestions

Demonstrate	• Show students a selection of textiles using as many techniques as possible. If you don't have all of them, show a selection of clear images in colour.
Discuss	• Ask the students their opinions and how they think they might use each individual technique.
Additional student activity	• Ask students to record their responses to the techniques in their notebooks.
Top tip	• Encourage students to begin thinking about their internally set assignment and which technique they will use for their portfolio.

2) Main lesson activity

To investigate, sample and research as many other construction techniques as possible so students have sufficient information and learning opportunities in order to inform and support their ideas regarding their internally set project.

Additional student activity 1	• Divide the students into groups and have them focus on creating sample pieces of knitting, crochet, embroidery, looping or knotting. Rotate the groups so all students explore each technique. Students enter their sample in their sketchbook, along with a record of their thoughts and ideas on how to develop the techniques further.
Plenary	• Provide opportunities for students to further advance their studies by asking them to include additional research into each technique, both traditional and contemporary, in their sketchbooks.
Demonstration 1	• Create a sample of wet felting using wool tops. This can be a messy exercise, so depending on time and resources, you can decide whether it is appropriate for your students.
Additional student activity 2	• Let students create a small sample of wet felting and record this in their sketchbook.

Demonstration 2	• Student Book, page 296 (Top tip): Adhering to health and safety rules, bond different surfaces together. Some applications will require fusible web, that is, paper to paper, and paper to cloth.
Top tips	• Bonding plastic to plastic does not require fusible web, as the heat of the iron is sufficient. However, whenever a hot iron is used, ALWAYS protect the ironing board and iron by covering or sandwiching the plastics between silicone paper. • The use of any form of heat, such as an iron, a hot-gun or a soldering iron, will produce fumes, especially when working with plastics. Always make sure that there is adequate ventilation and no one in the room suffers from breathing problems.

3) Plenary suggestions

Discussion	• Having explored and carried out several textile techniques, students should discuss the differences and uses of each one. Why might embroidery be more suitable for a project than weaving? Was one method easier, or more suitable for a certain approach – for example, is one method more accurate, or easier to replicate? Students should make notes in their notebooks.
Display	• Ask all students to create a temporary exhibition of their work on the wall to pool ideas. Encourage discussion about the display.
Consolidate	• Ask students to write up a summary of their answers to the above questions in their notebooks either for homework or as classwork.

Reflection

Ask students questions about their activities to check their progress and understanding. For example: What have you done? What went well? What have you learnt from this? What could be improved?

Collect students' work on a regular basis and ask yourself questions such as: What is going well? Are the students meeting their targets? Do students need more support?

Also consider these questions: Which resources could you retain or modify for future use? Which aspects of the assessment process have been met? Do you need to change or add to your plans to improve learning opportunities for students?

PROJECT WORK: INTERNALLY SET ASSIGNMENT

Suggested ideas

Although many textile applications are for practical purposes and date back to ancient times, many artists exhibit their work in galleries and museums, and textile design is globally recognised as an important form of artistic and visual communication.

In order for students to achieve the best grading opportunities, they will need to focus their project ideas and fully explore traditional and modern uses for their chosen technique.

Encourage students to look at the work of various artists such as Emily Eibel, Clyde Oliver, Jennifer L Porter, Sheila Hicks, Natalie Jones, Louise Bourgeois and Tracy Emin.

When researching historical and contemporary textiles, students should be able to make links into other areas of art and design, perhaps by identifying craft practitioners or fine artists who work with textiles.

Reflection

Ask students questions about their main activity to check their progress and understanding. For example: What have you done? Why have you done this? What have you learnt from this? What went well? What could be improved? Collect in student work on a regular basis. Spread out all tasks on a table. Ask yourself what is going well and what further resources or support your students require from you. Identify what aspects of the Assessment Objectives have been addressed.

UNIT 3: FASHION

LESSON 1	Initial ideas

These lesson plans will take students from thinking about inspiration and creating a mood board, to researching, creating and working with a brief, and finally to planning and carrying out a project using appropriate materials and techniques. Students will investigate the design and creation of clothing, and how people adorn their bodies with various accessories including shoes, bags, belts and headpieces. Students' journies will begin with a brief where the requirements of the unit, aims and objectives, will be set out clearly.

Classroom resources

- *Classroom arrangement:* Grouping tables to allow brainstorming and discussions on the themes may help if practical. Space will need to be cleared for later work, and if possible wall space should be available for displaying mood boards.
- *Materials and equipment:* Sheets of A3 paper for mood boards, reusable adhesive or packaging tape for affixing mood boards; a selection of fabrics and materials.

Research sources

- Fashion Institute of Technology
- Costume Institute, Metropolitan Museum of Art
- Fashion and Textiles Museum, London
- Fashion Museum, UK

LESSON TASKS

1) Starter suggestions

Additional student activity 1	• Ask students to brainstorm in groups to decide what theme they would like to tackle for their brief. Inspirations for a theme could include colours and patterns, historical costumes, local history or fashion, or the latest textile technology.
Top tips	• If you want to expand this activity, rotate themes between groups once each one has been explored. Choose suitable sized groups to allow sufficient time to complete the projects and rotate between the themes.
Demonstration	• Set a brief for student projects and discuss it with students. Make sure that they understand each element of the brief, such as timing, market, materials, cost, season and so on. For example, a simple brief could read: *Design an outfit or garment suitable for a young woman to wear at a family wedding.*
Advanced additional student activity 2	• Although you would usually set the brief, in later stages of the course, students may negotiate with you to lead this process. If suitable for your class, ask students to brainstorm in their groups again. This time, they need to develop a brief for their work within the theme they have chosen. Discuss what a brief might include, using the Student's Book for guidance and accepting suitable student suggestions. The brief for a fashion project could include, for example, design, target market, season, cost and occasion.
Top tip	• The brief is usually the start of any creative process. It should be seen as a set of instructions that leads into the project, which is a collection of work carried out to achieve the brief. A time scale should be set with each brief and must include plenty of opportunities for the student to meet the aims and objectives of the syllabus and must be designed to ensure that they can be met. The purpose of the brief is usually to inspire and outline the aims and objectives, as well as to give information about what the student is required to do.

2) Main lesson activities

Additional student activity 1	• Students should take their brief (their own one or one you have set) and use it as the start of the project to do thorough research. Research should be informative, inspirational, useful and, hopefully, fun. Using the project brief as a starting point, students should list every word they can think of that relates to the brief. They can also add images, which may also help in establishing a theme or concept. Encourage students to be open-minded and let their imagination wander into different areas, even unrelated ones. • Research into a suitable design may involve looking at the quality of the cloth, the drape, handle, texture, colour, pattern, surface interest and so on. The addition of 'season' to the brief will include another constraint, which will affect the nature of the research and the outcome. • An example could be 'Dress': long, floaty, tight, sleeves, wrap, colour, texture, beads, embroidery and recycle. • Each of these ideas could immediately spark further ideas: *Floaty:* Silk, chiffon, see-through, layered, lined *Long:* Floor length, mid-calf, handkerchief hem *Recycle:* Denim, embellish, leather, beads. • A mind-map may also give direction for further research, by allowing students to gather images, fabric swatches, construction techniques, sample processes and so on.
Top tip	• The addition of more constraints to the brief will result in more learning objectives being covered. However, too many constraints may inhibit the creativity of the student, so each brief should be carefully planned to achieve the necessary objectives.
Skills activity A	• Student's Book page 299. • Now that students have researched their theme and brief thoroughly, they can start to create a mood board to display their research, initial thoughts and response to the brief. Final mood boards can be displayed in the class to share ideas. By rotating the theme and brief, students can learn from previous groups' mood boards and progress in their understanding of the requirements of this task.
Demonstrate	• Show the class a mood board and/or design brief. Ask them what it contains and discuss how (and why) to put one together for fashion.

3) Plenary suggestions

Teacher	• If you have built up a store of previous mood boards, you could display these to students and ask them to try to identify the brief. Encourage them to look for ideas about materials, theme, season, cost, purpose and so on. Reveal the brief and ask students how well they think the mood board responded to it. • If you have mind-maps as well, you can cover up the central term and ask students to decide what the theme is. Can they come up with any further terms or ideas to respond to it?

Reflection

Students should review their mood boards and mind-maps to consider what they did well and what they found difficult. They could compare their moods boards with those from other groups and critique them.

As the teacher, consider how you created and set the brief, and which themes and categories worked well or less well with students.

LESSON 2	Fashion design

Now that students have looked at themes, briefs and research, and have displayed their initial ideas, it is important for them to consider the materials they will use. They should explore widely, considering any fabrics and materials they can find and assessing each one for its properties and uses.

Classroom resources

- *Classroom arrangement:* Storage space should be created for student work, as well as fabric materials.
- *Materials and equipment:* Selection of fabrics, scissors and pins.

Research sources

- Fashion Institute of Technology
- Costume Institute, Metropolitan Museum of Art
- Fashion and Textiles Museum
- Fashion Museum

LESSON TASKS

1) Starter suggestions

Demonstration	• Show students a range of materials from a classroom collection. Elicit responses from them about each one. Try to get students to respond in terms that relate to the initial briefs or suitability for different designs. For example: For which type of design would this material work best? Why would this material be or not be suitable for a certain project?
Student	• Give students time to explore the collection of materials, picking them up, sharing them and considering a few. Students can affix small amounts of materials to their sketchbooks and comment on their properties.

2) Main lesson activities

Additional student activity 1	• Students should now start exploring materials based on each one's purpose and function in relation to the brief. Encourage them to explore the materials they have and to research others, in order to determine what will work well for their project. Students should write down terms to describe the materials they have selected – for example fine, coarse, natural, synthetic, waterproof or translucent. They should explain why they have chosen each fabric, what it is being used for and why its properties make it suitable.
Additional student activity 2	• Students should plan their design, while looking back to their brief and mood board, and select fabrics to drape on the stand. They should record their progress at each stage, using photographs if possible. They should also note any changes in approach, design or material, and the reasons for these. Encourage students to explore variations, such as pleats, folds and different silhouettes. Remind them to use their Student's Book as a guide for building their garments on the stand, cutting, pinning and so on.

3) Plenary suggestions

Additional student activity	• Students should reflect on the whole project – from theme and brief to research, material selection and creation. They should record the process in their sketchbooks and note what they would change in any aspect if they did it again.
Reflective log	• Students should think back to their mood boards and compare their garments to their original ideas. Did they realise the brief? Have they selected the best materials for their garment? What would they change in the research, design and creation of their garment?

Reflection

Reflect on the briefs you set and the materials you have provided. Ask yourself these questions: How suitable was the brief? Did it engage students effectively and allow them to explore all elements of the syllabus? Was your collection of materials suitable? Which other materials could you have added?

Assessment of projects

When reviewing the project work, consider the following aspects of the four AOs:

- **AO1:** Observational drawings of relevant objects, ideas for designs, notes and photographs to document technical making processes and the relevance of the artists that have been researched.
- **AO2:** Exploration of relevant materials showing evidence of use of a range of media or approaches. Fabric samples that show growing refinement of practical skills.
- **AO3:** Development of ideas through the inspiration of the relevant artists stated above and any others as appropriate and demonstrating how research has been used to inspire and inform student work.
- **AO4:** Production of a sustained final outcome (garment) that realises intentions in supporting work and shows an understanding of visual language.

See page 305 in the Student's Book for a full-colour version of this student's work.

PROJECT BRIEF

Primary and secondary research and construction methods are explored in this project, with the final outcome being shown in Image 4. The initial research is based on the word 'wheel' and the student has presented the work creatively reflecting a wheel shape. For the design development, the student has sampled construction and decorative techniques, and has identified where changes need to be made.

Assessment
• **AO1:** *Record ideas, observations and insights relevant to intentions as work progresses.* The student began the project with a wide range of information, which could have taken many directions. Her inspiration has elements of shape and form and she has consciously used these throughout. She has made effective use of primary research. The shapes and positions of the decorative processes also reflect these observations. During the design development, various techniques were sampled and evaluated resulting in a change of technique. • **AO2:** *Explore and select appropriate resources, media, materials, techniques and processes.* An appropriate range of media has been used for the sketchbook and finished item. The techniques and processes sampled are considered and confirm the choice of materials for the chosen textiles. The initial development work shows an open approach, which gained focus following the planetarium visit. • **AO3:** *Develop ideas through investigation, demonstrating critical understanding.* This student demonstrates an open approach at the beginning of the project with a collection of research in various colours. She has clearly shown her intent to follow a particular colour palette. When working with shape, she has confirmed her original thoughts and followed through on the overall shape of the garment, as well as some of the decorative finishes. The student shows a critical understanding of shape and form in this garment and an excellent development of ideas. • **AO4:** *Present a personal and coherent response that realises intentions and demonstrates an understanding of visual language.* The project is consistent in maintaining a focus on curved and circular objects, but avoids a premature focus by gathering several sources for initial observation. The final outcome itself is a confident example of textile design. Consideration for light, shade, colour and texture are all present. A high level of observational ability is evident in the supporting studies and the outcome. There is an excellent realisation of intentions demonstrating effective understanding of visual language.

DEVELOPING WORK

A prescriptive approach at the beginning of the process will help instil in students the good practice of setting targets and the timescale in which to fulfil a brief. In addition, this pattern of research (gather – explore – sample – research – develop ideas – outcomes) will become second nature to them. To ensure that students are ready to complete the externally set assignment, it is important that, as well as having the relevant information, they also have the confidence to work independently under stress.

Many less able students will need your guidance and support throughout the course, and a teacher-led approach will continue to be necessary. However, more able students will prefer to take a more personal approach once they have been taught to do this. Encourage them to find their own direction, but supervise them closely to ensure that they do not stray away from the syllabus.

As students develop their skills and knowledge of textile design techniques, they should be able to refine their work and ideas, referencing historical, contemporary and technological influences. They should continue to explore and experiment with samples, design development, drawings and so on, and continually collect information. They also need to thoroughly document and photograph all their work.

Further projects
•   Suggested starting points for further projects: Developing design details on patterns Developing skills in patchwork and quilting Ethical fashions, how to reuse and upcycle clothing.

💡 Further research
•   *JJ Pizzuto's Fabric Science* (a comprehensive guide to current textiles and textile technology) •   *Sustainable Fashion and Textiles* by Kate Fletcher •   *How to be Creative in Textile Art* by Julia Triston, Rachel Lombard •   *Interpreting Themes in Textile Art* by Els van Baarl, Cherilyn Martin •   *The Textile Artist's Studio Handbook* by Owyn Ruck, Visnja Popovic

Checklist
✓   I have introduced students to the large variety of possible material and techniques available for textile design work within the constraints of what I can offer at my school or college.
✓   I understand how to help students choose a successful area of textile design that they can explore.
✓   I know what type of support work is required if my students choose to work in textile design.
✓   I understand how to teach students textile design ideas and a range of related disciplines.
✓   I know how to teach students to gather, research and record relevant information for making textile design work.
✓   I have enough knowledge, experience and understanding of textile design to successfully teach my students.

SCHEME OF WORK

INTRODUCTION

The scheme of work provides a framework for structuring your students' work and enables you to plan ahead with requirements for rooming and materials. It can be adapted to the changing circumstances of your department, but provides a starting point for organising the course.

DESIGN FACTORS

Before designing the course for your school, there are a variety of factors to consider:

1) Facilities

The art subject choices available at your school may be historical but will also be limited by the facilities available. For example:

- Digital facilities are often used heavily in graphic design and photography.
- Photography may benefit from a darkroom.
- Ceramics will require a kiln.
- Screen printing and intaglio require specialist equipment.

There are many other specialist rooms and equipment needed or preferred for different subjects. Rooms can be multi-purpose, but there is a limit to how easily a room can be swapped from one subject to another; a busy ceramics lesson might not leave a room dry and dust-free for a textiles lesson.

2) Teacher specialisms

Each teacher will have their own subject knowledge and skills. The Art & Design subject areas taught should match the skills and abilities of the staff. Staff will also often have skills in areas for which your department does not have facilities. The emphasis of the course you design may lean towards the strengths of the Art Department staff.

3) Location

The location of your school may limit or add to the options available for the course you design.

- Do you have access to outdoor areas for primary observation?
- Are there local galleries to visit?
- Is it easy for students to visit different environments in their free time?

COURSE AIMS

The aim of your course is to deliver the Art & Design syllabus. This covers a wide range of elements and you need to be clear that the essential areas will be covered in the course you design.

1) Introduce concepts and ideas

- Knowledge of artists and analysis of their work
- The synthesis of different ideas
- Collecting and recording primary and secondary resources
- The development process from initial idea to final outcome

2) Introduce materials and techniques

- Relevant subject materials
- Relevant techniques
- Assessment and judgement of which materials to explore further

3) Develop independent thinking

- Students need to develop independent ideas.
- They must be able to show a personal interest.
- They must show a sustained interest.

4) Develop visual understanding

- Through analysing their work
- Applying the elements of art
- Comparing their work to other artists or designers

5) Produce final outcomes for coursework and the externally set assignment with supporting work

- Produce a coherent visual statement

COURSE STRUCTURES

The course has three main sections:

- Part 1: Development of skills and approaches (approximately 90 hours)
- Part 2: Coursework project (approximately 40 hours)
- Part 3: Externally set assignment project

Each section builds on what has gone before.

PART 1	Course introduction

AREAS TO COVER

Several areas need to be introduced in the first part of the course:

Artists	Artists relevant to the broad subject area and the themes and media can be introduced to students. A range of cultures and historical periods should be included. Ways of analysing art including the elements of art are relevant here.
Materials	Students should gain some experience with the main materials they can use for the broad subject area. Students then have the knowledge to decide with which materials they want to develop further skills.
Techniques	Students should also gain experience with the main techniques they will use for the broad subject area. Students then have the knowledge to decide which techniques they want to use to refine their skills.
Concepts	Art themes such as portraiture, landscape and still life can be introduced, together with ways of thinking around open-ended themes. Students studying in design-based subject areas will also need to be introduced to working from design briefs.
Development skills	This is a challenging area for some students and short, guided projects can go a long way to helping them understand this process. Paintings from references and tonal studies help students to see how pieces of work can be connected.
Final outcome	Include final outcomes for some of the shorter-term projects to help students see how supporting work relates to a final piece of work.
Evaluation and assessment	Build in periods to evaluate and assess all work produced. Tutorials and peer group evaluation help students to better understand what they have achieved. Later in the course, the Assessment Objectives can be useful in promoting understanding of the coursework submission.
Externally set assignment paper preparation	Past papers or similar types of starting points can be a valuable exercise in preparing students for the externally set assignment. They can be used as open-ended starting points for shorter projects and help students to understand how to respond to the 'real' test paper.

EXAMPLE FRAMEWORK

There are many ways to design an Art & Design course, but you will need to introduce the concepts and skills that students require slowly so that they can be practised and become knowledge. This early stage is crucial to grounding students in the subject and building confidence. There are different approaches to consider but, in each case, small steps at first will prevent students from being overwhelmed with information, and allow them time to absorb new ways of working. The table below outlines an example framework for the first year of a course.

Unit	Hours	Description	Outcomes
Four short workshop introductions	6 6 6 6	Material- and technique-based projects that introduce themes and artists. For example: • Tonal portraits in charcoal or pencil • Surreal digital collage • Ink and wash urban landscape • Acrylic cubist still life.	• Individual pieces of work • Materials experiments with annotations • Observation and recording • Artist research
Three short projects of increasing length	8 10 12	Longer projects with more emphasis on student research and personal response, for example: • Artist-inspired interior painting • Fantasy character design • Open-ended starting points.	• Observation and recording • Artist research • Exploration of materials • Development of ideas • Small final outcome
Two longer projects	16 18	These projects can be very student-led where possible, but also provide a structure for less independent students. Starting points should be broad, but materials and techniques can be suggested for students still finding a personal direction for their work. For example: • The theme of 'Journey' • The theme of 'Generations'.	These projects should contain all the elements required to fulfil the Assessment Objectives. They are full projects, but may not be as lengthy or of the overall high quality aimed for in the coursework submission.

PART 2	Coursework project

See Part 1 Chapter 1 on page 32 in the SB.

The coursework submission should show students' strengths and build on the ability they have developed during the course. For some students, a personal direction and chosen subject will develop naturally from their previous work. However, many students find it easier to work from a more limited set of objectives. In this case, some open-ended starting points give students something to focus on and also give them practice for the test paper.

When preparing students for the coursework submission project, make the deadlines very clear and design a series of assessment points that will encourage students to get their work completed. If the coursework is completed on time, students will be able to focus fully on their test paper.

PART 3	Externally set assignment project

See Part 1 Chapter 2 on page 62 in the SB.

Before planning the externally set assignment project schedule, confirm suitable dates for the externally set assignment sessions with your school. You can then allocate the preparatory time appropriately from initial ideas to final development studies.

COURSE OUTLINES

In this section, you will find a course outline for each broad subject area:

- Painting and related media
- Printmaking
- Three-dimensional studies
- Photography
- Graphic communication
- Textile design.

These outlines refer to sections of the Teacher's Guide and the Student's Book. The guides are in no way prescriptive but should help you see how a series of activities and themes can be structured to cover the syllabus in the broad subject areas. They might provide a useful starting point for your planning or stimulate a series of totally different projects structured in an alternative way. There is no best way to design a course. Always take into account individual circumstances and student feedback, and adjust your plans accordingly.

The themes and projects outlined here are used to show how a course might be structured. The course you design should be centred on your own skill set, departmental resources and the particular requirements of your students.

STAGE 1: Introductory workshops

This stage consists of teacher-directed tasks to build skills and confidence. Students can focus on exploring materials and how to present their recording and research. Students are more familiar and confident with drawing techniques, so they are a good way to start the course. Following introductory workshops with sustained exercises gives students time to reinforce their learning, and begin to develop their own approaches.

Estimated teaching time	Topic	Suggested teaching activities / guidance	Student's Book and Teacher's Guide references
30 hours	Drawing lessons	• Introduce students to drawing materials and techniques of observation using tonal drawing followed by line drawing, washes and textural drawing. • Demonstrate techniques and show artist examples.	• Student's Book pages 179–187 • Activities: Tone, line, wash, texture • Teacher's Guide pages 91–96
	Drawing: Sustained exercise Still life	• By selecting their own objects for an exercise in chiaroscuro, students begin to select their own sources for observation. • The still life can be arranged with students. This provides an opportunity to discuss composition and views from different parts of the room.	• Student's Book page 180 • Activity: Still-life drawing • Teacher's Guide pages 96–97 • Lesson plan: Project suggestions
	Painting lessons	• Introduction to colour and painting starting with watercolour washes and developing into opaque tempera or acrylics. • Demonstrate techniques and show artist examples.	• Student's Book pages 184–197 • Activities: Colour, line and colour wash, opaque colour • Teacher's Guide pages 100–103
	Painting: Sustained exercise Organic forms	• Reinforce introduction to colour by creating abstracted compositions from observation of shells, bones and drift wood. Observational line drawings can be overlapped to create an abstracted composition for painting inspired by the example artists.	• Artists – Georgia O'Keefe, Paul Klee • Student's Book pages 116, 168-9, 182, 196 • Teacher's Guide pages 126, 130
	Portraits (if time, consolidate work so far with an additional workshop)	• Use photography and drawing to explore proportion and chiaroscuro. Then move into colour with a simple portrait using layers of acrylic paint or watercolour.	• Artists – Peter Blake, Chuck Close, Lucien Freud • Student's Book pages 78–79, 96, 104, 196–197 • Teacher's Guide pages 41, 70, 82, 100

STAGE 2: Short projects

Students have been introduced to materials and techniques, as well as to developing approaches to recording and presenting their work. The next stage of the course builds on this. More emphasis is given to development from personal observation and research.

Estimated teaching time	Topic	AOs	Suggested teaching activities / guidance	Student's Book and Teacher's Guide references
30 hours	Urban landscape	Record	• School buildings, town centre buildings, housing in home area	• Artists – Jeffrey Smart, Edward Hopper • Student's Book pages 84–85, 192–194 • Teacher's Guide page 102
		Explore	• Tonal drawing, paint handling, colour mixing	
		Develop	• Compositions from observed drawings and photographs	
		Outcome	• Colour painting	
	Surreal portraits	Record	• People, faces, objects, places	• Student's Book page 195 • Teacher's Guide page 96
		Explore	• Digital manipulation, collage, drawing	
		Develop	• Surreal combinations of objects, alternative compositions	
		Outcome	• Surreal portrait drawing *	

*This project could be extended to use colour using the student's preferred media. The subject matter can be broader if students are not comfortable with portraiture.

STAGE 3: Sustained projects

Some examples of possible projects are included below. At this stage in the course, students should be developing projects that have a strong personal element. Students may become very involved in a project and extend it to the end of the coursework period rather than doing two projects. Students need to present one coherent project with their portfolio. As students mature and develop their skills, some will be self-directed, while others will benefit from more structured projects initiated by you, the teacher.

Consider presenting a series of words or themes to students as starting points later in the course. This gives the students some practice in developing ideas in a similar way to the externally set assignment, but with useful guidance from you to help guide their focus.

Estimated teaching time	Topic	AOs	Suggested teaching activities / guidance	Student's Book and Teacher's Guide references
70 hours	Emotional portrait	Record	• Observation of friends and family in photography, drawing and painted sketches	• Student's Book pages 191, 194, 196–197 • Activity: Emotional portraits • Teacher's Guide page 102 • Lesson plan: Project suggestions
		Explore	• Coloured ink techniques, painting techniques	
		Develop	• Expressive face studies, colour palettes related to emotions	
		Outcome	• Colour painting	
	Bedroom	Record	• Students' homes can provide a sound basis for observation. The theme can be expanded to include different artists and rooms in the house.	• Student's Book page 189 • Activity: Bedroom painting • Teacher's Guide pages 96–97, 99, 102 • Lesson plan: Project suggestions
		Explore	• Digital manipulation, collage, drawing	
		Develop	• Surreal combinations of objects, alternative compositions	
		Outcome	• Surreal portrait drawing *	

The themes and projects outlined here are used to show how a course might be structured. The course you design should be centred on your own skill set, departmental resources and the particular requirements of your students.

STAGE 1: Introductory workshops

New skills and techniques are introduced during the technical lessons. These lessons allow students the chance to experiment and understand the process through demonstration, before being given a series of simple tasks to complete. It is important for students to keep the proofs from these sessions, and record and analyse their progress as close to the event as possible.

Estimated teaching time	Topic	Suggested teaching activities / guidance	Student's Book and Teacher's Guide references
4–5 hours per session	Technical lesson: Monoprinting	• Introduce students to the process of monoprinting. • Show the students some examples of monoprinting from Pinterest to give them an idea of how the process looks. • Set up your classroom for a very simple day of testing monoprinting techniques. • Explore the following techniques: Rolling up the plate Tracing images Experimenting with mark-making Wiping away Playing with different materials to print from, such as feathers, leaves, yarns, lace or nets. • Keep the prints to reflect on at the end of the session.	• Student's Book pages 204–207 • Teacher's Guide pages 130–133 *Use Pinterest for current examples of how artists use monoprinting in their own practice.*
	Technical lesson: Relief printing	• Introduce students to the process of relief printing. • Show the students some examples of relief printing from Pinterest to give them an idea of how the process looks. • Set up your classroom for a very simple day of testing relief-printing techniques. • Explore the process of relief printing and the different materials with which to print: Lino Wood Cardboard Foam board Erasers • Introduce the students to cutting tools and give them a series of prompts to follow. • Print the blocks and keep the proofs to reflect on at the end of the session.	• Student's Book pages 208–211 • Teacher's Guide pages 134–137 *Use Pinterest for current examples of how artists use relief printing in their own practice.*

	Technical lesson: Intaglio printing (etching)	• Introduce students to the process of intaglio printing. • Show the students some examples of intaglio printing from Pinterest to give them an idea of how the process looks. • Explore intaglio printing by producing a number of drypoint prints using acetate. • This session can be used to experiment with mark-making, inking up and printing the plate. • Keep the proofs to reflect on at the end of the session.	• Student's Book pages 212–215 • Teacher's Guide pages 138–141 *Use Pinterest for current examples of how artists use intaglio printing in their own practice.*
	Technical session: Screen printing	• Introduce students to the process of screen printing. • Show the students some examples of screen printing on Pinterest to give them an idea of how the process looks. • Explore screen printing by cutting simple stencil shapes and printing them (see Student's Book pages 216–217). • Encourage the students to cut letters and make up words to reinforce the understanding that screen printing is one of the few methods of printmaking that does not print in reverse. • Keep the proofs to reflect on at the end of the session.	• Student's Book pages 216–219 • Teacher's Guide pages 142–145 *Use Pinterest for current examples of how artists use screen printing in their own practice.*

STAGE 2: Short projects

Students have now been introduced to the tools, theory and process of printmaking. They should also have a record of their proofs, together with their reflection and evaluation notes on them. The short projects below are designed for students to practise their new skills, using the appropriate techniques for their work, and to become confident in managing an assignment brief.

Estimated teaching time	Topic	AOs	Suggested teaching activities / guidance	Student's Book and Teacher's Guide reference
10 hours	Monoprinting	Record	**Primary research** • Take some photographs to create a strong sense of light and shade. • Develop drawing using charcoal or soft pencil. • Develop a series of sketches which are quick and linear. • Try to keep the theme similar to give a sense of connection in the work produced.	• Student's Book pages 204–207 • Teacher's Guide pages 130–133
		Explore	**Secondary research** • Print out your photographs, blow up and edit sections you like. Review your work. Select the stronger drawn images you think would work as a print.	
		Develop	• Produce a series of monoprints using your body of work. • Trace and copy your photographs and drawings using cloths, your fingers, pens and pencils. • Review, reflect and evaluate the work you produce.	
		Outcome	• Series of proofs and final set of prints	
	Relief printing	Record	**Primary research** • Draw and photograph images, and select strong images from newspapers.	• Student's Book pages 208–211 • Teacher's Guide pages 134–137
		Explore	**Secondary research** • Review the work selected. Photocopy any coloured images into black and white. Crop and blow up images and select sections which have strong colour contrast and interesting mark-making or pattern.	
		Develop	• Cut and print the series of relief prints. • Concentrate on the pattern, then experiment with overprinting different colours.	
		Outcome	• Series of proofs and final set of prints.	

	Intaglio (etching)	Record	**Primary research** • Produce a series of drawings and photographs that have a strong linear quality. • Look at the etchings of Käthe Kollwitz for inspiration.	• Student's Book pages 212–215 • Teacher's Guide pages 138–141
		Explore	**Secondary research** • Review your photographs and drawings. Select the work you think will work in a drypoint or etching.	
		Develop	• Produce a set of drypoints of etchings. Concentrating on the line and composition of the plate. The drawing has to be accurate as the printed reversed image will emphasise any part of the drawing which is out of proportion or wrong perspective.	
10 hours		Outcome	• Series of proofs and final set of prints	
	Screen printing	Record	**Primary research** • Look at the work of Sister Corita Kent and her use of text in her work. Photograph, draw and copy text you find interesting from your surroundings. Look at advertising, street signs, graffiti, newspaper headlines.	• Student's Book pages 216–219 • Teacher's Guide pages 142–145
		Explore	**Secondary research** • Print out photographs and review all collected work, drawings and newspapers. Sort through what you find inspiring and select words, phrases, typefaces and letters that you enjoy.	
		Develop	• Play with colour. Blow up letters. Make words, sentences and new words. Link words and phrases with colour. • Use your developed research to produce a series of stencils with which to print.	
		Outcome	• Series of proofs and final set of prints.	

STAGE 3: Sustained projects

Some examples of possible projects are included below. At this stage in the course, students should be developing projects that have a strong personal element. Students may become very involved in a project and extend it to the end of the coursework period rather than doing two projects. Students need to present one coherent project with their portfolio. As students mature and develop their skills, some will be self-directed, while others will benefit from more structured projects initiated by you, the teacher.

Estimated teaching time	Topic	AOs	Suggested teaching activities / guidance	Student's Book and Teacher's Guide reference

70 hours	Monoprint	Record Explore Develop Outcome	• Examples of inspirational images appropriate to monoprinting:
			  Figurative
			  Light and dark
			  Urban landscape
			  Skyline
			  Outline
			  Organic form
			  Texture
			  Narrative
			  Mapping
			  Text
			• All the above themes could be used to produce a set of monoprints, but it is how the theme is used that is important: the image selection, the idea development and the type of printing technique applied.
			• All these stages need to be considered and reflected on.
				• Student's Book pages 204–207
				• Teacher's Guide pages 130–133

	Relief print	Record Explore Develop Outcome	• Examples of inspirational images appropriate to relief printing:
			  Figurative
			  Light and dark
			  Urban landscape
			  Skyline
			  Outline
			  Organic form
			  Texture
			  Narrative
			  Mapping
			  Text
			• All the above themes could be used to produce a set of relief prints, but it is how the theme is used that is important: the image selection, the idea development and the type of printing technique applied.
			• All these stages need to be considered and reflected on.
				• Student's Book pages 208–211
				• Teacher's Guide pages 134–137

Intaglio (etching)	Record Explore Develop Outcome	• Examples of inspirational images appropriate to intaglio printing: Figurative Light and dark Urban landscape Skyline Outline Organic form Texture Narrative Mapping Text • All the above themes could be used to produce a set of intaglio prints, but it is how the theme is used that is important: the image selection, the idea development and the type of printing technique applied. • All these stages need to be considered and reflected on.	• Student's Book pages 212–215 • Teacher's Guide pages 138–141
Screen print	Record Explore Develop Outcome	• Examples of inspirational images appropriate to screen printing: Figurative Light and dark Urban landscape Skyline Outline Organic form Texture Narrative Mapping Text • All the above themes could be used to produce a set of screen prints, but it is how the theme is used that is important: the image selection, the idea development and the type of printing technique applied. • All these stages need to be considered and reflected on.	• Student's Book pages 216–219 • Teacher's Guide pages 142–145

Chapter 10 — Three-dimensional studies

The themes and projects outlined here are used to show how a course might be structured. The course you design should be centred on your own skill set, departmental resources and the particular requirements of your students.

STAGE 1: Introductory workshops

Start by focusing on teacher-directed tasks to develop skills in handling materials safely and with confidence. Students can focus on exploring relevant materials and techniques and on recording the progress of 3-D work in stages. Introductory workshops aim to give students a basic understanding of techniques and processes on which they can build later. The Stage 2 short projects can be introduced at any appropriate point to reinforce previous workshops before moving on to new workshops with a different technique, material or focus.

Estimated teaching time	Topic	Suggested teaching activities / guidance		Student's Book and Teacher's Guide references
Throughout the workshops 7–8 hours	Recording and documenting 3-D form	• Give students opportunities to observe items such as 3-D artefacts, designs and models as appropriate to your course. Allow students to record their observations with methods such as drawing, photography and written analysis. • Ask students to photograph all relevant stages of making for any 3-D processes that they try. • Show students examples of technical notes and annotation relevant to the materials and techniques with which they are working. Ask students to present their own technical notes with images as appropriate to the workshops.		• Student's Book pages 222–223 • Teacher's Guide pages 149–150
	Sculpture	• Introduce students to a variety of possible sculptural materials. Show relevant examples of sculpture. • Examine the properties, qualities and possibilities of each material. • Demonstrate relevant techniques and processes such as carving, modelling and casting. • Allow students to make samples using a range of techniques.		• Student's Book pages 224–225 • Teacher's Guide pages 151–154
	Ceramics	• Introduce students to making and what it is like to work with clay. • Demonstrate relevant techniques such as pinching, coiling, slab building and slip casting. • Allow students to make samples using a range of techniques.	Ceramic surfaces and decoration: • Explain the processes of drying and firing clay. • Introduce students to glaze, using oxides, using decorating slip, using decals. • Allow students to make samples using a range of techniques.	• Student's Book pages 226–229 • Teacher's Guide pages 151–154

	Design-based topics	Product and craft design: • Introduce students to possible materials and techniques for product or craft design such as working with glass, wood, metal, plastics or papier mâché, wire. • Examine the properties, qualities and possibilities of each material. • Allow students to make samples using a range of materials.	Architectural and environmental design: • Introduce students to model-making, scale drawing and digital software appropriate to spatial design. • Make links as appropriate to relevant skills learnt in other areas of art and design such as papier mâché as a possible techniques for mask-making or textile skills for costume design. • Allow students to practise techniques or make test work as appropriate.	• Student's Book pages 238–247 • Teacher's Guide pages 165–172

STAGE 2: Short projects

Once students have been introduced to materials and techniques, as well as developing recording skills specific to 3-D processes, this stage builds on this with short technical or research projects. More emphasis is given to personal development and research. A technical project could be completed in lessons with the easier availability of materials, tools and equipment, while a research project can be completed as a series of homework tasks.

Estimated teaching time	Topic	AOs	Suggested teaching activities / guidance	Student's Book and Teacher's Guide references
20 hours	**Example of a technical project:** Ceramic slab-work (*this can be adapted for many different 3-D techniques*)	Record	• Examples of slab-built ceramics both historical and contemporary and across cultures.	• Student's Book pages 226–229 • Teacher's Guide pages 151–154
		Explore	• Roll out clay to make flat slabs. Experiment with how to cut, shape and bend slabs and how to join slabs together using slip.	
		Develop	• Sketch alternative designs for a slab pot or sculptural form made from slabs informed by researched examples.	
		Outcome	• Make a final outcome in clay using slab-building techniques.	
	Example of a research project: Sculpture (*this can be adapted for many other research topics appropriate to 3-D studies*)	Record	• Examples of sculpture both historical and contemporary and across cultures. Personal reflection and evaluation of the sculptures presented.	• Student's Book pages 224–225 • Teacher's Guide pages 151–154
		Explore	• Experiment with methods of presenting research using both digital and handmade techniques.	
		Develop	• Refine presentation skills to enhance and complement the content of the research.	
		Outcome	• A PowerPoint, mood board, slideshow or other appropriate method of research presentation on sculpture.	

STAGE 3: Sustained projects

Some examples of possible projects are included below. At this stage in the course, students should be developing projects that have a strong personal element. Students may become very involved in a project and extend it to the end of the coursework period rather than doing two projects. Students need to present one coherent project with their portfolio. As students mature and develop their skills, some will be self-directed, while others will benefit from more structured projects initiated by you, the teacher. Consider presenting a series of words or themes to students as starting points to focus their work (please refer to the Student's Book and Teacher's Guide for possible themes and starting points). This gives the student some practice in developing ideas in a similar way to the externally set assignment, but with useful guidance from the teacher to help support their focus.

Estimated teaching time	Topic	AO	Suggested teaching activities / guidance	Student's Book and Teacher's Guide references
70 hours	Sculpture	Record	• A wide range of examples of traditional methods and new technologies with a focus on space, mass and volume. Visit a museum or gallery to sketch and photograph. Relevant visual inspiration from a range of secondary sources.	• Student's Book pages 224–225 • Teacher's Guide pages 155–156
		Explore	• One or two specific materials and techniques explored in more depth. Make further samples and test out ideas.	
		Develop	• Sketch alternative ideas informed by research, exploration and evaluation.	
		Outcome	• A completed sculpture or series of sculptures photographed from a range of viewpoints.	
	Ceramics	Record	• Examples of inspirational images. Examples of methods for making and decorating ceramics.	• Student's Book pages 226–229 • Teacher's Guide pages 155–156
		Explore	• One or more making techniques in depth. Making alternative possibilities and refining ideas and skills. Try out various methods of decoration.	
		Develop	• Design drawings focusing on functional or decorative form informed by research and an awareness of aesthetics and some historical and cultural knowledge.	
		Outcome	• Finished ceramic sculpture or a functional or decorative ceramic outcome.	

	Theatre and set design and environmental and architectural design	Record	• Examples of inspirational spaces, environments or designs for performance.	• Student's Book pages 232–237 • Teacher's Guide pages 157–161
		Explore	• Photographs, digital work, models and scale drawings to help explore ideas.	
		Develop	• Awareness of role, function, location and audience.	
		Outcome	• A final 3-D model or digital final designs.	
	Product or craft design	Record	• Drawings and photographs of inspirational products or craft design. Insights into problem-solving and designing to a brief.	Student's Book pages 238–247 Teacher's Guide pages 165–172
		Explore	• Processes and techniques, domestic and industrial. Use of technology in the design industry and the possibilities of functional or decorative outcomes.	
		Develop	• Solve problems and try out alternative ideas related to the initial brief or problem.	
		Outcome	• A design solution that solves a problem or fulfils a design brief.	

Chapter 11 — Photography, digital and lens-based media

The technical lessons and project ideas outlined here are used to show how a course might be structured. The course you design should be centred on your own skill set, departmental resources and the particular requirements of your students. It is recommended that you regularly revisit the technical sessions in order to boost students' confidence and cement new knowledge.

STAGE 1: Introductory workshops

New skills and techniques are introduced during the technical lessons. You may want to sequence a few technical lessons and then set a mini project for students to test their new skills. It is not advised that students complete all of the technical lessons in one block, as they are unlikely to retain all of the information and they will need time to become confident with their new skills. Students need to record and analyse their progress during the technical sessions, as well as during sustained projects.

Estimated teaching time	Topic	Suggested teaching activities / guidance	Student's Book and Teacher's Guide references
3–4 hours per session	Technical lesson: Camera controls	• Introduce students to a manual DSLR camera. Cover aperture, shutter ISO and general handling of a camera. You may wish to also cover downloading of images, saving images and producing contact sheets.	• Student's Book pages 252–254 • Teacher's Guide pages 178–179
	Technical lesson: Composition	• Introduce students to photographic composition. Deconstruct photographs and discuss compositional rules, set compositional challenges. Extension activity, recreate a famous photograph.	• Student's Book page 255 • Teacher's Guide pages 180–181
	Technical lesson: Natural lighting	• Introduction to natural lighting. Experiment with natural lighting techniques and portraiture. Use a variety of lighting situations and reflectors to create a range of portraits. Extension activity, experiment with still-life objects and natural lighting.	• Student's Book page 255 • Teacher's Guide pages 182–183
	Technical lesson: Artificial lighting	• Introduction to artificial lighting. Experiment with artificial lighting techniques and portraiture. Use a variety of lighting situations and reflectors to create a range of portraits. Extension activity, experiment with still-life objects and artificial lighting.	• Student's Book page 255 • Teacher's Guide pages 182–183
	Technical session: Editing and printing	• Basic introduction to your school's editing software (Adobe Photoshop preferable). Introduce the basic tools to edit and resize an image ready to print. Print the images to exhibit in class.	• Student's Book pages 256–260 • Teacher's Guide page 185
	Technical session: Deconstructing films	• Introduce students to the elements of film-making through deconstructing a short film.	• Student's Book pages 261 • Teacher's Guide pages 186–187
	Technical session: Planning a film	• Take students through the steps of planning and making a short film. This should form the start of a sustained project.	• Student's Book pages 262–263 • Teacher's Guide pages 188–189

	Technical session: Shooting a film	• Show students the basics of shooting a film, as well as downloading and saving footage.	• Student's Book pages 262–263 • Teacher's Guide pages 188–189
	Technical session: Editing a film	• Show students the basics of using the school's editing software (Adobe Premier advised).	• Student's Book page 264 • Teacher's Guide page 185

STAGE 2: Short projects

Students have been introduced to the equipment, theory and techniques, as well as developing approaches to recording and presenting their work. Short projects are designed for students to practise their new skills and become confident in managing an assignment brief.

Estimated teaching time	Topic	AOs	Suggested teaching activities / guidance	Student's Book and Teacher's Guide references
30 hours	A different viewpoint	Record	• School buildings, local environment, home environment.	• Artists: Edward Weston Paul Strand Tokihiro Sato Andreas Gursky William Eggleston Uta Barth Paul Outerbridge • Student's Book pages 252–260 • Teacher's Guide pages 178–185
		Explore	• Composition, point of view, aperture, shutter speed, lighting, editing, printing.	
		Develop	• Explore chosen theme in a variety of locations, test shoot and revisit regularly, develop a style of editing to suit the theme and images.	
		Outcome	• Series of edited and printed photographs.	
	Portraits	Record	• People and associated objects.	• Artists: Seydou Keïta Steve McCurry Annie Leibovitz • Student's Book pages 252–260 • Teacher's Guide pages 178–185
		Explore	• Composition, point of view, aperture, shutter speed, lighting, editing, printing.	
		Develop	• Explore chosen theme in a variety of locations, test shoot and revisit regularly, develop a style of editing to suit the theme and images.	
		Outcome	• Series of edited and printed photographs.	

STAGE 3: Sustained projects

Some examples of possible projects are included below. At this stage in the course, students should be developing projects that have a strong personal element. Students may become very involved in a project and extend it to the end of the coursework period rather that doing two projects. Students need to present one coherent project with their portfolio. As students mature and develop their skills, some will be self-directed, while others will benefit from more structured projects initiated by you, the teacher.

Consider presenting a series of words or themes to students as starting points later in the course. This gives the students some practice in developing ideas in a similar way to the externally set assignment, but with useful guidance from you to help guide their focus.

Estimated teaching time	Topic	AOs	Suggested teaching activities / guidance	Student's Book and Teacher's Guide reference
70 hours	Inside outside	Record	• Exploration of the environment and objects, relevant research and documentation.	• Student's Book pages 252–260 • Teacher's Guide pages 178–185
		Explore	• Camera and lighting techniques, compositional techniques, editing techniques, documentation and analysis of the project.	
		Develop	• Multiple test shoots exploring and refining ideas, contact sheets, further research leading to the development of ideas, editing, improving techniques and camera skills.	
		Outcome	• A series of printed images.	
	My town	Record	• Exploration of the local environment, relevant research, planning and documentation.	• Student's Book pages 252–260 • Teacher's Guide pages 178–185
		Explore	• Camera and lighting techniques, compositional techniques, editing techniques, documentation and analysis of the project.	
		Develop	• Multiple test shoots exploring and refining ideas, contact sheets, further research leading to the development of ideas, editing, improving techniques and camera skills.	
		Outcome	• A series of printed images.	

The sequence of lessons outlined here is used to show how a course might be structured. The course you design should be centred on your own skill set, departmental resources and the particular requirements of your students. Many of the elements introduced in this section could be developed into sustained projects or technical lessons if you feel your students would benefit from them.

STAGE 1: Introductory workshops

The introductory workshops are designed to help students explore new skills and techniques. Skills should be reflected on and supported with relevant research. You may wish to spend time revisiting and improving skills sessions to embed knowledge and refine techniques.

Estimated teaching time	Topic	Suggested teaching activities / guidance	Student's Book and Teacher's Guide references
4–5 hours per session	Photomontage, collage, found image	• Before the first lesson, set a topic for research that can stimulate in-class discussion. Students develop photomontages of found images and collage materials to create compositions that convey the ideas generated at the start of the lesson.	• Student's Book pages 274–275 • Teacher's Guide pages 201–202
	Typography, typefaces, fonts, pictograms	• Experiment with fonts and typefaces: both digital and hand drawn. • Students should commit to their best idea and stick the image elements down into a completed photomontage. Work should be documented throughout the process.	• Student's Book pages 270–273 • Teacher's Guide pages 196–200
	Found images: Consider the use of found images for reference and for their own sake. As part of an artwork, develop students' appreciation of how image composition can be manipulated to aid story telling.	• Use found images as a quick way to explore composition, record each composition using a digital camera, and discuss the composition through analytical writing. Develop one composition as a final outcome.	• Student's Book pages 274–275 • Teacher's Guide pages 201–202
	Pictograms	• Explore pictograms and apply them to a real-life scenario. Use the techniques available in your school. A live brief will add purpose to this session.	• Student's Book pages 272–273 • Teacher's Guide pages 199–200
	Illustration	• This project uses observational drawing as a starting point for making illustrations suitable for a cookery book. As part of a broader graphic communication scheme of work, the images generated might also be used in subsequent packaging and advertising projects.	• Student's Book pages 274–279 • Teacher's Guide pages 201–203
	Game design – create a 3-D character	• An avatar or 'second life' personality can be created as an introductory activity for game design. Use various techniques available to create an avatar for an existing game.	• Student's Book pages 286–287 • Teacher's Guide pages 209–210

STAGE 2: Short projects

Graphic design depends on project briefs and clients. It may be worthwhile seeking some client briefs from other departments in your school or your wider community.

Estimated teaching time	Topic	AOs	Suggested Teaching Activities / Guidance	Student's Book and Teacher's Guide reference
30 hours	Food advertising or a designed spread suitable for a cookery book.	Record	• Research into advertising and cookery books, record observational drawings and ideas.	• Student's Book pages 274–279 • Teacher's Guide pages 201–203
		Explore	• Composition, materials, ideas, research.	
		Develop	• Revisit ideas and test pieces regularly, and develop a method of working to suit the theme and ideas. Refine techniques and processes leading to a final outcome.	
		Outcome	• Series or single spread suitable for a cookery book or standalone advert.	
	Avatar	Record	• Research into avatars and games characters, record observational drawings and ideas.	• Student's Book pages 286–287 • Teacher's Guide pages 209–210
		Explore	• Explore different methods of designing and developing an avatar. This should be informed by research.	
		Develop	• Refine early experimental pieces and investigate how to improve techniques and clarify ideas. This developmental work should be fully documented.	
		Outcome	• A developed avatar suitable for a game scenario.	

STAGE 3: Sustained projects

Students should, at this stage of their course, be independent and confident in their chosen projects. You may need to scaffold students' documentation and facilitate opportunities for them to meet mini deadlines and presentations.

Estimated teaching time	Topic	AOs	Suggested teaching activities / guidance	Student's Book and Teacher's Guide reference
70 hours	Client brief set by another school department or local business	Record	• Exploration of the client brief through relevant research and documentation.	• Student's Book pages 170–285 • Teacher's Guide pages 196–208
		Explore	• A variety of techniques and processes suited to the client's brief and initial ideas.	
		Develop	• Multiple test pieces into refined pieces suitable to meet the client's needs.	
		Outcome	• A piece of work that the client can use to meet their needs.	

The themes and projects outlined here are used to show how a course might be structured. The course you design should be centred on your own skill set, departmental resources and the particular requirements of your students.

STAGE 1: Introductory workshops

This stage consists of teacher-directed tasks to build skills and confidence. Students can focus on exploring materials and how to present their recording and research. As a foundation for the creative design process, it is recommended that students begin with a clear understanding of the properties of a wide range of textiles. Following introductory workshops with sustained exercises gives students time to reinforce their learning, and begin to develop their own approaches.

Estimated teaching time	Topic	Suggested teaching activities / guidance	Student's Book and Teacher's Guide references
3–4 hours per session	Identify fibres, yarns and fabrics	• Introduce students to a wide range of fibres, yarns and fabrics. • Examine suitability and fit-for-purpose and encourage students to suggest uses. • Examine wash care labels and discuss their importance. • Demonstrate a simple burn test.	• Activity: Identify labels • Activity: Displaying swatches of fibres, yarns and fabrics • Student's Book pages 294–295 • Teacher's Guide pages 222–223
	Setting a brief Themes and research Mind-maps	• Discuss with students the importance of setting and following a brief. Show students how to work to a theme and how to select and analyse information. • Display mind-maps to students and help them select appropriate information or images.	• Activity: Setting a brief; themes. • Activity: Designing a mood board • Link: Future projects – setting a brief • Student's Book pages 298–300 • Teacher's Guide pages 227–230
	Construction techniques Traditional and contemporary materials for weaving Traditional and contemporary materials for other techniques	• Introduce students to diverse ways of constructing fabrics. • Demonstrate how to make a simple weaving loom and construct a sample. • Introduce other construction techniques including knitting, crocheting and so on. • Discuss with students many different fibres and materials that can be used when producing fabrics.	• Activity: Researching weaving looms • Activity: Plain weaving sample • Activity: Making samples using other techniques (could be homework) • Student's Book pages 298–301 • Teacher's Guide pages 220–221

	Joining fabrics Draping qualities of fabric Design features/details	• Discuss and demonstrate ways of joining fabrics with stitch, embroidery, lacing, bonding and so on. • Demonstrate how different fabrics drape/handle on a mannequin. • Discuss design features and show designer examples. • Introduce students to applique and other ways of embellishing fabric.	• Activity: Draping on mannequin • Student's Book pages 295–297 • Teacher's Guide pages 225–228
	Dyeing fabrics Tie and dye Batik dyeing	• Discuss cold and hot water dyeing and range of methods. • Demonstrate tie-dye. • Demonstrate batik dyeing.	• Activity: Tie-dye • Activity: Batik dyeing • Student's Book pages 292–293 • Teacher's Guide pages 220–221
	Printing fabrics Silk screen printing Block making and printing	• Introduce silkscreen printing. Demonstrate how to make screen. • Introduce block printing. Demonstrate how to make printing block.	• Activity: Screen printing • Activity: Making printing blocks • Student's Book page 291 • Teacher's Guide pages 218–219
	Discharge printing Flock printing	• Demonstrate on different qualities of fabrics. • Discuss flock printing; students collect samples for sketchbook.	• Activity: Discharge print • Activity: Sketchbook and research project • Student's Book page 291 • Teacher's Guide pages 218–219
	Painting fabrics Silk painting	• Introduce a range of materials, for example fabric paints, painting pens. Demonstrate silk painting	• Activity: Prepare fabric for painting and demonstrate technique • Activity: Silk painting • Student's Book page 292 • Teacher's Guide pages 220–221

STAGE 2: Short projects

Students have been introduced to materials and techniques, as well as to developing approaches to recording and presenting their work. The next stage of the course builds on this. More emphasis is given to development from personal observation and research.

Estimated teaching time	Topic	AOs	Suggested Teaching Activities / Guidance	Student's Book and Teacher's Guide references
30 hours	Research project: Flock printing	Record	• Range of flock printing samples, fabrics, wallpapers, books and so on.	• Student's Book page 291 • Teacher's Guide pages 218–219
		Explore	• Ancient and modern methods of creating flock printing.	
		Develop	• Links with other areas of art and design.	
		Outcome	• Portfolio and range of sample piece, commercial and handmade.	
	Research project: Art, design and inspiration	Record	• Examples of ancient and modern textiles and visual communication.	• Student's Book pages 292–301 • Teacher's Guide pages 220–221
		Explore	• Work of textile artists and links with other areas of art and design. Museums and galleries.	
		Develop	• An understanding and appreciation of global production and uses of textiles.	
		Outcome	• Portfolio of inspiration for modern textiles – historical, contemporary, cultural, social.	

STAGE 3: Sustained projects

Some examples of possible projects are included below. At this stage in the course, students should be developing projects that have a strong personal element. Students may become very involved in a project and extend it to the end of the coursework period rather than doing two projects. Students need to present one coherent project with their portfolio. As students mature and develop their skills, some will be self-directed, while others will benefit from more structured projects initiated by you, the teacher.

Students should develop their own designs and although there are many overlaps in the course content, their final project should be from one specialism only. Consider presenting a series of words or themes to students as starting points later in the course.

Estimated teaching time	Topic	AO	Suggested teaching activities / guidance	Student's Book and Teacher's Guide references
70 hours	Constructed textiles	Record	• Fibres and fabrics used for textile production. Examples of traditional methods and new technologies.	• Activity: Exploring global uses of textiles; visual communication • Lesson plan: Identifying fabric properties and applications • Student's Book pages 294–297 • Teacher's Guide pages 222–226
		Explore	• Fabrics and dyeing processes used in fashion industry laser printing, *devoré*.	
		Develop	• Knowledge and skills in different techniques.	
		Outcome	• Portfolio or single completed item of individual design.	
	Fashion	Record	• Examples of inspirational images. Examples of fabrics, accessories and body adornment.	• Activity: Fashion design, garment construction. • Lesson plan: Working to theme, planning a brief • Student's Book pages 298–303 • Teacher's Guide pages 227–230
		Explore	• Historical, contemporary, cultural and social influences on fashion. Uses of modern and new technologies, and range of appropriate techniques.	
		Develop	• Design drawings, building a collection, decorative samples, design on mannequin. An awareness of fashion industry, textile design and fashion.	
		Outcome	• Finished garment or portfolio of original and individual designs.	
	Printed and/or dyed textiles	Record	• Examples of printed and dyed fabrics. Process for applying colour. Range of media, examples of small and large-scale productions.	• Lesson plan: Working to a theme, influences and fashion • Student's Book pages 290–293 • Teacher's Guide pages 218–221
		Explore	• Processes and techniques, domestic and industrial. Use of technology in the textile industry and the relationship between textiles and fashion.	
		Develop	• Knowledge and skills in different techniques like spraying, digital printing.	
		Outcome	• Portfolio of a range of processes, images and samples or single item of individual design.	

Cambridge International course terms

externally set assignment   this is the 8-hour test that students will sit at the end of their course

final outcome   this can refer to either the student's final work in their coursework project (A2 size), or the final piece that they create across the externally set assignment (A2 size)

portfolio   this is the material that students supply alongside their final outcome to support their coursework submission. It should be no more than four pages (eight sides) of A2

starting point   students will be presented with a range of starting points on their externally set assignment paper and must choose one to respond to in their final outcome

supporting studies   these are the supporting materials that students can take with them into the externally set assignment and which they will submit alongside their final outcome. They should be no more than two pages (four sides) of A2

theme   all coursework projects start with a theme, which may be set by you (as the teacher), the examining board or the student

A

abstract   a style of art where most things are not realistic or recognisable as something

acrylic   a plastic paint that mixes with water, but is water-proof when dry

aperture   the variable space inside of the lens that allows light into the camera

avatar   an image used to represent a person

B

bias   45 degrees across the grain of a woven fabric

bleed   in printing, this is ink that goes beyond the edge of where a sheet will be trimmed

block   a customised pattern

brush load   the amount of paint on a brush; too little creates a dry mark; too much, can drip or flood

C

CAD   computer-aided design

carding   the process of combing fibres

catwalk   a long stage walked by models during a fashion show

chiaroscuro   Italian artistic term for the contrast of light and dark

codes   signs in a film that create meaning for an audience; technical codes are how camera equipment is used to tell a story (for example, a shot of a scary character in a film would generally be shot from a low angle to make them seem more menacing); symbolic codes are used to communicate feelings (for example, a big close-up shot of a face and scary music can communicate fear)

coiling   rolling clay into long lengths like rope and wrapping or winding them together to form a design

collage   paper, photographs and/or fabric pasted onto a supporting surface

collection   a series of themed garments

colour wheel   relationship of primary and secondary colours in a circular diagram

colourfast   a colour that doesn't fade or wash out

complementary colours   opposite colours in colour wheel such as red and green

composition   the placement or arrangement of visual elements in a work of art

concept   an abstract idea or plan

constructive   adding to a material to build and shape it

conventions   elements generally expected from a particular genre of film, for example: in a horror film, you would expect to see dramatic lighting to create moody scenes and scary music

D

darts   stitched folds that shape a garment

deconstruct   to change the original material to create something new or different

decorative   no specific use other than being visually attractive

drape   the way a fabric hangs

drypoint   a technique used to draw into a soft surface using a sharp pointed needle or etching tool

E

editing cutting film footage to put shots into a coherent sequence

edition the total number of copies of a print

emulsion water-based paint

etching press a press made up of two polished steel rollers sitting on top of a metal bed, which are operated by a handle

exposure the amount of light that reaches the film or electronic sensor; how light or dark a picture is

F

fibres strands from which textiles are formed

first proof a print taken during the printmaking process to check the current state of the image while still being worked on by the artist

flash card a card with a few facts used to help with learning and remembering

flood the screen when you coat the top of the screen with ink without printing, which loads the image up with ink and stops the mesh drying out

font a set of text characters with the same size and style used in printing

form the shape and volume

found image existing images that are used to create a new artwork

free-motion stitching freehand darning or drawing on the sewing machine

functional useful, with a particular purpose or role

fusible webbing adhesive that melts when heated

G

gouge tool a hand chisel with a number of blades used to cut into different surfaces

grain the direction of the warp and weft fabrics

graphic design the process of visual communication and problem-solving using typography, photography and illustration

ground a waxy substance that covers and protects the printing plate and resists the corrosive liquid

gutta a latex substance

H

hand dry sheets of sized paper are placed on a flat surface and pressure is applied by rubbing a smooth, hard object across the surface of the paper

handle the feel of a fabric

harmonious colours colours next to each other in the colour wheel such as 'yellow, green, blue'

haute couture French for 'high fashion'; one-off designs produced by fashion houses

heavy gauge waxy paper best for cutting stencils used for screen printing

I

impasto thick paint that dries with a texture

ink up intaglio ink is applied to a plate and worked into the etched or cut surface; the surface is then carefully wiped away using scrim and tissue paper, leaving only the etched lines to print from

intaglio meaning 'to carve'; an intaglio print is the opposite of a relief print

ISO in traditional film photography, ISO refers to the sensitivity of the film to light; in digital photography, it refers to how sensitive your image sensor is to light

iterative step-by-step changes to improve a design

K

kinetic involving movement

L

lighting the use of natural and artificial light to create a specific effect or an particular atmosphere

loom a tool for weaving

lustre shine or gloss

M

maquette a small practice model

mid-tone the tonal value half-way between light and dark

monotype a one-off print made by painting ink or oil paint straight onto a plate, then pressing paper on the image

mood board a collection of imagery to inform a design

mordant a chemical that fixes the dye

motif a single image in a design

mould an object usually made of wood, plastic or plaster to hold the clay in a particular shape while it dries and stiffens; to press a material into a specific form or shape

N

nylon a flexible and strong artificial fibre

O

oil-based   ink or paint that requires a solvent to mix or clean it, such as white spirit, turpentine or methylated spirits

oil paint   paint that needs a solvent to mix with, and takes a long time to dry

opaque   solid; cannot be seen through

P

photographic film   film made of transparent plastic, with an emulsion of light-sensitive silver gelatin on one side

photomontage   a digital or handmade method of layering one or more images together to create a new image

pictogram   a pictorial symbol for a word or phrase

pigment   a substance used to give colour

pile   a raised fabric surface or nap

pinching   shaping the clay into a design by pressing with your thumb and fingers

plate   a surface made of acrylic glass, plastic, acetate, wood or aluminium on which to work to produce a print (the size of the plate will determine the size of the print)

positive and negative   contrasting empty and filled space

pret-à-porter   French for 'ready to wear' collections

primary   colours that cannot be mixed, namely red, yellow and blue

printing   the process used to transfer images or designs onto paper or material, or other substances

printing press   a hand-operated machine for printing on paper or fabric

proof   a print taken in the printmaking process sometimes called a trial impression

R

reductive   shaping a material by removing parts of it

reflectors   pieces of equipment used to bounce light into a shot, for example, to soften shadows on a face

registration mark   a mark used with printing to help ensure that the print is aligned properly

relief print   produced by cutting into a flat surface made from wood or linoleum using a gouge tool; the print is a negative image of what is cut away

trends   changes or crazes

representational   a style of art in which people and things are shown in a realistic way

rote learning   memorising information through continuous repetition

S

scale   the size of something

scribe   drawing tool often made of metal

scrim   a light gauze material made from cotton

script   the written text of a film or play

seams   a join of two fabrics

secondary   colours mixed from primary colours: orange, green, purple

selvedge   woven edge of the fabric

sequences   a series of scenes arranged in a specific order to form a unit

shape   external form, contours

shot list   a document that lists all the shots to be filmed or photographed

shutter speed   the amount of time for which your shutter is open, measured in fractions of a second

silhouette   the outline of a garment

slab building   building an object from flat sheets of clay

slip   liquid clay used to bond other clay surfaces together

sound   everything that the audience hears in a film, such as talking, sound effects and music

spinning   the process of twisting fibres together

squeegee   a rubber-edged tool used to spread ink or to push ink through a silkscreen mesh

stand   a mannequin

stencil   a sheet with a design cut out of it; card or plastic cut to prevent paint or spray going on parts of a picture

storyboard   a set of sketches or photographs showing what will happen in a planned film, animation, advertisement or video game

symbolic   represents or means something more

synthetic   artificial or chemical